Portraits of Conflict

FELIX HUGHES
Photo courtesy of the Old Court House Museum, Vicksburg

Portraits of Conflict

A PHOTOGRAPHIC HISTORY

OF MISSISSIPPI

IN THE CIVIL WAR

Bobby Roberts and Carl Moneyhon

The University of Arkansas Press
Fayetteville 1993

This book was designed by Chiquita Babb using the Minion typeface.

The paper used in this publication meets the minimum requirements of the American National Standard for Permanence of Paper for Printed Library Materials z39.48-1984. ∞

Library of Congress Cataloging-in-Publication Data

Roberts, Bobby Leon.
    Portraits of conflict: a photographic history of Mississippi in
the Civil War / Bobby Roberts and Carl Moneyhon.
      p. cm.
    Includes bibliographical references and index.
    ISBN 1-55728-260-9. — ISBN 1-55728-261-7 (pbk.)
    1. Mississippi—History—Civil War, 1861–1865—Pictorial
works. 2. United States—History—Civil War, 1861–1865—
Pictorial works. I. Moneyhon, Carl H., 1944– .
II. Title.
E516.9R64 1993
973.7'462—dc20   92-21637
                        CIP

In memory of First Lieutenant Pryor Lea Wheat, U. S. Army Infantry.

Born March 19, 1944, in Mississippi.

Killed serving his country in Vietnam on September 6, 1967.

Preface and Acknowledgments

The third volume of *Portraits of Conflict* focuses on Mississippi in the Civil War. Like the two previous books in this series, this story is about the individual soldiers and their experiences in the war. The linkage of photographic images with the narrative, we think, allows the reader to see the conflict at an individual's level. This combination humanizes the horror of a war which the very scale of combat and the number of deaths tends to mask. Whether or not a soldier lived, fought, or died in the critical Virginia Theater, with the Army of Tennessee, or at a Mississippi crossroads is immaterial for the story we seek to tell. Each life was important. Each contributed to a war that continues to have meaning for Americans, in part because it was fought by many and its impact was felt across the nation.

The reader will not find photographs like those modern Americans are used to seeing. The technology of the period made it impossible to capture the moment of battle, and in that sense, these photographs do not speak for themselves. They must be seen in the context that we have tried to provide: the stories of war and battle, the statistics of nineteenth-century military conflict, the casualties of war. In this way, the reader transcends both the limits of photographic technology and the coolness of print and visualizes the human dimension of this great national war.

This is not a collection of all of the Mississippi-related photographs that we located; many others were generously offered for use, and numerous other images were examined in archives across the nation. What we offer here are those men whose stories best fit into the course of the war in Mississippi as interpreted by other scholars. We did not seek to provide a new scholarly analysis, but to write an overview of the work that has been done since the war and to integrate, as well as possible, the most recent scholarship into our experiment in pictures and words.

⌐

Several repositories in Mississippi contain important collections of Civil War materials. The staff at the Mississippi Department of Archives and History assisted us in locating many primary sources for this study; we are especially indebted to Forrest Galey and Elaine Owens for helping us find a number of important Civil War–era images among the department's photographic holdings. On more than one occasion, Elaine graciously responded to our phone requests for information that we needed to complete our research. The Old Court House Museum at Vicksburg also contains many excellent images. We spent hours talking with the museum director, Gordon Cotton, about our project. The director helped us better understand the nature of the war in Mississippi, and we wish to thank him for his assistance. The University of Mississippi has an important collection of pre–Civil War campus photos, and we would like to thank Sharron Sarthou of the John Davis Williams Library for helping us locate the images. We also appreciate the efforts of Les Wyatt of the University of Mississippi, for making arrangements for us to obtain copies of those photographs. Several years ago Les and the authors worked together on the faculty at the University of Arkansas at Little Rock. This project gave us an opportunity to renew an old friendship. The Grand Gulf Military Monument Park contains many interesting photographs, and we wish to thank Ellen and Tommy Presson for providing us access to those images. Beauvoir, the Jefferson Davis Shrine, contributed several photographs to this study; the authors appreciate Thomas M. Czekanski for providing prints of those images. Mary Lohrenz of the Mississippi State Museum furnished us with copies of images and helped us locate other photographs that are in private hands. Sandra E. Boyd of the McCain Library at the University of Southern Mississippi provided us with the excellent image of Isom Herrington. Florence McLeod Hazard of The Columbus and Lowndes County Historical Society sent us the postwar image of S. D. Lee. We appreciate their contributions to our research.

In the spring of 1990 Bobby Roberts traveled to northeast Mississippi searching for photographs. Despite the cold and constant rain, it was a rewarding trip. The staff at the Marshall County Museum allowed the author complete access to the museum's images, many of which had never been published. Tommy Covington of the Ripley Public Library has collected many excellent sources on the county, and he helped the author locate several images that appear in this volume. Margaret Rogers, director of the Northeast Mississippi Museum at Corinth, spent several hours showing the writer the materials in the col-

lection; she also allowed the author to copy the two fine ambrotypes of her relatives that appear in this volume. Margaret later provided the author with several important documents about her ancestors' experiences in the war, and she also suggested that the author contact Doug Locke, a local reenactor. Doug furnished an interesting image of Eleazer Kirkland that we plan to use in a future book on Tennessee and gave the author the name of Ronnie Fullwood of Selmer, Tennessee, who furnished the image of William Fullwood. The trip through northeast Mississippi yielded many important sources for this volume, and the author wishes to thank all those persons who helped him.

Images that are important for documenting the photographic history of the war in Mississippi are located in collections in other states. The United States Army Military History Institute at Carlisle Barracks, Pennsylvania; the Library of Congress; the National Archives; the Naval Historical Center; the Historic New Orleans Collection; the Chicago Historical Society; the Indiana Historical Society; the Indiana State Library; the Kentucky Historical Society; the Bentley Historical Library at the University of Michigan; the American History Center at the University of Texas, Austin; and the Kean Archives in Philadelphia all contain extensive holdings of Mississippi-related photographs. Each institution provided important images for this study. The authors would especially like to thank Michael Winey, curator of the Special Collections Branch at the United States Army Military History Institute. Mike previously assisted us with *Portraits of Conflict: Louisiana* by introducing us to the MOLLUS, Mass., Collection, which is the best single source for images of Federal soldiers. Mike has also collected prints from hundreds of individuals, and several of those copies appear in this volume. Mary Ison of the Prints and Photographs Division of The Library of Congress helped the authors locate the L.C. images in this volume. We appreciate her interest and support of this project.

Two important sources for photographs of Southern soldiers are the Confederate Memorial Hall in New Orleans and the Museum of the Confederacy in Richmond. Pat Eymard, director of Confederate Memorial Hall, provided invaluable assistance on our study of Louisiana and allowed us to publish the image of Samuel McNulty in this book. We appreciate her help and encouragement. Corrine P. Hudgins of the Museum of the Confederacy was most helpful in our search for photographs of Mississippians, many of which appear in this volume. The Museum also furnished images for our earlier volumes on Arkansas and Louisiana. We wish to thank Betsy Louis of the J. Paul Getty Museum, Malibu, California, and Joanna Norman of the Florida Photographic Collection, Florida State Archives, Tallahassee, Florida, for furnishing copies of J. D. Edwards' photographs for this book.

Our search for Mississippi-related photographs led us back to several other institutions that had provided material for our earlier works. Faye Phillips and her staff of the Louisiana and Lower Mississippi Valley Collection at Louisiana State University worked closely with us on the Louisiana book and provided the same quality service to us on our research on Mississippi. Bill Meneray and his staff at the Special Collections Department at Tulane University ably assisted us with our earlier research on Louisiana and provided the image of Andy Swain for this study. We would also like to thank the staff of the Arkansas History Commission for helping us locate several important Mississippi-related images in their collections. The authors are always looking for images of Arkansans, and we wish to express our gratitude to Victor Wallen of Old Washington State Park (Arkansas) for providing us with the negative of Col. Henry P. Johnson.

Public repositories contain thousands of important Civil War photographs, but many excellent images are in private collections. This photographic history could never have been completed if dozens of collectors were not willing to share their images with us. Eleven collectors of Civil War material have been our constant companions and advisors in the search for Civil War photographs. They are Gary Hendershott (Little Rock), Roger Davis (Keokuk, Iowa), Lawrence "Larry" Jones (Austin, Texas), George Esker (Metairie, Louisiana), J. Dale West (Longview, Texas), John Wernick (Hampton, Illinois), Richard Holloway (Washington, D.C.), Eugene Groves (Baton Rouge), Skip Mayorga (North Little Rock), Herb Peck, Jr. (Nashville), and Tom Sweeney (Republic, Missouri). Roger and Gary have been helping the authors since 1983 and have provided images for all three volumes in this series. We wish to express our thanks to them for their continued support. Roger also told his fellow collector, Mark Warren of Bloomfield, Iowa, about our research, and we thank Mark for furnishing photos for our latest effort. Larry, John, Richard, Gene, and Dale provided images for at least one of our earlier works, and we appreciate their contributions to this volume. George, who helped us with the Louisiana volume, gave us several fine images for our current book; we are especially pleased to print his unpublished image of William Thompson Martin. Tom Sweeney also advised us on our Louisiana research, and we thank him for allowing us to publish the excellent images of the Duval brothers. We also consulted with Herb on our two previous volumes, and we wish to thank him for allowing us to publish the image of T. R. McGuire. Finally, we wish to thank another old friend, Skip Mayorga, for providing the image of the 13th Illinois Infantry.

Several new friends and Civil War collectors also helped with this project. Richard Carlile of Dayton, Ohio, has many fine Civil War images; we are indebted to Rick for furnishing his prints for this book. We would also like to thank Dale Snair of Atlanta, Georgia, for responding to our ad for help in *Military Images*. Dale lent the authors negatives of a number of images in this study and solved several questions that arose during our research. His assistance was most welcome. Don W. Scoggins (Longview), Thomas Wixon (Pascagoula, Mississippi), Kevin Hooper (Penny Farms, Florida), Daniel Stari (Baton Rouge), and John H. Luckey (Richardson, Texas) are all active collectors who made substantial contributions to this volume. We appreciate their help and encouragement.

We were especially pleased with the support given by persons who still have family photographs in their possession and who gladly shared them with us. We would like to thank the following Mississippians for furnishing images to the authors: Mary Johnson (Forest), Mrs. Britt Barron (Boonesville), Mrs. Sam W. Crawford (Hamilton), Lee O. Jordon (Gulfport), Ruth Bullard Carr (Jackson), Joseph Henry Mitchell and Nelda Spell Mitchell (Collins), Edwin H. Davis (Rienzi), Margaret Ann Peel (Houston), William E. Stewart (Natchez), and Joyce Aycock (West Point).

Individuals with Mississippi roots who live in other

states also made important contributions to this study. We wish to thank Sallie Harrison (Houston), Harvey B. Steele (Sidney, Arkansas) and Edna Lee Sullivan (North Little Rock), Judge Henry Woods (Little Rock), Eugene Wilson (Franklin, Tennessee), and Mrs. Barry Vaught of Columbus, Georgia, and other members of her family for adding their photographs to this study.

We would also like to thank John Bigham of the South Carolina Confederate Relic Room and Museum for responding to our advertisement in *Military Images*. Through his efforts we obtained permission from Sarah Escott and Sue Cathy to use the image of George Snow and his diary. Snow's diary is an important document on the war in Mississippi; we hope that some day it will be edited and published. We also thank J. B. Harvey, the historian of Old Marion, Mississippi, for furnishing us with extensive documentation on events in Lauderdale County and for providing us with the print of his ancestor, A. T. Harvey. J. B. is currently working on a history of Old Marion, and we have no doubt that it will be an exhaustive and important study of the town. We also thank Charles Sullivan of the Mississippi Gulf Coast Community College at Perkinston, Mississippi, who helped us locate several photographs and is dedicated to locating the graves of Mississippi's Confederate dead. Ron Miller of Natchez also helped the authors identify several images of the town. We would also like to thank Lois C. Benton and Mrs. Peel Cannon for giving us permission to publish the Moore brothers images.

Oftentimes a particular Civil War image cannot be found without the assistance of many persons. We wish to thank Harry Roach, editor of *Military Images;* John Voight of the Gettysburg National Military Park; Mary Anna Rogers; and Frances Maginnis for helping us locate and acquire a copy of the image of John Alemeth Byers.

Sometimes luck plays a role in locating photographs. For almost two years one of the authors had been trying to locate the owner of the Robert Jarman image which appeared in a 1973 issue of *Civil War Times Illustrated.* At the time of its publication, the owner, Frances Evans, lived in Okolona, Mississippi, but she had since moved. In the last months of this project, the author was having lunch with his friend Dwight Blissard and remembered that Dwight was originally from Okolona. When asked if he knew a Mrs. Evans, Dwight responded that she had been his high-school teacher and that she now lives in Tupelo, Mississippi. Within a week the author had a copy of the Jarman image and has since enjoyed several phone conversations with Frances Evans.

Several members of the Arkansas General Assembly are interested in the Civil War, and two shared their family photographs with us. Ernest Cunningham, past speaker of the house, and his wife, Cathy, furnished the copy of Joseph W. Cunningham. Representative Charles Stewart, chairman of the House Revenue and Tax Committee, provided the image of Albert O. McCollum. We appreciate their help and also their continued support for the University of Arkansas Press.

We would like to thank Linda Pine, Joy Geisler, and Paula Kaizer for allowing us to use the darkroom facilities of the University of Arkansas at Little Rock Archives and Special Collections Department. Without their cooperation we could not have reproduced most of the photographs that appear in this volume. The authors also appreciate the assistance of their good friend and long-time morning-coffee colleague, Prof. Phillip Kehler of the U. A. L. R. Department of Earth Sciences, who was kind enough to critique the geological descriptions of the Vicksburg region.

Despite the best intentions of the director of the Central Arkansas Library System (CALS) not to burden the staff with his interest in the Civil War, he was not entirely successful. His administrative assistant, Larrie Ohlemeyer, helped type and proof the hundreds of letters that this project generated. Each morning she could look forward to the author eagerly inquiring if any new photographs had arrived in the mail. Valerie Thwing, our Inter-Library Loan Department librarian, located dozens of esoteric sources from across the nation. The requests were never easy, and we usually needed the documents immediately. Valerie unfailingly filled every request. CALS' assistant directors, Linda Bly and Bob Razer, patiently listened to frequent babblings about the Civil War and competently managed the library while the director was away on research trips. The director greatly appreciates his staff's tolerance and help with this project.

We would like to thank Kathy Williams, a friend of

the director, and Patricia Moneyhon. Kathy proofread the chapters written by the director. She corrected many awkward sentences and misspelled words that crept into the manuscript. Her criticisms were always penetrating and constructive; any inconsistencies that remain are due to the vanity of the authors. Patricia gave yeoman service on this third volume, reading galleys and page proofs and helping with the numerous details necessary to finishing any book like this. Patricia and Kathy graciously allowed us to periodically disappear on long research trips, and they suffered through many conversations about the manuscript. We appreciate their support of this study of the Civil War in Mississippi.

Finally we would like to thank Miller Williams, director of the University of Arkansas Press, for supporting this series on the Civil War. After the first book the authors were ready to quit, but Miller persuaded us to continue our work. We appreciate his confidence in this project. We would also like to thank Debbie Bowen and Chiquita Babb, who have worked with us on this series. Debbie has had the difficult task of editing the manuscript. Her suggestions have been excellent, and she has corrected many mistakes in spelling and grammar that would have seriously weakened the volume. Chiquita has been responsible for the layout of these volumes; her talent for composition is evident in the final design of our studies. We appreciate the support of the entire staff of the Press and look forward to working with them on later volumes in the series.

Key to Photographic Locations

L.L.M.V.C., L.S.U.: Louisiana and Lower Mississippi Valley Collection, Hill Memorial Library, Louisiana State University, Baton Rouge, Louisiana

M.D.A.H.: Mississippi Department of Archives and History, Jackson

U.A.L.R.: University of Arkansas at Little Rock, Archives and Special Collections

U.S.A.M.H.I.: The United States Army Military History Institute, Carlisle Barracks, Pennsylvania. MOLLUS, Mass., refers to the Military Order of the Loyal Legion of the United States—Massachusetts Commandery Collection.

Contents

Portraits of Conflict

Chapter 1

Civil War Photography in Mississippi

In 1860 photography was well established in Mississippi, and a large number of men engaged in that trade across the state. In the United States Census of that year, eighty-five men listed occupations associated with photography. Forty of them were unmistakably photographers—twenty-nine daguerreotypists, eight photographers, and three ambrotypists. Forty-five others were artists, a trade that often involved photography as well. J. A. and N. F. Hawkins were typical of the artist-photographer. The two may be found as artists in the 1860 census, but their Gallery of Fine Arts advertised that they also made photographs. Their patrons could not only have a photograph made, but could also have it "colored in oil by the *Finest* and most successful *Portrait Painter* now in the South."[1] There was even one amateur photographer who would leave a legacy of images: Edward C. Boynton, professor of sciences at the University of Mississippi.

Natchez had the largest concentration of photographer-artists before the war, with six listed in the manuscript census. Vicksburg and Columbus, considerably smaller communities, had five. Jackson had only two. Photography was a young man's trade for the most part. The oldest listed in the census were J. B. Kuner, a forty-three-year-old artist from Bavaria, and John S. Claiborn, a forty-three-year-old artist from Virginia. Others came mainly from outside of Mississippi: Bavaria, Prussia, Canada, England, Ireland, Alabama, Connecticut, Illinois, Kentucky, Massachusetts, Missouri, Ohio, and Virginia were the original homes of photographer-artists in the four largest towns. Only two, Theodore J. Keenan of Natchez and E. H. Mullen of Columbus, were native Mississippians.[2]

Mississippi photographers offered the latest techniques available. In 1860, L. Anderson and Thomas Poindexter offered Jacksonians "PHOTOGRAPHS of all styles from a *Visiting Card* to *Life Size*, either plain or *Colored in Oil*," and proclaimed that Poindexter was "one of the most widely known portrait painters of the Southwest."

Anderson and Poindexter also pointed out that their pictures were "ACTUALLY MADE AND FINISHED IN THE ROOMS AND ARE *not* sent to New Orleans, Memphis, or elsewhere to be photographed from an ordinary ambrotype."[3]

An 1860 advertisement in a Jackson newspaper provides an indication of some of the conditions of the photography business. The photographer, B. F. Boyd of Memphis, announced his intention to sell his "established sky light gallery, (formerly Teliga's) over J. W. Shaw's store." While Boyd was probably putting the best possible light on the business since he was trying to get rid of it, the advertisement is suggestive. Boyd noted that he paid ninety-six dollars per year in rent for these rooms. Profits could be made despite the overhead. "A good artist," he stated, "can make $3,000 a year in this Gallery." Boyd offered the business for five hundred dollars.[4]

These men were available in 1861 to capture the images of the thousands of Mississippians who went off to war. Unfortunately, most of their work remains anonymous. Of all of the photographers at work in 1860, only H. D. Gurney, a thirty-eight-year-old Massachusetts native who owned Gurney's Photograph and Fine Art Gallery at Natchez, left identifiable wartime work. The legacy of these photographers was, for the most part, the individual portraits that they made.[5]

There were some exterior scenes of Mississippi troops during the war, but almost all such Confederate images were made by New Orleans photographer Jay D. Edwards. Edwards photographed the men of the 9th and 10th Mississippi infantries who were at Pensacola in the spring of 1861. One of Edwards' photographs of Co. B of the 9th Infantry became the basis for a sketch by Theodore Davis that accompanied pieces on conditions in the South written by William H. Russell in 1861. The artist's rendition of the photograph was published in *Harper's Weekly* on June 22, 1861.[6]

As in the other Southern states, Confederate photography did not continue long after the beginning of the war. Many of the younger photographers may have enlisted in the army. Older ones found that they could not continue to take pictures because the Federal blockade cut off the supplies that they needed for their work. No images were found that could be identified as having been made by a photographer working in Confederate territory within the state after 1861.

Confederate photographers were, however, replaced by Yankee photographers. As the Union forces moved into Mississippi, they were accompanied by men photographing the Union soldiers. At Corinth, G. W. Armstead, Griswold White, and the firm of Howard & Hall carried on wartime business. D. P. Barr, Charles N. Bean, J. E. Joslyn, J. W. Young, William K. French, and photographers named Bishop, Herrick, and Needles worked alone and as partners at various times in Vicksburg after its capture. At Natchez, N. H. Black, Gurney, and Hughes and Lakin took pictures during the war. Le Clears Photographic Palace was one of the few firms working at wartime Jackson. Little is known about any of these individuals except for J. E. Joslyn. J. W. Young advertised, when he opened the Washington Photograph and Ambrotype Gallery at Vicksburg, that he had hired Joslyn and that the new photographer had been associated with Anthony and Matthew Brady's studios on the East Coast.[7]

The wartime galleries in Union-occupied areas made their money selling photographs of outdoor scenes, prominent military leaders, and the soldiers themselves to the fighting men, who apparently were avid collectors of such materials. French & Co. of Vicksburg announced in their advertisement that they had photographs of many of the prominent generals for sale. The Washington Photograph and Ambrotype Gallery offered a wide variety of photographs and a means to encourage their purchase when it

4

advertised, "All negatives made at this establishment will be carefully preserved until after the war, when a catalogue of the same will be published and distributed throughout the United States, thus enabling our patrons, as well as their friends, to order any number of cards they may desire."[8]

The Northern photographers brought with them the latest developments in equipment and were able to produce large numbers of inexpensive photographs. Herrick's Excelsior Gallery at Vicksburg advertised that it offered clients "sphereotypes—, Vitrotypes, Photographs, Ambrotypes, and Daugurrotypes [sic]." Prices were cheap. At the war's end, Joslyn, Smith, and Young at Vicksburg offered *cartes de visites* for only fifty cents per card.[9]

Together, Confederate and Union photographers left a rich legacy of the images of war in the state of Mississippi. The nature of their contribution is limited in some ways. Unlike the modern photographer, they could not capture fully the immediacy of war and its carnage. With the exception of Corinth, there are no pictures of the death and destruction of the battlefield. The Mississippi pictures, however, particularly the portraits of the officers and men who fought the war, leave their own contribution to our perception of the war. They capture the images of the men who carried out the grand schemes of the generals and political leaders, whose actions and whose deaths created the grand patterns of Civil War history. These photographs help us to see the human dimension of war that history might otherwise forget.

Edward C. Boynton, a native of Vermont and graduate of West Point, began teaching chemistry, mineralogy, and geology at the University of Mississippi in 1856. Interested in photography, Boynton experimented with the wet-plate collodion process in his photos of scenes at the University of Mississippi, including this self-portrait. When the war broke out, Boynton returned to the North but left his collection of glass-plate nega- tives. In a note written on September 6, 1861, he stated his intention to "return, or send to Oxford to reclaim my other effects and this box, when tranquillity [sic] is restored."[10] Although he photographed none of the war, Boynton did capture scenes of Oxford and its students on the eve of war. *Photo courtesy of Archives and Special Collections, John Davis Williams Library, University of Mississippi*

EDWARD CARLISLE BOYNTON
copy print from glass negative

Boynton took this photograph of the University of Mississippi's class of 1861, possibly in the spring of the year. Many of these young men enlisted in the University Greys or the Lamar Rifles, both of which were mustered into service in late April 1861. Thirty-seven students served in the Greys, Co. A, 11th Mississippi Infantry, and the unit participated in most of the battles of the Army of Northern Virginia. Of all the members of the company, only two of the men who originally enlisted would be left when it disbanded. *Photo courtesy of Archives and Special Collections, John Davis Williams Library, University of Mississippi*

CLASS OF 1861, UNIVERSITY OF MISSISSIPPI
copy print from glass negative

While many contemporary Northern photographers posed their subjects in front of elaborate scenes, Mississippians appear universally in formal portraits with plain backgrounds, as in this photograph of Pvt. Joseph H. Mitchell made by an unknown photographer early in the war. Mitchell, who enlisted in the J. W. Thompson Invincibles, later Co. E, 23rd Mississippi Infantry, was mustered in at Iuka in the autumn of 1861. In this photograph he was wearing his militia uniform, which was brown with black trim, instead of the later Confederate gray uniform. He is carrying a foot artillery sword, inappropriate to his infantry service, suggesting that it and the pistol may have been photographer's props, a common practice. *Photo courtesy of Ripley Public Library*

Joseph Henry Mitchell
copy print of unknown original

This photograph, by an unknown artist, of Alfred Cox Smith was probably made about the time of his enlistment. Smith was a member of the Swamp Rangers, eventually Co. I, 22nd Mississippi Infantry. The twenty-one-year-old farmer joined his unit in June 1861 and was appointed first sergeant. His uniform reflected parts of the uniform pre-scribed by the Mississippi Military Board. Hats were to be broad-brimmed black felt, looped up on three sides and ornamented with cord, tassel, and plume. For fatigue duty a red flannel shirt was in order. Smith was carrying a Model 1840 noncommissioned officer's sword, appropriate to his rank. *Photo courtesy of Dale S. Snair*

JOHN BENJAMIN STEWART
copy print of unknown original

ALFRED COX SMITH
copy print of unknown original

This photograph of Pvt. John B. Stewart also shows a typical undress uniform common to Mississippi soldiers at the beginning of the war. According to family tradition, the forty-nine-year-old farmer from Tippah County enlisted in F. A. Montgomery's Bolivar Troop, later Co. A, 1st Battalion Mississippi Cavalry, as a replacement for his son, who had small children at home. Stewart appears to carry a foot artillery sword, although this may be a variation on the Bowie knife car-ried by troops throughout the South when the war began. *Photo courtesy of Sallie Harrison*

9

There were few photographs of Mississippi troops other than in individual portraits. The photographer who took the greatest number of group photographs was J. D. Edwards of New Orleans, who was with Gen. Braxton Bragg's army at Pensacola. This photograph captures a group of privates of the 9th Mississippi around a campfire. From the left they include James Pegues, Kinloch Falconer, John Fennel, James Cunningham, Thomas W. Falconer, James Simms, and John T. Smith. Kinloch Falconer rose to the rank of major and became assistant adjutant general in the Army of Tennessee. *Photo courtesy of the Library of Congress, LC B8184-1794*

Co. B, 9th Mississippi Infantry
albumen print
J. D. Edwards

10

The members of Co. B, 9th Mississippi Infantry, received national attention as "Rebel Troops at General Bragg's Camp" when the Edwards photograph was used as the basis for a drawing by Theodore Davis to accompany reports in *Harper's Weekly* about the war in western Florida. For artistic purposes, Davis rearranged the positions of the men from the Edwards photograph, but he included all of them in what was as close to a photojournalistic portrait as was possible at the time. *Photo reproduced from* Harper's Weekly, *June 22, 1861, p. 395*

Co. B, 9th Mississippi Infantry
woodcut
Theodore Davis

The work of photographers behind Northern lines was well documented and often included portraits of themselves or of their studios. This image is of the Armstead & White studio at Corinth, showing the opening to the roof that allowed the fullest amount of light into the studio for making portraits. George Armstead himself is standing at the rear of the studio on the far left. Armstead & White took several outdoor scenes of Corinth and the surrounding area during the Federal occupation.

ARMSTEAD & WHITE STUDIO
copy print from Francis T. Miller,
The Photographic History of the Civil War

This scene is apparently of the outskirts of Corinth. It is typical of the work of Armstead & White and shows the rich detail made possible by the photographic techniques of the day. Beginning with a crisp negative made with the wet-plate collodion process, the photographer could then make any number of equally crisp paper prints from the original. *Photo courtesy of the Chicago Historical Society, no. ICHi-08017*

SCENE OF CORINTH
carte de visite

Federal photographers left a large number of photographs of Vicksburg. These two, by unknown photographers, are typical of this work and show scenes of the river and wharf area. *Photos courtesy of U.S.A.M.H.I., MOLLUS, Mass., Collection*

The firm of Joslyn & Smith established their Washington Gallery on the third floor of this building at Vicksburg. In addition to numerous scenes and individual portraits, they took this picture of their own establishment. *Photo courtesy of the Library of Congress, LC B816-8685*

WASHINGTON GALLERY, VICKSBURG
carte de visite

14

VICKSBURG SCENES
cartes de visites

GROUP SCENE
carte de visite

The photographers at Vicksburg also captured group scenes. This *carte de visite* was of the camp of the 94th Illinois Infantry. The subjects captured were Maj. John McNulty, Brig. Gen. William W. Orme, two unknowns, Mrs. McNulty, Mrs. Hudson Burr, and another unknown. *Photo courtesy of U.S.A.M.H.I., Dave Charles Collection*

A. E. HURLEY
carte de visite
D. P. Barr

UNKNOWN GROUP OF SOLDIERS
carte de visite
Washington Gallery

The photographers at the Washington Gallery captured this group of soldiers, members of an unknown regiment, while they were on duty at Vicksburg. *Photo courtesy of Richard F. Carlile*

As everywhere, at Vicksburg the bread and butter of the photographer was the individual portrait. Typical of this work is this portrait made by D. P. Barr of Lt. A. E. Hurley of the 50th U.S. Colored Infantry. *Photo courtesy of John Wernick*

17

Chapter 2

Mississippi Goes to War

During the sectional crisis of the 1850s, Mississippi was one of the centers of Southern-rights activism, with its politicians standing alongside those of South Carolina as strident defenders of the South and its institutions. The public stance of the state's politicians reflected the social and economic developments that had taken place in the 1850s that firmly linked the state to the economy of cotton and the system of slavery. This linkage ensured that with the election of Abraham Lincoln, the Republican candidate for president in 1860, and the secession of South Carolina, Mississippi would soon be one of the leaders in the formation of a new Confederacy. The Southern identity of the state also meant that Mississippians would enlist in great numbers in support of the Southern cause, defending the state and the new nation from what they characterized as Northern aggression.

A major factor determining Mississippi's course in 1861 was its development during the 1850s as the leading plantation state in the South.

The state's farms extensively cultivated cotton, the crop that was the basis for the South's antebellum plantation economic life. In the 1850s the state led the Union in bales of cotton produced. By 1859 the 1,202,507 bales that were ginned placed the state over three hundred thousand bales ahead of the nearest competitor, Alabama, and accounted for over 22 percent of the cotton produced in the United States. Although cotton was grown throughout the state, most of it was cultivated along the deltas of the Yazoo and Tombigbee rivers and their branches. In 1859 Yazoo, Hinds, Madison, Lowndes, and Noxubee counties were the five top producers and accounted for nearly 23 percent of the state's entire crop.

Population expanded along with economic opportunities. In 1816 a special census taken as a prelude to statehood listed the state's population at 75,492 inhabitants. By 1840 the total population had expanded to 375,651 inhabitants, and growth continued through the next two decades.

On the eve of the Civil War the census showed that the state had a population of 791,305. Indicative of the growing importance of the cotton economy was the fact that the state's black slave population was increasing during these years at a faster pace than that of whites. By 1840 the census showed that the majority of the people in the state were slaves. By 1860 the population of Mississippi consisted of 353,899 whites and 437,404 blacks. Most of the latter were slaves, but the black population did include 773 individuals who were free.

While plantation agriculture and slavery were increasingly important for Mississippi, these developments do not indicate everything that was taking place in the state, nor that the white population resided primarily on large plantations. The majority of whites were not planters. In the farm regions 63 percent of the farms were under one hundred acres in size. Small farmers with no slaves dominated the pine hills of the interior and could be found throughout the state. Towns such as Columbus, Holly Springs, Jackson, Natchez, Port Gibson, and Vicksburg had populations of craftsmen and workers whose interests also were not closely linked with those of the large planters. In the 1850s, however, few of these people challenged the idea that their futures were linked to the expansion of cotton and slavery. In 1861 social differences among the state's citizens did not prevent secession, and many of the state's yeoman farmers and town workers rushed to fill the companies organizing for the fight. White Mississippians spoke almost with a single voice when they confronted the sectional discord that led ultimately to war.

Many of Mississippi's most prominent political leaders stridently supported the protection of what they considered to be the South's unique institutions and were early proponents of secession or other militant action to ensure their goals. Through the 1850s the most outspoken advocate of Southern rights was John A. Quitman. Quitman, Mexican War hero and perennial state office holder, supported nullification in 1832–1833, opposed the compromise of 1850, advocated secession in 1851, and continued to back such action until his death in 1858. Others followed in Quitman's footsteps. John J. Pettus became a major advocate of Southern rights and ran for governor in 1859, promising to arm the state in preparation for what he considered to be inevitable secession and war. In Washington, D.C., United States Senator Albert G. Brown was a major advocate of secession and strongly anti-Northern. Senator Jefferson Davis had become more moderate during the decade, but he was throughout the period after the Compromise of 1850 a prominent advocate of states' rights.

The threat to states' rights that all feared finally appeared to be realized in the attack in Virginia of John Brown upon the Federal arsenal at Harpers Ferry in the fall of 1859. At that time the state legislature appropriated money to arm volunteer companies and created the Volunteer Military Board that consisted of the captains of these companies. Defensive in nature, the new units and the companies of the regular militia provided the basis for the military organizations that would respond to the call for troops once the state seceded in the spring of 1861.

From the viewpoint of the state's political leaders, the ultimate cause for action came in 1860 with the election of Abraham Lincoln. Following Lincoln's election, prominent secessionists immediately called for action. Governor Pettus met with the state's congressional delegation on November 22, 1860, to discuss how to respond to Lincoln's election. Despite some concern expressed by Senators Brown and Davis and Congressman L. Q. C. Lamar that the state not act on its own, the conference decided to call the legislature into session and advised immediate secession. When the legislature assembled at

Jackson in December, its members called for a state convention to meet on January 7, 1861, to consider the relationship between the state and the nation, and they set December 20, 1860, as the date of elections for the delegates.

In the ensuing campaign, divisions within Mississippi society became apparent, but the large majority of delegates favored secession—either immediate or in concert with other Southern states. The delegates showed their future course of action on the first day of the convention when they elected William S. Barry, a strong disunionist, president. Barry was authorized to appoint a committee of fifteen to draft an Ordinance of Secession. The committee, headed by Congressman Lamar, reported the Ordinance on January 9. Those who favored delay in order to ensure action was taken with other Southern states tried to block the committee's report by attempting to amend it, but with no success. The convention was dominated by immediate secessionists; the cooperationists were able to get no more than twenty-nine out of ninety-nine votes cast on a proposal to submit the Ordinance to a popular vote.

At least initially, the vote for secession brought Mississippians of all backgrounds together in support of what for a time was the Republic of Mississippi. Once the state had seceded, it ordered local military companies to take action against Federal installations in the state. On January 20 Mississippi state troops seized the naval works at Ship Island off the southern coast of the state. Units of the Jackson Artillery were ordered to Vicksburg, where they joined that city's volunteer companies in fortifying Fort Hill north of the city in order to keep Northern troops from moving down the Mississippi River to resist state operations in Louisiana. To assist in efforts to seize the forts and naval yards at Pensacola, Governor Pettus ordered seven volunteer companies to Florida on January 11, 1861. Companies from Chickasaw, Lowndes, Noxubee, and Clark counties left for Mobile on that day and arrived at Pensacola by January 14. On January 17 they organized Abert's Regiment, named for its colonel, Charles A. Abert. This unit never fought and was mustered out in February 1861 after being replaced by new regiments organized under an ordinance creating the Army of Mississippi.

On January 23, the state convention moved to create the Army of Mississippi for the self-protection of the state. Senator Jefferson Davis was commissioned to major general of the army. There were four brigadier generals—Earl Van Dorn, Charles Clark, James L. Alcorn, and Christopher H. Mott. These men, plus Governor Pettus, constituted the Military Board. The board quickly organized the army, even adopting a state uniform consisting of gray frock coats and trousers, trimmed in red for the infantry, yellow for the cavalry, and orange for the artillery. The hats of the army were to be of black felt, looped up on three sides, with horsehair pompoms for enlisted men and plumes for officers. In the first six months, membership on the board changed rapidly as Davis moved on to the Confederate presidency and as his successors, Van Dorn and Clark, took commissions in the Confederate army. In July 1861 Reuben Davis became major general of the state's army.

Under the Ordinance of Secession, Mississippi began to organize eight regiments of infantry. The names of the companies that gathered at muster points to form these regiments indicated the pride of the men in their homes and in their leaders. Typically, the 2nd Regiment included the Tishomingo Riflemen, the O'Connor Rifles, the Town Creek Riflemen, the Joe Matthews' Rifles, the Calhoun Rifles, the Magnolia Rifles, the Pontotoc Minute Men, the Conewah Rifles, the Cherry Creek Rifles, the Iuka Rifles, and the Liberty Guards. Others took more fanciful or more politically germane names such as the Reub

Davis Rebels and the Mississippi Yankee Hunters of the 1st Infantry, the Red Rovers and Pettus Rebels of the 5th Infantry, the Jeff Davis Sharpshooters of the 7th Infantry, and the True Confederates, Moody True Blues, Tullahoma Hard Shells, Southern Sentinels, and Confederate Guards of the 8th Infantry.

The Army of Mississippi did not exist for long. Elsewhere politicians formed the new Confederate States of America, and Mississippi's Jefferson Davis was named its provisional president. While the formal process of ratifying the new government proceeded slowly, the Confederate government began to act with Davis's inauguration on February 18. Mississippi was *de facto* part of a new union. Militarily, the state's entry into the Confederacy meant that most of the troops already called up and future enlistments would be placed in the service of the regular Confederate army. The state received its first call for recruits for Confederate service on March 9, 1861, when Governor Pettus was asked to send fifteen hundred men to Pensacola to help reduce Fort Pickens, which remained in Federal hands. In March, the state sent twenty companies to Pensacola. These were organized into Col. J. R. Chalmers' 9th Regiment and Col. S. M. Phillips' 10th Regiment in April and transferred into the Provisional Army of the Confederate States on April 14.

President Davis issued the first general call for troops to be sent for Confederate service in the midst of the crisis at Fort Sumter. On April 8 he asked for three thousand men, then for an additional five thousand men following the attack on Sumter. On May 21, 1861, Pettus ordered fifty companies to muster at Corinth. Out of these companies the 14th, 15th, 16th, 17th, and 18th regiments were formed. Two regiments were organized at Corinth after additional requests were made in June. Following the units sent to Pensacola, the first unit to leave the state would be Col. William C. Falkner's 2nd Regiment of

state troops, sent to Virginia in May, shortly followed by Col. William H. Moore's 11th Infantry. According to Dunbar Rowland's *Military History of Mississippi, 1803–1898*, ultimately twelve infantry regiments, two infantry battalions, one legion, and two batteries of artillery served in Virginia. Thirty-four infantry regiments plus a number of combined regiments and battalions served in the Army of Tennessee and various Western armies. Fourteen cavalry regiments, with additional battalion and partisan units, and fifteen artillery batteries and battalions also were attached to the armies in the West.

The motivations of the men who joined in 1861 varied with each individual, but most appear to have perceived a real threat to their freedom and to their state. Pvt. Robert A. Moore of the Confederate Guards, Co. G, 17th Mississippi, from Holly Springs wrote that "our country calls & he that would not respond deserves not the name of man & though we fall, we fall battling for our rights & are determined to have them or die in the attempt." Henry A. Garrett, a law student at the University of Mississippi who joined the Adams Troop, Jeff Davis Legion, considered himself to be fighting for a "holy and just cause." Caleb B. M. McCaleb, who was helping to organize the University Grays at Oxford, informed Governor Pettus that his company consisted of fifty men "as enthusiastic as those who love freedom should be. . . . Our motto is 'Ducit amor Patrie'—'the love of my country leads me.'"[1]

Confederate soldiers first encountered military life at the camps of instruction established across the state. At the beginning of the war most of the regiments were mustered in and began their training at Corinth, Iuka, or Enterprise. Wherever they were sent, the new soldiers quickly experienced a lifestyle that few had encountered before. LeGrand J. Wilson wrote of the camp of the 1st Mississippi Infantry at Iuka:

Camp life grows monotonous in a short time. The novelty soon wears off, and its routine duties become tiresome indeed. We were in camp during July and August. Reveille at 5 A.M., roll call; breakfast 7; surgeon's call, 8; guard mounting 9; squad drill or drilling in the manual of arms to 10; company drill to 11; recess—dinner 12 M. From 2 to 4, company and regimental drill, which generally prolonged to 5; dress parade 6; supper 7; taps 9. Thus the days came and went, and our military education progressed.[2]

Henry A. Garrett wrote simply that "the first taste of a soldier's life was not very palatable."[3]

Whether the life was "palatable" or not, Mississippians rushed to join the Confederate army. In 1860 the state's male population between the ages of fifteen and fifty was 88,286; ultimately, perhaps as many as 75,000 Mississippians served in the Confederate service during the war. As early as September 1861, the state had some 25,000 men in uniform. Wiley P. Harris wrote to his friend Jefferson Davis on September 30, "You would be struck with the aspect our State now presents. Except in the principal towns the country appears to be deserted. There are not more men left than the demands of society and the police of the slave-holding country actually require."[4]

These men soon discovered that war was much more than they initially perceived. In addition to the boredom of the camp and the thrill of battle, there was also misery and death. Disease would be the first real threat that the Mississippi soldier faced. In the instruction camps, men who were thrown together in large numbers contracted diseases against which they had developed no immunity—measles, mumps, chicken pox, and whooping cough. LeGrand Wilson of the 1st Mississippi recorded that at Bowling Green in three months beginning in September 1861 the 3rd Mississippi lost 61 men and the 1st Mississippi, 43, from measles alone. In the field, suffering from inadequate food and quarters, troops faced a second assault by diseases such as dysentery, diarrhea, typhoid, and malaria. Although the estimates are inadequate because of

Confederate records, a report made in 1866 by the United States Provost Marshal General placed the number of Mississippi troops who died from disease at 6,807.[5]

Others would die in battle. Perhaps the first Mississippians to face enemy fire were the soldiers of the 2nd and 11th Infantry regiments, who, as part of the brigade of Brig. Gen. Bernard Bee, helped repel a Federal assault and save the day for the Confederacy at Manassas on June 21, 1861. Suffering 25 dead and 82 wounded, they earned the accolade of Gen. Thomas J. Jackson, who reported that they had stood "like a stone wall" against the Federals. First Manassas, or Bull Run, would be only the beginning of Mississippi's battle casualties. Again, accurate figures of Mississippi's dead killed in battle cannot be obtained, but the United States Provost Marshal General tabulated 8,458 deaths of soldiers who were killed in battle or died subsequently from their wounds. This amounted to over 11 percent of those who served in the Confederate forces; when combined with those who died of disease, the figures represent over 19 percent of the men in service. These figures, however, do not do justice to what individual Mississippi units would suffer. The 6th Mississippi Infantry had the distinction at Shiloh of being the unit that would suffer the worst casualties relative to the number of men engaged in battle of any of the state's regiments—losing over 300 men killed and wounded out of 425 who went into battle—over 70 percent of its force. Other units with casualty rates over 50 percent included the 16th Infantry, which suffered over 63 percent casualties at Antietam, and the 29th Infantry with over 52 percent at Chickamauga.[6]

In 1861, however, few men fully realized what they faced. William Howard Russell of the London *Times* recorded the optimism and false assumptions many of the recruits brought with them to this war when he wrote of a train load of volunteers headed for the front. They were a company "armed with rifled pistols and enormous bowi-knifes, who called themselves 'The Toothpick Company.' They carried along with them a coffin, with a plate inscribed 'Abe Lincoln, died—,' and declared they were 'bound' to bring his body back in it, and that they did not intend to use muskets or rifles, but just go in with knife and six-shooter, and whip the Yankees straight away."[7] The war would not present such an easy victory.

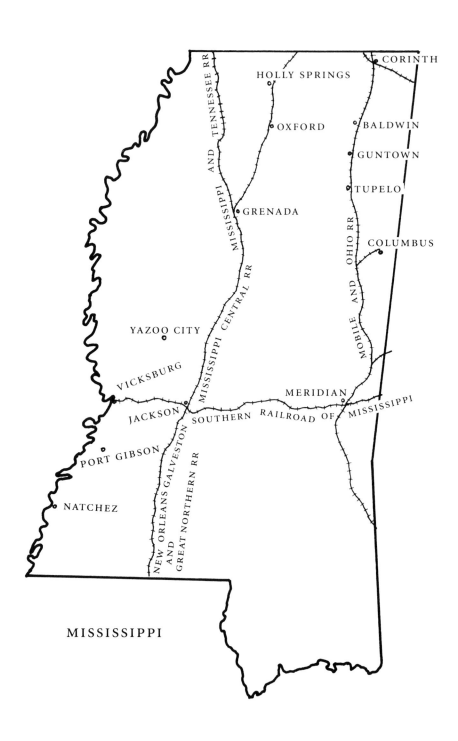

John A. Quitman
copy print of unknown original

John Quitman was in many ways representative of the secession impulse in Mississippi. Although born in the North, he moved to Natchez in 1821. He became a planter, practiced law, and rose to political leadership—serving in the state constitutional convention of 1832, in the state legislature, as governor, in Congress, and in various courts. He added a reputation as a military leader in the Texas Revolution and in the Mexican War, where as a brigadier general he led a division in the assault upon Chapultepec.

In the 1850s Quitman was a major proponent for secession of the Southern states to counter the growing antislavery sentiments expressed in the North. When he ran for governor in 1851, he campaigned on a platform urging secession and the unification of the slaveholding states in a new nation. In an 1856 debate in Congress on slavery in the Federal territories, Quitman said of the growing sectional tension, "It is a battle for victory or death. In this struggle either *you* must conquer, and crush *us,* or *we* must succeed in defending the rights and privileges of our section. As the contest now stands, it is a war to the knife."[8]

Quitman never saw his ambitions realized. Although he had paved the way for secession in 1861, Quitman died on July 17, 1858. Others were left to pick up his role as a leader of secession. *Photo courtesy of M.D.A.H.*

ALBERT GALLATIN BROWN
copy print of unknown original

Quitman was not alone in his radicalism.
Albert G. Brown, elected to the United States
Senate in 1853, had been a major proponent
of Southern rights and territorial expansion,
and he pushed the state toward secession.
Raised on his family farm in Copiah County,
Brown had achieved prominence in the state
as an attorney and politician, and he became
a spokesman for the economic interests of
his state. As a politician Brown had opposed
the Compromise of 1850, had urged the
annexation of Cuba, and had become a
spokesman for the expansion of slavery. In
1860 he believed the time for action had
come, the election results convincing him
of inevitable Southern secession. Like more
moderate politicians, however, he was
unsure of how the state should proceed. At a
speech given in Jackson he finally concluded
that there was no further hope in the Union.
Brown told his audience, "The Union is
dead and in process of mortification. . . . and
nothing now remains but to bury the rotten
carcass."[9] *Photo courtesy of M.D.A.H.*

26

JEFFERSON DAVIS
copy print

Quitman and Brown represented the more radical secessionists within Mississippi. Jefferson Davis was probably more typical of the state's leadership in his moderate states'-rights position. A planter and successful politician, Davis was the state's most visible leader nationally. He had been United States Senator from 1847 to 1850, secretary of war in the cabinet of Franklin Pierce from 1853 to 1857, then senator from 1857 to secession. During the 1850s Davis was a strong advocate of the protection of Southern rights, but he looked for ways to maintain the South's position while remaining in the nation. Indicative of the way that events in 1859 and 1860 unified Mississippi leaders, however, Davis's position changed after Lincoln's election and after congressional efforts to address Southern grievances collapsed. On December 14, 1860, Davis wrote:

The argument is exhausted. All hope of relief in the Union through the agency of committees, congressional legislation or constitutional amendments, is extinguished, and we trust the south will not be deceived by appearances of the pretence of new guarantees. In our judgment, the Republicans are resolute in the purpose of granting nothing that will or ought to satisfy the South. We are satisfied the honor, safety, and independence of the Southern people require the organization of a Southern confederacy—a result to be obtained only by separate State secession— that the primary object of each slaveholding State ought to be its speedy and absolute separation from a Union with hostile States."[10]

Photo courtesy of M.D.A.H.

JOHN J. PETTUS
copy print of unknown original

Leadership of the state into secession fell to the lot of Governor John J. Pettus. Pettus was a planter from Kemper County and a successful lawyer. His bid for governor in 1859 was based on a strong states'-rights platform. Following Lincoln's election, the governor called a conference of the state's congressional delegation. Despite support for moderation by Senators Brown and Davis and Representative Lamar, the conference ultimately advised immediate secession. Pettus called a special session of the legislature, then urged them to action. "If we falter now," he told them, "we and our sons must pay the penalty in future years, of bloody, if not fruitless efforts to retrieve the fallen fortunes of the State, which if finally unsuccessful must leave our fair land blighted—cursed with Black Republican politics and free negro morals, to become a cess pool of vice, crime and infamy."[11] The legislators promptly called for an election on December 20 for delegates to a state convention to consider the relationship of the state to the Union. *Photo courtesy of M.D.A.H.*

LUCIUS QUINTUS CINCINNATUS LAMAR
copy print of unknown original

L. Q. C. Lamar, another moderate Mississippian, was charged by the president of the convention with chairing the committee to draft the Ordinance of Secession. Lamar was an attorney and a professor of mathematics at the University of Mississippi who had pursued a successful political career in the 1850s. He was elected to Congress in 1858 and in 1860 he had been one of the few Mississippians who opposed the withdrawal of the Southern faction from the national Democratic convention. While not opposed to secession following Lincoln's election, he did urge caution and opposed any action without careful planning and cooperation among the Southern states. The majority favored action, however, and Lamar's committee reported its work quickly. The Ordinance proclaimed that "all the laws and ordinances by which the said State of Mississippi became a member of the Federal Union of the United States of America be, and the same are hereby repealed, . . .[The state] shall from henceforth be a free, sovereign and independent state."[14] *Photo courtesy of M.D.A.H.*

MISSISSIPPI STATE HOUSE
carte de visite

The convention assembled in the representatives' chamber at the statehouse on January 7, 1861. The election had returned a majority in favor of immediate secession. Ninety-nine men gathered in the hall, sitting at what one reporter described as plain, black-painted wooden desks with chairs of "great, square, faded mahogany frames, stuffed and covered with hair cloth." Before them sat the president who sat behind an "old-fashioned mahogany pulpit" in a recess in the wall flanked by two Ionic columns. To the president's right was a portrait of Senator George Poindexter and an open fireplace above which was a copy of the Declaration of Independence and a lithograph of the Medical College of Louisiana. To his left was another fireplace, also surmounted by a copy of the Declaration.[12] Edmund W. Pettus reported to Governor A. B. Moore of Alabama that the delegates represented some of the "most distinguished men of the State." He described its deliberations as being conducted with "order, dignity, and solemnity fitting the deliberations of a sovereign people changing their form of government."[13] *Photo courtesy of M.D.A.H.*

Lamar's committee report was acceptable to the majority of delegates. Samuel J. Gholson, representing Monroe County at Jackson, was one of the leaders of the secession movement and possessed sentiments typical of most of the members. A former state legislator, a former congressman, and at this time a Federal court judge, Gholson had supported secession in the state Democratic convention of 1860. At Jackson he was named temporary chairman of the convention and had called the convention to order before being replaced by the permanent president, William S. Barry. The judge added his own touch of drama to the convention's proceedings on January 11, the day that the delegates finally considered the Ordinance of Secession. In secret session, the delegates recognized the independence of South Carolina, then received the resignation of Gholson as a Federal judge. They then took up the Ordinance. *Photo courtesy of U.S.A.M.H.I., MOLLUS, Mass., Collection*

SAMUEL J. GHOLSON
copy print of unknown original

AMELIA GLOVER ALCORN
AND JAMES L. ALCORN
copy print of unknown-sized daguerreotype

Not all of the members of the secession convention favored immediate action by the state. Edmund Pettus determined that a minority opposed separate action, although no one favored remaining in the Union. James L. Alcorn, the representative from Coahoma County, shown in this picture with his wife circa 1851, was one of the more moderate members of the assembly. A wealthy planter, Alcorn had served in

the state legislature and had been a prominent Whig during the antebellum years. Opposition to immediate secession proved fruitless, however, and Alcorn announced his conversion to the majority's position on the roll call on Lamar's resolution. Giving his wildly applauded vote, Alcorn said, "Mr. President: I have thought that a different course in regard to the settlement of this great controversy should have been adopted, and to that end I have labored and spoken. But the die is cast—the Rubicon is crossed—and I enlist myself with the army that marches on Rome. I vote for the ordinance."[15] *Photo courtesy of Kathryn S. Vaught*

William T. S. Barry, president of the convention, hinted at the future promised by the action of the delegates in his closing address, delivered after passage of the Ordinance. The forty-year-old Barry was a native of Mississippi, the child of a prosperous planter at Columbus and a graduate of Yale College. He had been a prominent Democrat in the 1850s and had been one of the delegates who walked out of the Charleston Democratic convention in 1860. Barry and those with him had been successful in sundering the Union. He warned, "you have accomplished the work of destruction; but the courage, the thought, the wisdom, necessary to destroy are not always equal to the task of re-building. More is required in the future than has been in the past. . . . What lies before us will test the heroism, the higher, the nobler qualities of our race, inherited from revolutionary sires."[16] *Photo courtesy of M.D.A.H.*

WILLIAM T. S. BARRY
copy print of unknown original

LAMAR M. FONTAINE
copy print of unknown original

The Secession Convention's actions set off a mad celebration across the state, even though the enthusiasm of some was questionable. Governor Pettus ordered the military to prepare for immediate action. Everywhere militia companies prepared for war, and young men optimistically joined units, fearing that the war might be over before they had a chance to fight. Lamar Fontaine was typical of these young men, enrolling in Capt. Robert A. Smith's Mississippi Rifles at Jackson on March 27, 1861. Fontaine's spirit was obvious when he wrote that he had signed up for "Forty years or the War," although his unit was enlisted for only twelve months.[17] *Photo courtesy of the Old Court House Museum, Vicksburg*

Mobilization of an army required more than simple enthusiasm. Mississippi volunteers went off to battle under a variety of conditions and circumstances. Most soldiers joined companies recruited at the local level, then moved to camps around the state where the companies were placed into regiments and then into Confederate service. Pvts. Robert and Samuel Dilley from Yazoo County were typical. They enlisted in the Satartia Rifles at Satartia in April 1861. In May, this company marched to Camp Clark near Corinth, where it was organized as

Co. I of the 12th Infantry. For the next two months they were trained in military life. For many the training required a discipline they had not experienced before. A member of another regiment, the 17th Infantry, recorded in his diary that his regiment had "had the rules & regulations of the army read to us this evening." He matter-of-factly observed, "They seem very tight."[18] In July, the Dilley brothers and their regiment boarded trains and headed for the Virginia theater of battle for the duration of the war.
Photo courtesy of the J. Dale West Collection

ROBERT W. DILLEY AND SAMUEL W. DILLEY
copy print of unknown-sized ambrotype

34

JOHN FREDERICK WILSON
copy print of unknown-sized ambrotype

For some Mississippians the path to battle proved a hard one. John Wilson, a farmer from near Liberty in Amite County, joined Sam J. Nix's Liberty Guards on April 29, 1861. The company mustered into Confederate service in July and was sent to Iuka to join a regiment. The members expected to join the 20th Infantry, but arrived at camp to find it already full. Captain Nix went to Richmond and had the Guards organized as an independent company. In September they were ordered to Memphis to join the 22nd Mississippi Infantry. At some point, however, the company was transferred to the 4th Louisiana Infantry, and then to the 9th Louisiana under Col. Henry W. Allen. Wilson and the rest of the Guards served with this unit until the end of the war when the 9th surrendered at Gainesville, Alabama. *Photo courtesy of Eugene D. Wilson*

ROBERT ENOS BAKER
copy print of unknown-sized tintype

The experience of Lt. Robert Enos Baker reflected the problems military officials faced early in the war. Baker, a planter, joined the Reuben Davis Rebels near Aberdeen in November 1861 in response to a call by Governor Pettus for sixty-day volunteers to serve in Kentucky under Gen. Albert Sidney Johnston. Known as the Army of Ten Thousand, these units were to furnish their own clothing, blankets, cooking utensils, and arms. Most of them headed for Kentucky armed with double-barrelled shotguns and hunting rifles. Baker's company became Company H of William S. Patton's 5th Infantry, Army of Ten Thousand. Commanders in the field were reluctant to use these volunteers for anything but garrison duty, since they had almost no training, and Baker and his unit were assigned to the fortifications at Bowling Green. The men suffered severely from disease during the winter of 1861–62, but took no part in any fights. Baker and the others returned to be disbanded that February. In April 1862 Baker joined Co. C, 43rd Infantry. *Photo courtesy of Mrs. Sam W. Crawford*

AUSTIN A. TRESCOTT
painting

For most Mississippians the earliest focus
of the war was to protect the Mississippi
River; the second was to capture Fort
Pickens, the Federal fort at Pensacola. The
new Confederacy would have to maintain
control over the lower Mississippi River
and remove Federals from positions in
Louisiana. To assist Louisiana troops in their
capture of the arsenal at Baton Rouge and
forts on the lower Mississippi, Governor
Pettus in early January 1861 ordered local
volunteer companies to keep any hostile
forces from descending the river. Austin A.
Trescott was a member of the Vicksburg
Southrons. On January 11, these militia units
fired what may have been the first shots in
Mississippi when they forced the *O. A. Tyler*
to turn about. Trescott and others would
soon join different units—Trescott serving
during the war as a private in Co. A
(Volunteer Southrons), 21st Infantry. *Photo
courtesy of the Old Court House Museum,
Vicksburg*

On January 11, 1861, Governor Pettus moved to help the governor of Alabama capture Federal installations at Pensacola. Seven companies from throughout the state were sent. On arriving at Pensacola, they camped near Fort Barrancas and on January 17 organized a regiment under Col. Charles A. Abert. William D. Lyles was named surgeon of the regiment. Thus he became one of the earliest Mississippians to see service outside the state—even though his unit was operating as a state regiment. Officials of the new-born Confederacy desired that no action be taken against Fort Pickens. As a result, Abert's regiment saw no action and was finally mustered out in February. *Photo courtesy of the Grand Gulf Military Monument Park*

WILLIAM D. LYLES
carte de visite

In March 1861 Mississippi troops returned to Pensacola in a further effort to seize Federal installations at that port. Twenty companies were rushed to the area and encamped on Pensacola Bay at Camp Davis near Fort Barrancas. They joined a Confederate army under Gen. Braxton Bragg, and their goal was the seizure of Fort Pickens in Pensacola harbor. Among the units was Co. K, 10th Mississippi Infantry, the Port Gibson Rifles. J. D. Edwards took this picture of the men of that unit in their camp shortly after their arrival that spring. A member of the 10th Mississippi in the Vicksburg Hill City Cadets described the situation in a letter home: "The place selected for our camp is beautiful indeed—about 75 yards from the beach, in a cool, shady place. . . . We have a fine time—go bathing in the bay every day—sometimes two or three times a day—go clear out and let the waves wash us back on shore. Fish—there is no end to them; I caught seventy-five in about ten minutes this evening. Oysters, plenty at 15 cents a hundred opened."[19] *Photo courtesy of the J. Paul Getty Museum*

PORT GIBSON RIFLEMEN
salt print
J. D. Edwards

Edwards captured another image of the Port Gibson Riflemen in camp, showing their tents, weapons, and uniforms, which, other than their dress uniforms, usually amounted to the civilian clothing they had brought with them. These men immediately began constructing batteries to shell Fort Pickens. William Howard Russell found working parties composed of volunteers from Mississippi and Alabama and described them as "great long-bearded fellows in flannel shirts and slouched hats, uniformless in all save brightly burnished arms and resolute purpose."[20] *Photo courtesy of the Florida Photographic Collection, Florida State Archives*

PORT GIBSON RIFLEMEN
salt print
J. D. Edwards

ARTHUR NEWTON BULLARD
sixth-plate tintype

Arthur Newton Bullard was one of the hundreds of young Mississippians at Pensacola. He had joined his father's unit, the "Ben Bullard Rifles," later Co. B, 10th Mississippi Infantry, when it was organized in Itawamba County, and he accompanied it to Pensacola in March. In a letter on April 10, 1861, James Bullard informed his wife that their son was "on guard on the walls of the Fort[.] I think he is doing well[.] [H]e seems to be satisfied & his health is as good as it has ever been."[21] Arthur Newton was discharged shortly afterward, however, to assist his mother on their farm. *Photo courtesy of Ruth Bullard Carr*

JAMES G. BULLARD
sixth-plate tintype

Arthur Newton Bullard's father, James G., had been a farmer living five miles west of Fulton. His brother was a prominent merchant and had been a member of the Secession Convention; James G. raised the Ben Bullard Rifles in honor of his brother and was elected captain. Through the summer of 1861 he would write to his wife, informing her of the situation in Pensacola and instructing her on business matters. In one letter he touched on why he had decided to join the army, reflecting the concerns of many others who had marched away to war that spring. He wrote: "I am determined no one shall ever say your husband was a coward and I know you had rather I should serve my country when she needs my services than like a coward to stay at home & cry peace peace when the enemy is on our very border."[22] *Photo courtesy of Ruth Bullard Carr*

The Jeff Davis Rifles, Co. D, 9th Mississippi Infantry, of Holly Springs was another Mississippi unit captured by Edwards. This image was No. 26 of the thirty-eight he offered for sale in New Orleans in the spring of 1861. By May 1861 the 9th had settled down to building batteries, and one member of the regiment wrote to the Natchez newspapers: "[A]ll have learned the science of shovel and barrow pretty thoroughly. I and several others have the idea to establish ourselves as levee contractors when we return."[23] *Photo courtesy of M.D.A.H.*

JEFF DAVIS RIFLES
copy print
J. D. Edwards

Fidel E. Jordan, a twenty-six-year-old farmer from Newton County, joined the Pinckney Guards on August 12, 1861. The company became Co. B, 8th Mississippi Infantry, and was rushed to reinforce Bragg at Pensacola. By the time the 8th Infantry arrived, the place where most Mississippians thought they would first see battle had been relegated to a backwater. The 8th participated in several artillery exchanges, but little else. In August, Bragg himself had written, "We are just lying upon our oars waiting events which seem to be indefinitely postponed here by occurrences elsewhere."[24] In May 1862 the 8th and other regiments moved to Mobile, Alabama. Federal forces remained in control of Fort Pickens until the end of the war. *Photo courtesy of Lee O. Jordan*

Fidel E. Jordan
copy print of unknown-sized tintype

Chapter 3

Mississippians in the Army of Northern Virginia

By January of 1861, several of Richard Bridges' classmates at the University of Mississippi had already begun preparing themselves for military service, but he had not yet joined their ranks. For the next few months Bridges remained aloof from the activities of his friends, telling his sister that he was "of a peaceful nature," preferring to shoot squirrels rather than his Northern brothers. After the Confederate attack on Fort Sumter, war fever swept through Mississippi, and Bridges rushed to join his friends in the University Greys. By mid-May 1861, Bridges was in Virginia with the 11th Mississippi Infantry. Now his "peaceful nature" was gone. "With God and . . . right on our side we can defy the angels of the infernal regions, let alone the legions of Abraham Lincoln. With such a cause," he informed his sister, "I will fight until the frosts of three score years and ten shall whiten my locks."[1]

Bridges' thoughts were not unlike those of many young Mississippians who were suddenly caught up in the romantic ideal of war; their innocence had yet to be challenged by the grim realities of military operations in the mid-nineteenth century. They did not know that campaigning meant making long marches in the summer heat and spending cold winter nights in makeshift shelters. They did not know what it was like to be without shoes and on short rations. They could not know that over two thousand Mississippians would die fighting with the Army of Northern Virginia and that thousands of others would be disabled by horrible wounds and diseases. Like Private Bridges, most of the young Mississippians believed that the war was going to be a short, glorious adventure. That romantic ideal soon died on the battlefields of Virginia.

The first Mississippians to fight in Virginia were members of the 2nd, 11th, 13th, 17th, and 18th Mississippi Infantry regiments. On July 21, 1861, eighty-four of their number were casualties in the First Battle of Bull Run. A sixth regiment, the 19th Infantry, was also in Virginia at that time, but it did not reach the battlefield until the next day. By the end of the year the 12th, 16th, and 21st Infantry regiments, the 2nd Mississippi Battalion, several independent infantry companies, and at least three cavalry companies were also serving in the state. In 1862 a tenth unit, the 42nd Infantry, arrived from Mississippi. Early in 1863 Confederate authorities created another Mississippi regiment by consolidating the 2nd Battalion with a number of independent companies to form the 48th Mississippi Infantry. The final Mississippi regiment to serve with the Army of Northern Virginia was the 26th Infantry, which joined Lee on April 12, 1864. In addition, the Madison Light Artillery, the Confederate Guards Artillery, and the Jeff Davis Legion also saw action in Virginia. The combined strength of all these units totaled perhaps sixteen thousand men.

After First Bull Run, the Mississippians saw no more hard action until October 21, 1861, when soldiers from the 13th, 16th, and 17th regiments helped rout the Union forces at Ball's Bluff, Virginia. The Mississippi regiments remained in northern Virginia until the spring of 1862, when Gen. Joseph E. Johnston began withdrawing his forces southward to block Maj. Gen. George B. McClellan's Federal army which was landing in the Virginia Peninsula. By the end of April the 2nd, 11th, 12th, 13th, 17th, 18th, 19th, and 21st regiments, along with the 2nd Mississippi Battalion, were in the Peninsula. Meanwhile, the 16th Infantry marched to join Maj. Gen. Thomas "Stonewall" Jackson in his famous 1862 Valley Campaign.

McClellan began his long-awaited advance on May 4, 1862, only to find that Johnston's forces had retreated from their entrenchments between the Warwick River and Yorktown. The next day two Federal divisions attacked the Confederate rear guard in its entrenchments at Williamsburg. Johnston's forces managed to hold their positions, but the fight cost him 1,251 casualties,

including 141 Mississippians from the 19th Infantry and the 2nd Battalion. Johnston continued to retreat until he reached the suburbs of Richmond.

On May 31, 1862, Johnston attempted to take the offensive by striking at two isolated corps south of the Chickahominy River near Fair Oaks. All the Mississippi units were in line during the battle, but only the 12th Infantry and the 2nd Battalion suffered heavy casualties. The two units lost a total of 280 men in a series of aggressive assaults by Maj. Gen. Daniel Harvey Hill's Division.[2] The Battle of Seven Pines was indecisive, but it nevertheless had one important result: Johnston was wounded, and the next day Gen. Robert E. Lee assumed command of the army.

On June 25, 1862, Lee launched a series of punishing attacks against McClellan's forces and drove the Union army back down the Peninsula. At the beginning of the Seven Days' Campaign, there were two Mississippi brigades in the Army of Northern Virginia. The larger of the two brigades contained the 13th, 17th, 18th, and 21st Mississippi Infantry regiments. The brigade's commander was Brig. Gen. Richard Griffith, a Mississippi politician and friend of Jefferson Davis. The second Mississippi brigade contained the 12th and 19th regiments and the 2nd Mississippi Battalion. Its commander, Brig. Gen. Winfield Scott Featherston, was also a Mississippi politician with ties to the president of the Confederacy. Two Mississippi regiments, the 2nd and 11th, were brigaded together with the 4th Alabama and the 6th North Carolina. These four regiments were under the command of Col. Evander M. Law. The 16th Mississippi, which had recently returned from the Shenandoah Valley with Jackson's army, served in Brig. Gen. Isaac Trimble's brigade.

On June 27, 1862, the 2nd and 11th Mississippi regiments lost a total of 55 men killed and another 272 wounded at Gaines Mill. Featherston's brigade also fought at Gaines Mill, and they were badly mauled three days later at the Battle of Frayser's Farm. His regiments suffered 666 casualties in the two battles. Griffith's brigade was not actively engaged in the Seven Days' Campaign until June 29, 1862, when he and a few other Mississippi soldiers died at Savage's Station. Col. William Barksdale, another Mississippi politician and friend of Davis's, then assumed command of the brigade. On the evening of July 1, 1862, Barksdale's men participated in Lee's final attempt to destroy the Union army at Malvern Hill. The brigade, advancing under "a terrible fire of shell, grape, canister, and Minie balls" was shot to pieces, losing approximately 500 men before it withdrew.[3]

The Peninsular Campaign was over and Richmond was safe, but the cost had been enormous. In a week Lee's army had suffered nearly twenty thousand casualties and over fifteen hundred of these were Mississippians.[4]

Before Lee began his next campaign, he reorganized the Army of Northern Virginia and assigned all the Mississippi infantry to Maj. Gen. James Longstreet's Corps. Featherston kept the 12th and 19th regiments and the 2nd Battalion; he also received command of the 16th Mississippi, which had been in Jackson's Corps. Barksdale, who had recently been promoted to brigadier general, retained command of the 2nd Mississippi Brigade, which still contained the four regiments that had fought together in the Seven Days' Campaign. The 2nd and 11th Mississippi regiments remained in Law's brigade.

Lee, believing that McClellan was safely contained in the Union fortifications around Harrison's Landing, Virginia, detached Jackson with 24,000 men to counter a second Federal advance in northern Virginia by Maj. Gen. John Pope. After indecisive fighting at Cedar Mountain on August 9, 1862, Pope eventually fell back to the Rappahannock River. The Union command now realized the danger of dividing their forces

and ordered McClellan to withdraw from the Peninsula and unite with Pope. Lee, hoping to destroy Pope's army before McClellan came to his aid, sent Jackson on a fifty-mile flanking march to get astride Pope's line of communications at Manassas Junction. He then ordered Longstreet's 30,000-man corps to rapidly march to Jackson's aid. On the morning of August 29, 1862, Jackson's men held Pope's army at bay on the old Bull Run battlefield until Longstreet arrived. The next day Longstreet's Corps, including Featherston's and Law's brigades, struck the left flank of the Union army as it was attempting to dislodge Jackson from his positions. The Confederate assault was irresistible, and only a stubborn Union defense near Henry House Hill saved the Federals from a complete disaster. Casualties among the Mississippians amounted to only 41 killed and 295 wounded. Barksdale's brigade did not participate in the Second Battle of Bull Run.

On September 4, 1862, Lee's victorious army crossed the Potomac River and invaded Maryland. He hoped to draw the Union army out of Virginia and win a decisive battle on Union soil. One of Lee's first objectives was to open a supply route through the Shenandoah Valley by capturing the garrison at Harpers Ferry, West Virginia. On September 9, 1862, Lee gave Jackson almost half of the 55,000 men in the Army of Northern Virginia and sent him to capture the garrison. Among the troops that marched with Jackson was Maj. Gen. Lafayette McLaws' Division, which contained Barksdale's brigade. Harpers Ferry surrendered on September 15, 1862; by then Lee's weakened army was cornered, and Lee was preparing to give battle along Antietam Creek. The next day Barksdale's brigade rushed forward with the rest of McLaws' Division to rejoin the Army of Northern Virginia before it could be destroyed by vastly superior Union forces. On the long march Barksdale's men dropped out of ranks from fatigue, but approximately 900 weary Mississippians reached the battlefield at dawn on September 17, 1862.

That morning a low fog hung over the Maryland countryside as the bloodiest day of the Civil War began. The Mississippi regiments lost 852 men as the aggressive but uncoordinated Union assaults were blunted by fierce fire from the Rebels. The battle died down that evening after the combatants had suffered a total of over 26,000 casualties. Lee's army had been defeated, but it had avoided annihilation. On September 18, 1862, the battered armies watched each other, but neither side renewed the attack. That evening Lee began withdrawing his beaten army southward and eventually established a defensive position along the Rappahannock River in the vicinity of Fredericksburg, Virginia.

Shortly after the Battle of Antietam, Confederate authorities decided to form a third brigade of predominately Mississippi units. In November 1862 the 2nd and 11th regiments left Lee's army and marched to Richmond. There they were brigaded with the 42nd Mississippi Infantry and the 55th North Carolina. The 42nd Regiment, with one thousand men, had been organized in Oxford, Mississippi, in May 1862, and since July it had been training near Richmond. The commander of the new brigade was Jefferson Davis's nephew, Brig. Gen. Joseph R. Davis. On December 13, 1862, the brigade was transferred to North Carolina where they remained until they were moved back to Virginia in the spring of 1863. In June 1863 Davis's brigade joined the Army of Northern Virginia.[5]

While Davis was busily organizing his new command, the other two Mississippi brigades were entrenched at Fredericksburg awaiting attack. For weeks Barksdale's Mississippians had been digging into concealed positions in the town. On December 11, 1862, the Federals began constructing pontoon bridges across the Rappahannock River, but Barksdale's riflemen

held up their operations until that afternoon. Barksdale's men then withdrew to join Lee's main defensive line on Marye's Heights. On December 13, 1862, Maj. Gen. Ambrose Burnside threw his infantry against Lee's lines in a series of suicidal assaults that cost him more than twelve thousand casualties. Lee lost fewer than five thousand men; the casualties among the two Mississippi brigades were negligible.

In the winter of 1863 the 2nd Mississippi Battalion and several independent companies were organized as the 48th Infantry. The regiment was sent to Fredericksburg where it joined Featherston's old brigade, now commanded by Brig. Gen. Carnot Posey of Wilkinson County, Mississippi. In late April 1863 Posey's men were among the troops that Lee hastily moved eastward toward Chancellorsville to check a Union attempt to outflank the Confederate army. Barksdale's brigade and several other units remained in Fredericksburg to defend against a possible Union advance from that direction.

Lee was badly outnumbered, and the Union move toward Chancellorsville surprised him, but he quickly regained the initiative. During the first four days of May 1863, Lee used speed, daring, and surprise to tactically defeat his opponent in a series of brilliant maneuvers around Chancellorsville and Fredericksburg. Barksdale's and Posey's brigades were engaged in bitter fighting during the campaign; they were fortunate to lose only 438 men out of a total of 13,000 casualties in the Army of Northern Virginia.

Lee had won a great victory at Chancellorsville, and he was determined to once again take the offensive. By June 3, 1863, he had pulled together all the troops that could be spared from other sectors, and his army was on the move. Barksdale's Mississippians still remained in Longstreet's Corps, but Posey's brigade had been transferred to Lt. Gen. Ambrose P. Hill's Corps. Davis's brigade, which had previously been stationed near Richmond, was in Maj. Gen. Henry Heth's Division, which was also with Hill's Corps. In less than a month all three Mississippi brigades would be in a desperate fight around the little Pennsylvania town of Gettysburg.

On July 2, 1863, Barksdale's brigade participated in Longstreet's assault against the Union left. Barksdale died leading his men through the Peach Orchard. His commander, Maj. Gen. Lafayette McLaws, later remembered that he saw Barksdale "as far as the eye could follow, still ahead of his men, leading them on."[6] The brigade had mustered 1,590 men before it advanced into the Peach Orchard. When the Battle of Gettysburg ended, 569 of these soldiers were either dead or wounded. Posey's men played a minor role in Longstreet's attack; his four regiments suffered only 83 casualties in the Gettysburg Campaign.

Davis's brigade went into action on July 1, 1863, and it suffered sizeable casualties in the early fighting just west of Gettysburg. On July 3, Davis's command was one of the ten brigades that Lee assigned to attack the center of the Federal line. About 3 P.M. the battle line began moving across the open fields toward Cemetery Ridge. Within minutes the brigades were being ripped apart by Union artillery fire, but the troops re-formed ranks and moved forward. Soon the Union infantry fire added to the carnage. A few soldiers actually reached the ridge, but they were driven back, and the remnants of 12,500 assault troops streamed across the field. In three days of fighting, Davis's three Mississippi regiments lost a total of 709 men. Most of the Mississippians had died trying to storm Cemetery Ridge.

The next day both armies remained motionless—their energy spent from inflicting a total of 51,000 casualties on each other. That evening, Lee began withdrawing toward Virginia. The battle of Gettysburg had cost the eleven Mississippi regiments at least 1,361 men; the regiments could never recover from such losses.

By the first week in August, Lee had his infantry south of the Rapidan River. There he reorganized his army and replaced the six generals who had been killed at Gettysburg. Among the Mississippi brigades only Barksdale had to be replaced. Lee promoted Benjamin Humphreys, colonel of the 21st Mississippi, to the rank of brigadier general and gave him Barksdale's old command. All three Mississippi brigades remained intact and were left with their respective corps.

Despite the horrible losses at Gettysburg, Lee still felt confident in the power of the Army of Northern Virginia, enough so to detach Longstreet's Corps, including Humphreys' brigade, for service elsewhere. By September 9, 1863, the corps was pulling out of the line for its new assignment with the Army of Tennessee. Longstreet's men went on to serve at Chickamauga and Knoxville; they did not fight again with the Army of Northern Virginia until the Battle of the Wilderness in May 1864. Longstreet's nine months' service in Georgia and Tennessee cost the Mississippi regiments at least another seven hundred casualties.

The other two Mississippi brigades remained with the Army of Northern Virginia as it maneuvered against the Union forces in Central Virginia. Neither Lee nor the commander of the Army of the Potomac, Maj. Gen. George G. Meade, seemed capable of seizing the initiative during the remainder of the year. The Mississippi brigades participated in several minor actions during those months; their losses were insignificant except for the death of General Posey, who was mortally wounded at Bristoe Station.

On April 30, 1864, Lieutenant General Grant, who now commanded all the Union armies, rode over to Meade's camp. Meade walked outside, shook Grant's hand, and invited him to his quarters. There the two men sat down, lit their cigars, and began planning the campaign for the Army of the Potomac. Grant's instructions to Meade that morning were clear and unambiguous: "Wherever Lee goes, there you will go also."[7] Grant planned to use his superior manpower to batter Lee's forces into submission; the Army of Northern Virginia was still a formidable foe, but it was Grant's strategy of attrition that eventually destroyed the Confederacy's greatest army.

When Grant began his advance into the Wilderness on May 5, 1864, Humphreys' brigade of Longstreet's Corps was marching toward the battlefield and would arrive there the next day. Posey's old brigade, now commanded by Brig. Gen. Nathaniel Harris of Natchez, Mississippi, and Davis's command, which had been strengthened recently by the 26th Mississippi, were with Lee's army as it deployed for battle.

Between May 5 and June 14, 1864, the two armies mauled each other in a series of bloody battles at the Wilderness, Spotsylvania Courthouse, North Anna, and Cold Harbor. During the campaign, Grant kept trying to march around Lee's right flank; each time the Confederate commander parried the Union thrust. However, every movement took the Army of the Potomac closer to Richmond. The Mississippi regiments suffered at least fourteen hundred casualties in the campaign. On June 14, 1864, Grant finally broke off contact with Lee's army and managed to cross the James River before Lee could react. By June 15, 1864, Grant was south of Richmond at Petersburg, and he finally had Lee's army pinned down.

For the next nine months, two of the three Mississippi brigades remained in their positions along the Richmond-Petersburg line. In July 1864 Humphreys' brigade was detached and sent to the Shenandoah Valley to reinforce Lt. Gen. Jubal Early's Corps. Early hoped to repeat Jackson's 1862 exploits, but his command was practically destroyed at Cedar Creek on October 19, 1864.

Humphreys had been seriously wounded prior to the battle, and his brigade was now commanded by Col. William F. Fitzgerald. The survivors of Early's Corps returned to Richmond in December 1864, and the Mississippi brigade, which now numbered less than eight hundred effectives, entered the defenses.

On April 2, 1865, Grant finally broke through the Richmond-Petersburg line, and Lee began his final retreat. On April 8, 1865, Lee's small army was cornered near Appomattox Court House. The next morning Lee attempted to break out of the trap; when the attack failed he decided to surrender. On April 12, 1865, the remaining soldiers of twelve Mississippi regiments stacked arms with the rest of the Army of Northern Virginia. The Mississippians numbered only 698 officers and men.

Private Bridges' old company, the University Greys, had proudly marched off to war in the spring of 1861 with 136 men. At Appomattox, only one soldier from the company remained in the ranks. Bridges, who had vowed to fight for three score and ten years, had been dead for almost a year when the lone soldier of the University Greys surrendered. On May 5, 1864, a Minié ball had struck Bridges in the left leg. The next morning the surgeon amputated the mangled limb, and Bridges was in agony until his death on June 2, 1864. Louisa Smith, who had helped nurse the wounded soldiers, wrote Bridges' sister to tell her about his death. "He was," she wrote, ". . . fast sinking. As I sat by him he opened his eyes and said 'Oh Mrs. Smith as I slept I dreamed I saw my Mother . . .'" Louisa was not there when Bridges died, but, she noted, "the nurse told me he passed away peacefully being unconscious for some hours preceeding [sic] his death."[8] Many Mississippi families had received such sad news from Virginia during the war. Those few Mississippians who had survived to surrender with Lee now began the long trek home.

DEWITT CLINTON FARMER
copy print from *Confederate Veteran,*
Vol. VII (April 1899)

Twenty-three-year-old Dewitt Clinton
Farmer was single and farming when he
decided to join the Noxubee Rifles on April
25, 1861. The unit became Co. F of the 11th
Mississippi Infantry, and Farmer's regiment
was one of the first Mississippi units to reach
Virginia. At the First Battle of Bull Run,
on July 21, 1861, Brig. Gen. Bernard Bee's
brigade contained the 4th Alabama, the 2nd
Mississippi, and companies A and F of the
11th Mississippi Infantry.

Early in the battle, the green Confederate
troops broke under attack and streamed
back toward Henry House Hill. There Brig.
Gen. Thomas Jackson had established a new
defensive line. Bee, attempting to stop the
retreating Confederates, urged them to rally
on Henry House Hill, exclaiming, "There
stands Jackson like a stone wall." Bee's words
gave Jackson the sobriquet "Stonewall," but
more important, the reassuring presence
of fresh troops calmed the frightened
Confederates. They began falling into line of
battle. Around 2 P.M. nearly 10,000 Union
troops tried to storm the hill. The fighting
raged until about 4 P.M. when the disorganized Union infantry panicked and began
heading toward Washington. Bee died in
the initial assault on Henry House Hill, and
his brigade suffered 421 casualties. Farmer
escaped injury, but the two companies from
the 11th Mississippi had 28 men wounded in
the fighting.

JOHN R. MOORE
copy print

Pvt. John R. "Soker" Moore's regiment, the 17th Mississippi Infantry, also fought at First Bull Run. However, Moore, like many of his fellow soldiers, was ill when the battle took place. Almost as soon as the 17th arrived in Virginia, measles swept through its ranks. Moore contracted the disease, and by June 24, 1861, he was seriously ill with an infected spleen. The surgeon recommended that Moore be discharged and sent home. His father, Austin E. Moore, traveled to Virginia to get his son. "Pa brought me nothing," complained Soker's brother, Pvt. Robert A. Moore, "but a bottle of whiskey." On Wednesday, August 21, 1861, Soker and his father left for Mississippi. "I hated to see them leave," remarked his brother.[9]

Few troops from rural areas such as Mississippi had been exposed to communicable diseases as children. With proper care, measles was not usually fatal, but the disease was dangerous to troops living in cramped conditions with only rudimentary medical services. Most of the young soldiers who contracted measles in the first months of the war recovered and returned to their units, but some, such as Pvt. John Moore, were disabled and had to be discharged from the army. *Photo courtesy of the Museum of the Confederacy, Richmond; original owned by Mrs. Peel Cannon*

WILLIAM F. PARKS
copy print

William F. Parks was forty-four years old when he enlisted as the second sergeant in the Confederate Guards, which became Co. G of the 17th Mississippi Infantry. After the First Battle of Bull Run the regiment went into camp at Leesburg, Virginia. The boredom of camp life often led to gambling, drinking, and occasional fights among soldiers. On the morning of August 22, 1861, several men in Co. G had to break up a fight between Parks and another soldier.[10]

About 4:30 P.M. on October 21, 1861, Parks' regiment received orders to march to the support of Confederate forces that were engaging a Union brigade at Ball's Bluff. The 17th Mississippi made the two-mile march in about twenty minutes and quickly deployed alongside two other regiments. The line then advanced and drove the Union brigade back toward a seventy-foot bluff overlooking the Potomac River. The seventeen-hundred-man Federal brigade lost more than nine hundred men in the battle. Among the dead was the brigade's commander, Col. Edward D. Baker. Parks' regiment lost only eleven men.

The battle was strategically insignificant. However, Baker was still a U.S. Senator; his death, coupled with the second humiliating defeat in Virginia, outraged the Radical Republicans in Congress. On December 20, 1861, Congress created the Committee on the Conduct of the War. Its members would spend much of their time attacking both Lincoln's war policies and the Democratic generals that he promoted. *Photo courtesy of Richard F. Carlile*

George W. King was only nineteen years old when he enlisted as a private in the Raymond Fencibles. The Hinds County unit became Co. C of the 12th Mississippi Infantry, and the regiment was en route to Virginia at the time of the First Battle of Bull Run. King remained with his company until January 1862 when he extended his enlistment for two years. He received a fifty-dollar bounty and a two-month furlough for reenlisting. King was on furlough when Maj. Gen. George B. McClellan began landing troops on the Virginia Peninsula in March 1862. Gen.

Joseph E. Johnston countered McClellan's slow advance by constructing a series of entrenchments that ran across the Peninsula from Yorktown to the Warwick River. In April, King rejoined his regiment in the Yorktown-Warwick River defenses. The 12th Mississippi had yet to see any action when Private King died at Yorktown from disease on April 12, 1862. On May 4, 1862, McClellan finally advanced against Johnston, who withdrew without a fight and retreated toward Richmond. *Photo courtesy of the Old Court House Museum, Vicksburg*

GEORGE W. KING
copy print

MARION B. HARRIS
copy print

At the beginning of the Civil War, many Southerners such as Marion B. Harris of Warren County, Mississippi, proudly wore a red, white, and blue cockade to symbolize their support of the new Confederacy. In Europe these cloth loops had originally been used to pin or "cock" up the side of a hat, but the rosettes soon became fashionable as a party badge. During the French Revolution, supporters of the new order adopted the red, white, and blue cockade as one of their symbols, and French soldiers wore the tricolor badge when they conquered most of Europe. To young men like Harris the cockade symbolized both their support of the secession movement and their hopes for its ultimate victory.

On May 3, 1861, Harris enrolled in the Warren Rifles, and he became second lieutenant of the unit. At Richmond, Virginia, Harris and his fellow soldiers were accepted into the Confederate army as Co. C, 19th Mississippi Infantry.

On May 5, 1862, the leading elements of McClellan's army clashed at Williamsburg, Virginia, with Johnston's rear guard. Harris and five hundred other men of the 19th Mississippi were deployed behind a rail fence when the fighting began. The Confederates held their position throughout the day and withdrew that evening in good order. Fifteen men from the 19th Mississippi were killed at Williamsburg, and another eighty-five soldiers were wounded. Harris was not hurt, and his commander complimented him for his performance during the regiment's first major engagement. *Photo courtesy of Dale Snair*

ELI PEEL
carte de visite

McClellan cautiously followed the retreating Rebels, and by May 23, 1862, his forward elements could see the church spires in Richmond. Johnston now had no choice except to try to drive the enemy back before the capital of the Confederacy fell, and on May 31, 1862, he attacked two Union corps that were temporarily isolated south of the Chickahominy River.

Eli Peel joined the 11th Mississippi at Okolona, and he had recently been promoted to first sergeant of Co. C. His regiment was part of Brig. Gen. William Henry Chase Whiting's Division. Johnston's attack almost immediately broke down as unclear marching orders snarled the advancing troops. Whiting's Division did not get into action until 4 P.M., some three hours after four Rebel brigades had already begun fighting on his right. Fresh Federal troops checked Whiting's attack and wounded Sergeant Peel. Intermittent fighting continued the next day, but Johnston had failed to win a victory at Seven Pines.

Johnston himself was wounded about the time that Peel fell, and Gen. Robert E. Lee assumed command of the Army of Northern Virginia. Lee was determined to attack as soon as possible, and he set about organizing an offensive. *Photo courtesy of Margaret Ann Peel*

WILLIAM THOMPSON MARTIN
half-plate ambrotype

Lee wanted to attack McClellan north of the Chickahominy River, but he needed accurate information about the disposition of Union troops in that sector. He was especially interested in knowing if the Union's right flank was vulnerable and if the main Federal supply depot at White House on the Pamunkey River was secure. On June 12, 1862, Lee sent Brig. Gen. J. E. B. Stuart and 1,000 cavalry troopers on a raid to gather that information. Lt. Col. William T. Martin, a Natchez lawyer, led one of the three detachments in Stuart's command. Martin handpicked 250 men from his cavalry regiment, the Jeff Davis Legion, for the expedition. During the next four days, Stuart's column, in perhaps the most famous raid of the Civil War, covered 150 miles as the cavalrymen rode completely around McClellan's army. Martin's troopers protected the rear of the column. There they gathered up prisoners captured by their comrades and completed "the destruction of the enemy's property commenced by those in advance . . ."[11]

The raid confirmed Lee's belief that he could attack McClellan's right flank, but it also caused the Federal commander to relocate his supply line to Harrison's Landing near Malvern Hill. Lee began his offensive north of the Chickahominy River on June 25, 1862. *Photo courtesy of George Esker*

William Whiting of Biloxi, Mississippi, graduated from West Point in 1845, and his grades were better than all the cadets who had preceded him at the academy. Whiting was posted to the engineering corps, which was considered the elite branch of the army. He spent most of his antebellum military career supervising river improvements and building fortifications. Whiting entered the Confederate service as a major of engineers, but he was almost immediately promoted to brigadier general and given command of an infantry division.

Whiting's division was north of the Chickahominy River, but it saw only limited action at Mechanicsville on June 26, 1862, when Lee's first attack misfired. On June 27, heavy fighting began about 2 P.M. near Gaines Mill, but Whiting's Division did not begin deploying until two hours later. Whiting found Confederate troops retreating all around him as he sent his two brigades forward to assault the enemy. Whiting's men scrambled through the brush, crossed a ditch in front of the Federal positions, and lunged headlong into the Union breastworks. The charge cracked the Union defenses, and the Federals began withdrawing. In three hours of fighting Whiting's two brigades suffered 1,016 casualties, but he had made a significant contribution to the Confederate victory at Gaines Mill. *Photo courtesy of the Library of Congress, no. B8171-3241*

JOHN HOLMES
copy print from Luke W. Conerly,
Pike County Mississippi, 1798–1876

John Holmes mustered into the Confederate service as a private at Holmesville, Mississippi, on April 23, 1861. His unit, the Quitman Guards, became Co. E of the 16th Mississippi Infantry, and on April 26, 1862, Holmes was elected lieutenant of his company.

Holmes's regiment was the only Mississippi command that fought with Stonewall Jackson in his celebrated 1862 Shenandoah Valley Campaign. On April 30, 1862, the 16th Mississippi joined Jackson in the valley and subsequently helped tie down thousands of Federal troops that McClellan needed in the Peninsula. On June 17, Jackson broke off contact with the enemy and began moving eastward to reinforce the Army of Northern Virginia.

On June 27, 1862, the 16th Mississippi fought at Gaines Mill as part of Brig. Gen. Isaac Trimble's brigade. Trimble began his final advance during the waning minutes of the battle. He could hear other retreating Southerners crying "You need not go in; we are whipped; you can't do anything." Some of Trimble's men shouted for the beaten soldiers to "Get out of our way; we will show you how to do it." The brigade supported Whiting's successful attack. Trimble praised the 16th Mississippi and the 21st North Carolina for their "intrepid bravery and high resolve" during the final charge.[12] In fifteen minutes, the two units lost eighty-five men. Holmes was wounded during the attack and remained hospitalized until July 13, 1862.

WILLIAM HENRY CHASE WHITING
copy print

JOSEPH C. WHITE
sixth-plate ambrotype

Early in 1861 Joseph C. White lived in Woodville, Mississippi, where he was a musician in the Woodville Republicans. On March 5, 1862, he mustered into state service as a private in the Natchez Fencibles. One month later the militia company transferred to the Confederate army as Co. B of the 12th Mississippi Infantry. The regiment organized at Corinth, and it is likely that this picture was taken there. White's accoutrements and the placard "Jeff Davis and the South" appear in at least six other photographs. White apparently had no desire to be an infantryman, and on April 22, 1862, the colonel of the 12th Mississippi wrote President Davis to ask for White to be made principal musician of the regiment.

The 12th Infantry was part of Featherston's Mississippi brigade, and before Davis's reply reached White, the men were ordered into combat. Featherston's regiments suffered heavy casualties at the Battle of Gaines Mill on June 27, 1862. Three days later they were again engaged at Frayser's Farm. The two days' fighting cost the 12th Mississippi 225 casualties, but White was uninjured. On July 1, 1862, he received his transfer to the regimental band.[13] *Photo courtesy of the Northeast Mississippi Museum Association, Corinth; original owned by Frank Johnson*

Third Lt. William P. Smith, a merchant from Ponotoc, Mississippi, had joined the New Albany Greys when he was thirty-five years old. The Greys became Co. K of the 21st Mississippi Infantry. Smith's regiment arrived in Virginia in the summer of 1861, and it was first engaged in heavy fighting at the Battle of Seven Pines. There the 21st Mississippi had 41 men killed and another 152 soldiers wounded.

On the morning of July 1, 1862, Smith's company was deployed in front of Malvern Hill, which was occupied by thousands of Union infantry and over one hundred artillery pieces. Throughout the morning the Southern regiments arrived in piecemeal fashion. About 3 P.M. a single Rebel brigade began advancing, but they were quickly pinned down. A little more than an hour later 5,000 more Confederates were fed into the assault, but they too were stopped cold. About 6:30 P.M. Barksdale's Mississippians, which included the 21st Infantry, began advancing with seven other brigades in Lee's last attempt to crush the Federals on Malvern Hill. A devastating sheet of "grape shot, canister, and small-arms" fire engulfed the 21st Mississippi Infantry as it made two attempts to storm Malvern Hill.[14] The regiment, like all the other Southern units, was driven back with bloody losses. In less than an hour the 21st Mississippi lost 106 men, but Smith was unharmed. *Photo courtesy of the Museum of the Confederacy, Richmond; original owned by the Library of Congress*

WILLIAM P. SMITH
copy print

WILLIAM S. PATTON, JR.
carte de visite

William S. Patton, Jr., chose to serve in a Louisiana unit even though he was the son of a prominent politician from Marion, Mississippi. Patton grew up in Lauderdale County, Mississippi, and later graduated from Baltimore Dental College. He then moved to Homer, Louisiana, to begin his practice. On May 1, 1861, Patton became an officer in the 2nd Louisiana Infantry, which may well have included more soldiers from different states and countries than any other unit in the Confederate army. During the war 1,297 soldiers joined the 2nd Louisiana; at least 655 of these men listed their birthplace as another state, and an additional 102 men were foreign-born.

The 2nd Louisiana arrived in Virginia during the spring of 1861; and, even though Patton liked the Louisianans, he decided to seek a transfer to a Mississippi regiment. On May 12, 1862, Patton wrote his mother and asked her to contact his father, William S. Patton, Sr., who was then an officer in the 37th Mississippi. He hoped that the elder Patton could use his influence to get him transferred to that regiment.[15] Patton was shot and killed at Malvern Hill before the transfer could be arranged. Twenty-nine of his comrades in the 2nd Louisiana also died there, and another 152 were wounded. It was the largest loss in any of Lee's regiments at Malvern Hill. The Seven Days' Campaign ended with a defeat at Malvern Hill, but Lee's aggressive offensive had saved Richmond. *Photo courtesy of Dale Snair*

WALTER SCOTT BUFORD
copy print from Thomas P. Buford, comp.,
*Lamar Rifles, a History of Company G,
Eleventh Mississippi Regiment, C.S.A.*

After the Seven Days' Campaign, Lee sent
Jackson northward with twenty-four thou-
sand troops to deal with a second Union
army under the command of Maj. Gen. John
Pope. In a series of swift marches, Jackson
destroyed Pope's supply depot at Manassas
Junction and then fell back on the old Bull
Run battlefield. There he had to hold the
Federals until he could be reinforced by
thirty thousand troops under Major General
Longstreet. On August 29, 1862, Jackson
battled the Federals to a standstill; that after-
noon the leading elements of Longstreet's
Corps began arriving on the field.

Pvt. Walter Scott Buford was with Co. G,
11th Mississippi Infantry, when it went into
action that evening. Buford was a nineteen-
year-old student living in College Hill,
Mississippi, when he joined the Lamar Rifles
on August 9, 1861. Buford saw his first action
during the 1862 Peninsular Campaign.

On the evening of August 29, 1862, his
brigade, after "delivering volley after volley"
against a Union battery, overran the position
and captured one of the pieces.[16] The next
day Buford was mortally wounded during
Longstreet's crushing assault against the left
flank of the Union army. Twenty-one other
Mississippians from the regiment perished
with Buford, and another eighty-seven were
wounded during the two days' fighting.

Thomas H. Chilton
copy print from J. Harvey Mathes,
The Old Guard in Grey

The spectacular victory at Second Bull Run opened the way for Lee's first invasion of the North. On September 4, 1862, Lee crossed into Maryland with 55,000 veteran soldiers. One of the men that marched with the Army of Northern Virginia was Pvt. Thomas Chilton.

When the war began, Chilton was a nineteen-year-old sophomore at the University of Mississippi. The company that Chilton eventually joined, the Lamar Rifles, consisted largely of students at Oxford, Mississippi. Young Chilton delayed joining the army because he had been elected by his classmates to speak at the summer commencement. However, the enthusiasm for the war among the students was so great that most had already joined the army; graduation was accordingly suspended. Chilton finally joined the Lamar Rifles, which was now Co. G of the 11th Mississippi Infantry, at Bristoe Station, on August 9, 1861. He had most likely traveled to Virginia with Walter Scott Buford. Chilton was with the 11th Mississippi when elements of the Army of Northern Virginia reached Hagerstown, Maryland. There the quartermaster managed to procure a few badly needed shoes for the troops. The department issued only two pair to Co. G and Chilton, whose feet were bleeding, was fortunate enough to secure new footwear. He slipped on the oversized shoes and continued on the march that eventually led to Antietam, where he was wounded.[17]

Joseph A. Taylor was twenty-two years old when he enrolled in William Lowry's company at Oxford, Mississippi. The unit quickly became known as the University Greys, because it was made up almost entirely of students. On December 18, 1861, Taylor was elected second lieutenant of the University Greys, which subsequently became Co. A, 11th Mississippi Infantry.

On the morning of September 17, 1862, the 11th Mississippi was part of Brig. Gen. John B. Hood's Division that fought near Dunker Church on the Antietam battlefield. Hood's two brigades were attacked by "an immense force of the enemy, consisting of not less than two corps" of Federal troops. "It was here," wrote Hood, "that I witnessed the most terrible clash of arms, by far, that has occurred during the war." The battle raged until the afternoon as Hood's brigades held their positions against heavy odds. The 11th Mississippi suffered 104 casualties at Antietam, including Lieutenant Taylor. On March 10, 1863, Taylor wrote Confederate authorities and tendered his resignation "on account of the loss of my left arm."[18] *Photo courtesy of M.D.A.H.*

Joseph L. Taylor
copy print

65

Twenty-one-year-old John C. Lowe was farming in Lauderdale County, Mississippi, when the Civil War began. He enlisted on March 23, 1861, in the Alumutcha Infantry, which mustered into the Confederate service as Co. E, 13th Mississippi Infantry.

A week before the Battle of Antietam, Lee detached McLaws' Division, which included the 13th Mississippi, to help Stonewall Jackson capture Harpers Ferry. On September 15, 1862, the 13th Mississippi took light casualties when Jackson forced the surrender of the Union garrison. The next day McLaws received orders for the division to move rapidly to support Lee's outnumbered army at Antietam Creek. McLaws' men were fatigued and had had no sleep for twenty-four hours, but they took up the march. The division reached Lee's beleaguered forces on the morning of September 17, 1862. McLaws' Division had been so weakened by stragglers that he did not have enough men to make "a continuous line." Nevertheless, they stood their ground against "lines of the enemy apparently double and treble" with supporting artillery. McLaws held his ground, but the division suffered 1,119 casualties.[19] Lowe's left arm was shattered during the fighting, and he was left behind when Lee retreated on the evening of September 18, 1862. The arm had to be amputated, and Lowe was discharged from service on April 12, 1863. *Photo courtesy of Richard F. Carlile*

Twenty-three-year-old William Lowe, like his younger brother, John, was farming in Lauderdale County when the war began. He, too, mustered into Co. E, 13th Mississippi Infantry, on March 23, 1861. Prior to Antietam, William had seen action at First Bull Run, Ball's Bluff, Frayser's Farm, and Malvern Hill. His regiment suffered 148 casualties in the four battles.

Hundreds of exhausted soldiers dropped out of the ranks of the 13th Mississippi as it marched from Harpers Ferry to Antietam. On September 17, 1862, the regiment took only 202 men into battle. William Lowe was not hurt during the fight, but his regiment lost 62 men. He survived five major battles, only to die of dysentery in a Richmond hospital on December 7, 1862.

A third Lowe brother, George W., enrolled in Co. E, 13th Mississippi Infantry, on November 5, 1862. The eighteen-year-old farmer served with the regiment until his capture near Petersburg on April 6, 1865. The youngest Lowe was described by his commander as "a splendid soldier."[20] *Photo courtesy of Richard F. Carlile*

66

The bloody battles of the summer and fall of 1862 drove home the horrors of **war to** many heretofore enthusiastic young soldiers. Thomas Fondren McKie was only sixteen years old when he joined the University Greys on March 1, 1862. On the evening before he enlisted, McKie's mother cried and pleaded with him to withdraw his name, but McKie would not do it. Throughout the summer of 1862 he campaigned with Co. A of the 11th Mississippi Infantry. By the fall McKie was suffering from diarrhea and regretted his rash decision to join the army. "Mother," he wrote, "I want you to write to President Davis to get me off; say to him that I joined contrary to your will and that I am a minor and that you desire me at home and are compelled to have me." He begged her to "do it immediately."[21] McKie's plea went unheeded, and he remained with his regiment. McKie was later mortally wounded at Gettysburg and died on October 16, 1863.

THOMAS FONDREN McKIE
copy print from Maud Morrow Brown,
The University Greys

WILLIAM D. LOWE
sixth-plate tintype

After the defeat at Antietam, Lee's army occupied positions around Fredericksburg, Virginia, on the south bank of the Rappahannock River. Since November 25, 1862, Pvt. Robert Moore of Co. G, 17th Mississippi, and most of Barksdale's brigade had been in the village, guarding against any Union attempt to cross the river. The weather was bitterly cold, and on December 6 a soft layer of snow fell on the shivering Confederates. The ill-clad men gathered around their fires trying to stay warm.

On the morning of December 11, 1862, a heavy fog hung over the river as the Federals began throwing pontoon bridges across the stream. Moore's regiment fired on the soldiers from concealed positions in houses. Federal artillery blasted the buildings, but the gunners could not dislodge the Mississippi sharpshooters. Finally Union volunteers crossed the stream in boats and drove the defenders out. About 8 P.M. Moore's regiment withdrew to the main Confederate line on Marye's Heights. Eight men of the regiment had been killed; eight were wounded; and thirty-four were missing. On December 12, Moore waited in line "expecting the ball to open tomorrow." He was not disappointed. On December 13, 1862, Burnside ordered attack after attack against the entrenched Confederates. By the end of the day over six thousand Union casualties littered the front slopes of Marye's Heights. Moore's unit had thirteen more men wounded in the fighting on December 13.[22] *Photo courtesy of the Museum of the Confederacy, Richmond; original owned by Lois C. Benton*

CARNOT POSEY
copy print

Lee had won an easy victory at Fredericksburg, and the new Federal commander, Maj. Gen. Joe Hooker, had no desire to repeat the mistakes of his predecessor. He planned to leave a covering force to distract Lee and then move the bulk of the Union army upriver. If all worked well, Hooker would cross the fords without Lee knowing it and swoop down on the flank of the unsuspecting Confederates.

Brig. Gen. Carnot Posey, of Wilkinson County, Mississippi, a Mexican War veteran and ex-U.S. Attorney, commanded a brigade of Mississippians that watched the fords above Fredericksburg. On April 29, 1863, he learned that the Union army was crossing in strength. Posey reported the information to his superiors and withdrew to the vicinity of Chancellorsville.

Lee now understood the intent of Hooker's movement, and he began deploying his forces to meet the new threat. On May 2, 1863, Posey's brigade helped hold the Union army in place, while Jackson took twenty-six thousand men on a long march around the right of the Federal army. By twilight he was behind the right flank of Hooker's men. About 6 P.M. Jackson slammed into the unsuspecting Federals, and the entire right flank crumbled. The next day Posey's brigade joined in the advance, pushing "through a dense wood and over a wide abatis and into the trenches of the enemy, driving him off with much slaughter and capturing many prisoners."[23]
Photo courtesy of the Museum of the Confederacy, Richmond

WALTER W. ADAMS
copy print

While Posey led his men to victory, Barksdale's brigade fought for its life a few miles away at Fredericksburg. When Lee decided to concentrate against the Union forces near Chancellorsville, he stripped the Fredericksburg defenses of everything but one division and Barksdale's four Mississippi regiments. Pvt. Walter Adams was with Barksdale's brigade in Co. A, 21st Mississippi Infantry, during the fight for Fredericksburg.

Adams was twenty years old when he joined the Volunteer Southrons on May 15, 1861. Most of the men were from Vicksburg, Mississippi. Private Adams went on to fight at Malvern Hill, Antietam, and Fredericksburg. The three battles cost his regiment a total of 214 men.

On May 3, 1863, Barksdale held a three-mile front; the 21st and 18th Mississippi were deployed on Marye's Heights. At daylight the Federals began attacking, and Barksdale's men repulsed two assaults. Around 8 A.M. twenty-six thousand men began moving toward his positions. The Mississippians stopped two of the columns, but the third force broke into their positions on Marye's Heights. There the men "resisted to the death with clubbed guns."[24] Barksdale's men retreated to the crest of Lee's Hill where they waited for another attack. It never came; the next morning the Union forces withdrew across the Rappahannock River. Adams was not hurt, but his regiment lost twenty-eight men in the defense of Marye's Heights.
Photo courtesy of the Old Court House Museum, Vicksburg

Lee had won his greatest tactical victory at Chancellorsville, and he began preparing for a second invasion of the North. By mid-June 1863 Lee's army of seventy-six thousand confident veterans was moving down the Shenandoah Valley toward Pennsylvania. Pvt. Joseph T. Steele of Senatobia, Mississippi, was with Co. B, 42nd Infantry, as his unit marched through the rolling Pennsylvania countryside. His unit was part of Maj. Gen. Henry Heth's Division.

Early on July 1, 1863, two of Heth's four brigades received orders to investigate reported Union activity in the small town of Gettysburg. Two miles from the town the brigades ran into Union infantry. At approximately 10:30 A.M. the 42nd Mississippi, along with the rest of Brig. Gen. Joseph Davis's brigade, began advancing toward the enemy. The Federals put up a stubborn resistance; they were driven from the field but fell back to a stronger position along a railroad embankment. Davis's brigade drove into the second Union position and again forced the enemy to retreat. However, the Confederates themselves were soon flanked by a large body of infantry. Every effort was made to withdraw the brigade, but Steele and a number of other soldiers were captured. Later that evening Heth's two brigades were reinforced, and the Rebels fought their way into the suburbs of Gettysburg. There the exhausted men rested. The first day of the Battle of Gettysburg was drawing to a close. *Photo courtesy of Harvey B. Steele and Edna Lee Sullivan*

WILLIAM BARKSDALE
albumen print

Before the Civil War William Barksdale was editor of the Columbus (Mississippi) *Democrat* and a member of the U.S. Congress. Barksdale used both platforms to vehemently defend states' rights, and he was pleased when Mississippi left the Union. Barksdale was later appointed colonel of the 13th Infantry and led his regiment at First Bull Run. After the death of Richard Griffith on June 29, 1862, he assumed command of the brigade. Barksdale then led his Mississippians at Malvern Hill, Antietam, Fredericksburg, and Chancellorsville. His leadership was exemplary, and the brigade earned a reputation as a hard-fighting unit.

On July 2, 1863, Lee ordered a general attack against the left wing of the Federal army. Barksdale's brigade was deployed near a peach orchard, and he was impatient to advance; the men shared Barksdale's enthusiasm as they waited in the ranks. About 5 P.M. Barksdale received orders to move forward. The general, mounted at the head of the brigade, removed his hat, uncovering his long white hair, and ordered the Mississippians forward. Barksdale fell mortally wounded while leading his men in the Peach Orchard.

J. C. Lloyd of the 13th Mississippi was later crossing the deserted orchard when he heard someone crying weakly for water. Lloyd found the stricken general; he tried to slake Barksdale's thirst, but the water poured out through a bullet hole in the dying Mississippian's mouth.[25] *Photo courtesy of U.S.A.M.H.I., MOLLUS, Mass., Collection*

Pvt. Billy Blake of Holmes County, Mississippi, arrived on the Gettysburg battlefield with Co. C, 18th Mississippi Infantry, a little after dark on July 1, 1863. His regiment was part of Barksdale's brigade. On July 2, Blake and the other Mississippians advanced into the Peach Orchard; it was held by eleven Union regiments and three artillery batteries. In places the Federals fought from behind stone walls and buildings. The battle was bitter and often hand-to-hand, but Barksdale's Mississippians drove the defenders back and followed them into a wheatfield. However, the attack finally stalled, and the Rebels were forced back into the Peach Orchard.

Barksdale's Mississippi brigade lost 791 of 1,590 soldiers in the battle. Their losses were the heaviest of that day's fighting and were also the fourth largest number of casualties of any Confederate brigade that fought at Gettysburg. The 18th Mississippi mustered 350 men before it advanced into the Peach Orchard; the infantry lost 134 men in the fight.

When Lee's beaten army withdrew on July 5, 1863, 224 of Barksdale's wounded were left behind. One of these men was Private Blake, whose leg was later amputated at the hip by Union surgeons.

JOSEPH R. DAVIS
albumen print

Joseph R. Davis of Woodville, Mississippi, began his military career on January 31, 1861, as captain of the Madison Rifles. Davis's men mustered into the Confederate army on April 14, 1861, as Co. I, 10th Mississippi Infantry; he became lieutenant colonel of the regiment. On August 31, 1861, Davis was promoted to colonel and assigned as aide-de-camp to his uncle, President Jefferson Davis. In the summer of 1862 the president nominated his nephew for brigadier general, but the Senate, amidst cries of nepotism, rejected the nomination. However, the president finally prevailed, and on September 15, 1862, his nephew's promotion was approved.

Davis was given command of a new brigade which contained the 2nd, 11th, and 42nd Mississippi regiments and the 55th North Carolina Infantry. Many of the men were veterans, but Davis, despite having served in the army for over two years, had seen almost no combat. His inexperience was evident on July 1, 1863, when two of his regiments were mauled at the Gettysburg railroad embankment. On July 3, 1863, Lee, having previously failed to turn the Union flanks, decided to launch a massive assault against the Federal center. Davis's brigade had suffered significant casualties two days earlier, but it was nevertheless part of the twelve thousand troops assigned to attack the center of the Federal line. *Photo courtesy of U.S.A.M.H.I., MOLLUS, Mass., Collection*

Jeremiah Gage, a native of Richland, Mississippi, was a twenty-one-year-old student at the University of Mississippi when he joined the University Greys. The unit became Co. A, 11th Mississippi Infantry; Gage subsequently fought at First Bull Run, Seven Pines, and Gaines Mill.

On July 3, 1863, Corporal Gage was with Davis's brigade as the men waited in a line of trees on Seminary Ridge. Around 2 P.M. approximately 160 Rebel artillery pieces began shelling the center of the Union line. Dozens of Union guns on Cemetery Ridge returned the fire. Gage was lying on the ground waiting for the order to advance when he was struck by an artillery fragment. The mortally wounded soldier was taken to the rear. Before Gage died, he wrote his mother the following letter:

This is the last you may ever hear from me. I have time to tell you that I died like a man. Bear my loss as best you can. Remember that I am true to my country and my greatest regret at dying is that she is not free and you and my sisters are robbed of my worth whatever that may be. I hope this will reach you and you must not regret that my body can not be obtained. It is a mere matter of form anyhow. This is for my sisters too as I can not write more. Send my dying release to Miss Mary . . .

At the bottom of the page he added, "This letter is stained with my blood."[26] Gage was one of the first Mississippians to die in the most famous charge of the Civil War. *Photo courtesy of Archives and Special Collections, John Davis Williams Library, University of Mississippi, Oxford*

JEREMIAH GAGE
copy print

HENRY DAVENPORT
quarter-plate ambrotype

Henry Davenport of Jacinto, Mississippi, mustered into the Tishomingo Riflemen on April 30, 1861. Davenport was a twenty-five-year-old college student at the time of his enlistment. The Tishomingo Riflemen became Co. A of the 2nd Mississippi Infantry, and the regiment arrived in Virginia in May of 1861. On July 12, 1861, Davenport was promoted to second lieutenant. Nine days later the 2nd Mississippi lost 107 men at First Bull Run; it is doubtful that Davenport participated in the battle, since he had been detached as a recruiting officer. Davenport was not recommissioned when the regiment reorganized on April 22, 1862, so he returned to Mississippi. On May 14, 1862, he was elected captain of Co. E, 42nd Mississippi Infantry. The regiment, with over one thousand men, arrived in Richmond, Virginia, on July 2, 1862.

Captain Davenport's company went into the Battle of Gettysburg on July 1, 1863, with forty-two men; only seven soldiers remained in the ranks that evening. The rest were casualties in the fighting around the railroad embankment. Around 3 P.M. on July 3, Captain Davenport led the seven men out of the woods on Seminary Ridge.[27] There the assaulting brigades stopped and carefully aligned their ranks. The mile-long line then began moving toward Cemetery Ridge. Davenport was badly wounded during the charge and was subsequently captured by the Union army. Only two of his men returned with the beaten Confederates. Davenport died two weeks later in a Federal hospital. *Photo courtesy of Margaret Rogers*

Pvt. Adoniram J. Farmer was an eighteen-year-old student when he joined the Noxubee Rifles on April 25, 1861. His outfit became Co. F, 11th Mississippi Infantry. Farmer and his brother, Dewitt, (see p. 51) had fought at First Bull Run almost two years earlier, and on July 3, 1863, they marched together toward the waiting enemy. The regiment came under a crushing artillery fire when it was about halfway to Cemetery Ridge; the men closed ranks and continued forward. Soon rifle fire began taking its toll, but the soldiers continued to advance. Miraculously, a few soldiers from the 11th Mississippi reached the stone wall on Cemetery Ridge, but the fire was so heavy that "any further effort to carry the position was hopeless."[28] The beaten brigade retreated in confusion across the field.

Adoniram Farmer and 31 other members of the 11th Mississippi were dead; another 170 men were wounded. Dewitt survived the deadly charge and led his company during the retreat from Gettysburg.

In three days of fighting Barksdale's and Davis's brigades had suffered a total of 1,466 casualties. Only two North Carolina brigades lost more men. Posey's Mississippi brigade had suffered very little, losing only 83 men. Gettysburg cost Lee at least 23,000 soldiers; neither his army nor the two Mississippi brigades could replace such horrible losses. It had been a terrible defeat.

ADONIRAM J. FARMER
copy print from *Confederate Veteran*,
Vol. VII (April 1899)

ROBERT K. HOUSTON
copy print

Lee's battered regiments were back in Virginia by mid-July, but morale was low, desertions were rising, and the Army of Northern Virginia numbered no more than thirty-five thousand men. Stragglers continued to return to their regiments, but it would be months before the once-powerful army regained even a semblance of its former strength. Many regiments, such as the 42nd Mississippi, which suffered at least two hundred casualties at Gettysburg, would never completely recover.

Thirty-one-year-old Pvt. Robert K. Houston of Fulton, Mississippi, was married and farming when he decided to join Co. E, 42nd Infantry, on May 14, 1862. Houston fought at Gettysburg and remained with his regiment the rest of the year. During that time Lee and Meade cautiously maneuvered against each other. On October 14, 1863, Houston fought at Bristoe Station where his regiment lost thirty-one men. The engagement cost the Confederates thirteen hundred casualties and was the largest battle that the Army of Northern Virginia fought from the Battle of Gettysburg until May 1864. Despite the lack of action, desertions continued to plague Lee's army. On February 7, 1864, Houston was listed as absent without leave, and he apparently never returned to his regiment. *Photo courtesy of Mrs. Britt Barron*

Thomas P. Buford was farming near College Hill, Mississippi, when he enlisted in the Lamar Rifles. On April 12, 1861, the unit mustered into the Confederate service as Co. G, 11th Mississippi Infantry. After the Battle of Seven Pines, Buford became ill with bronchitis and was furloughed to his home in Mississippi. He did not recover from the illness until early in 1864.

On May 4, 1864, the regiment was camped at Orange Court House, Virginia; twenty miles to the east, Lee was concentrating his army in a densely wooded area known as the Wilderness. That day Buford's regiment received orders to immediately join the Army of Northern Virginia. On May 5, 1864, the 11th Mississippi led Heth's Division up the Orange Plank Road and into the Wilderness. At about 9 A.M. the 11th Mississippi encountered enemy skirmishers, and the men deployed for battle. Soon, Union infantry came up and fighting erupted all along the line. The tangled brush made it difficult to coordinate any attack, and the heavy smoke from fires caused by the discharge of weapons quickly made conditions even worse. By 5 P.M. over thirty-eight thousand Federals were blindly struggling with fourteen thousand Confederates who held Lee's right flank. At nightfall the Rebels still held their positions, but they were badly shaken and low on ammunition. The next morning Buford was shot through his left thigh when a massive assault demolished Lee's right flank.

THOMAS P. BUFORD
copy print from Thomas P. Buford, comp., *Lamar Rifles, a History of Company G, Eleventh Mississippi Regiment, C.S.A.*

NATHANIEL HARRIS
albumen print

The Union attack on May 6, 1864, put the Army of Northern Virginia in mortal danger; it was able to resist total destruction only because Lee himself had been planning an offensive against the left wing of the Federal army and had therefore assembled fresh infantry behind his own right flank. Brig. Gen. Nathaniel H. Harris commanded four Mississippi regiments which made up a part of the force that Lee used to counter the Union attack.

In 1861 Harris, a twenty-seven-year-old Vicksburg attorney, helped organize the Warren Rifles, which became Co. C of the 19th Mississippi Infantry. Harris was elected captain of the company, and on May 5, 1862, he was promoted to major. He was wounded twice during the Peninsular Campaign. By the spring of 1863 he was colonel of the regiment. On January 20, 1864, he was promoted to brigadier general and given command of a brigade of Mississippians.

Harris remained in reserve on the morning of May 6, 1864, while Longstreet's Corps moved through the shattered Confederate right flank and went into action. Around 3 P.M. Longstreet sent Harris's Mississippians and three other fresh brigades against the left flank of the Federal army. Harris's infantry captured 150 men and forced the Federals on his front to fall back.[29] However, the Confederates became disorganized, and the attack sputtered out. Around 4:15 P.M. the Rebels resumed their assault, only to be stopped by the Federal infantry. *Photo courtesy of U.S.A.M.H.I., MOLLUS, Mass., Collection*

The Union army had been checked at the Wilderness, but Grant had no intention of abandoning the offensive. He planned to move around Lee's right flank, and on May 7, 1864, he sent two corps on a march toward the road junction at Spotsylvania Courthouse. When Lee learned about the maneuver he immediately sent troops eastward to occupy the crossroads before it could be seized by the Federals.

In May 1861, Thomas J. Hardin of Marshall County, Mississippi, mustered into service as captain of Co. I, 19th Mississippi Infantry. Hardin went on to serve in most of the Army of Northern Virginia's campaigns. By January 1864, he was the lieutenant colonel of the regiment. After Harris was promoted to brigadier general, Hardin was commissioned colonel of the 19th Mississippi.

On May 9, 1864, Hardin commanded the regiment as it marched rapidly toward Spotsylvania Courthouse. His men arrived in time to help block Grant's flanking movement, and the Confederates began building a series of strong fortifications. On May 12, 1864, four Union corps attacked a Confederate salient known as the Mule Shoe. The columns swept over the breastworks and were on the verge of shattering Lee's entire position. All available troops, including Hardin's regiment, rushed toward the Mule Shoe. Hardin and twenty-one other men from the 19th Mississippi died defending the salient. *Photo courtesy of Judge Henry Woods*

82

The struggle for the Mule Shoe lasted almost
twenty-four hours, and some of the most
vicious fighting of the war occurred there.
Hour after hour the soldiers battled at close
quarters. At times the men bludgeoned
each other with their weapons or fired into
the entrenchments at point-blank range.
Throughout most of the fight a cold,
drenching rain fell and eventually filled the
bottom of the trenches with muddy water.
Wounded and dead men were trampled into
the soggy ground.[30] One of the men fighting
to save the Mule Shoe was Pvt. John LeRoy
Williams of Sardis, Mississippi.

Williams was twenty-eight years old
when he joined the Sardis Blues on April 20,
1861. The Sardis Blues became Co. F, 12th
Mississippi Infantry. Williams was wounded
during the Peninsular Campaign and later
fought at Fredericksburg, Chancellorsville,
Gettysburg, and the Wilderness.

The 12th Mississippi went into action on
May 12 at 7 A.M. and fought until approxi-
mately 3:30 A.M. the next day. Williams'
brigade commander, Brig. Gen. Nathaniel
Harris, reported that the firing was so heavy
that "trees 22 inches in diameter were hewn
to splinters and felled by the musketry."[31]
Williams died in the battle for the Mule
Shoe, but the Confederates sealed the breach
and saved the Army of Northern Virginia.
*Photo courtesy of U.S.A.M.H.I., John L.
Williams II Collection*

ROBERT F. WARD
copy print from J. Harvey Mathes,
The Old Guard in Grey

Grant's attempt to turn Lee's flank by marching to Spotsylvania Courthouse had failed, but the maneuver set the pattern for the ensuing campaign. During the following weeks, as Lee parried Grant's flanking movements, men such as Lt. Robert F. Ward found themselves alternating between rapid marches and long hours of digging defenses.

In 1861, Ward was nineteen years old and living in Senatobia when he became the first sergeant in Co. I, 9th Mississippi Infantry. After serving a year, Ward joined the 42nd Infantry and was elected first lieutenant of Co. B. On May 22, 1864, the 42nd Mississippi was near Hanover Junction, where Lee had again blocked Grant's attempt to turn the right flank of the Army of Northern Virginia. The next day the men came under heavy artillery fire. On May 24, they improved their entrenchments. The Federals threw out heavy skirmishers during the next two days, but no major engagement occurred. When the Confederates probed the Federal lines on May 27, 1864, they discovered that Grant had moved to the left in yet another flanking movement. Ward was soon marching to block the Federal maneuver. Since the Battle of the Wilderness Ward's regiment had suffered 119 casualties. Grant's offensive was grinding up depleted units like the 42nd Mississippi, and Lee had no way to replace his losses.

Grant's third flanking move ended near Cold Harbor, Virginia, where the Army of Northern Virginia blocked the way to Richmond. Grant, who was now frustrated by his continued inability to move around Lee's right flank, decided to attack the Rebels' fortified lines. Pvt. Frank L. Hope of Co. G, 11th Mississippi Infantry, was behind the fortifications at Cold Harbor when Grant launched his attack.

Hope, a farmer from College Hill, had enlisted in the army on April 26, 1861. He had been severely wounded at Seven Pines and did not rejoin his company until shortly before the Gettysburg Campaign. Since then Hope had seen action at Bristoe Station, the Wilderness, and Spotsylvania Courthouse.

At 4:30 A.M. on June 3, 1864, three Union corps moved toward the Rebel entrenchments. Hope's regiment occupied the center of the line, which was being assaulted by Maj. Gen. Horatio Wright's Corps. By 8 A.M. his men had made fourteen unsuccessful advances against the Confederate center. At least two thousand of Wright's soldiers fell in the assaults. In less than an hour Grant lost over seven thousand soldiers. Confederate losses were about fifteen hundred. Hope was not among the thirty-seven casualties of the 11th Mississippi Infantry.

FRANK L. HOPE
copy print from Thomas P. Buford, comp.,
*Lamar Rifles, a History of Company G,
Eleventh Mississippi Regiment, C.S.A.*

CORNELIUS ROBINSON NESMITH
copy print

On the evening of June 12, 1864, the Union army began pulling out of Cold Harbor; the next day, Lee's men discovered that the enemy had vanished. Lee seemed baffled by Grant's sudden disappearance, and he had no true picture of where the Federals had gone until June 15, when they emerged south of the James River near Petersburg. During the next three days, Lee got enough men south of the river to contain the Federal army, but he was pinned in a defensive position protecting the vital rail links to Richmond. He would remain there until April 2, 1865.

Cpl. Cornelius Robinson Nesmith was with the 12th Mississippi when the regiment arrived in the Petersburg trenches on June 18, 1864. Nesmith, a native of Port Gibson, had joined the Claiborne Guards on May 10, 1861. His unit became Co. K of the 12th Mississippi Infantry, and it had been fighting in Virginia since July 1861.

Between June 1864 and April 1865, at least twelve major engagements and hundreds of other minor fights occurred near Petersburg. By the end of 1864, the 12th Mississippi had seen action at Weldon Railroad, the Crater, Darbytown Road, and Reams' Station. Nesmith was wounded on Friday, August 21, 1864, in the fighting at Weldon Railroad. As late as March 10, 1865, regimental muster roles still listed Nesmith as "furloughed, wounded."[32] *Photo courtesy of the Grand Gulf Military Monument Park*

James R. Bell
copy print from *Confederate Veteran,*
Vol. XIV (May 1906)

James R. Bell, a native of Holmes County, joined the colors in the spring of 1861. He had originally mustered into service as the first lieutenant of the Satartia Rifles, which became Co. I of the 12th Mississippi Infantry. Bell saw action in the Peninsular Campaign and was wounded at Seven Pines. Early in 1864 Bell was promoted to major, and he served with his regiment in the Petersburg defenses. Grant's basic strategy was to pin Lee while he extended the Union lines to eventually cut the Confederate railroads to the south and west of Richmond. On August 18, 1864, Union forces seized a section of the Weldon Railroad near Globe Tavern. The next day, five brigades of Rebel infantry tried to retake the vital position. The Confederate infantry, including the 12th Mississippi, failed to drive the Federals away on August 19, 1864. The Rebels attacked again two days later. In that fight the 12th and 16th Mississippi regiments had 6 field officers, 15 line officers, and 101 enlisted men captured. Major Bell was among the prisoners.

In slightly less than five weeks the 12th Mississippi had suffered ninety-three casualties, and all their field officers were either dead or missing. Even if the Confederacy could have replaced its losses, it could not replace the experience of veterans such as Major Bell, who was known as a "faithful and efficient officer."[33]

On June 11, 1864, Lee detached Lt. Gen. Jubal Early's Corps and sent it to operate in the Shenandoah Valley. Pvt. John Byers was with Brig. Gen. Benjamin Humphreys' Mississippi brigade, which joined Early in late July 1864.

Byers was farming near Water Valley, Mississippi, when he enlisted in the Panola Vindicators. The twenty-five-year-old private was with the unit on June 7, 1861, when it joined the Confederate army as Co. H, 17th Mississippi Infantry. When Byers was in the 1862 Peninsular Campaign, he had this ambrotype made by Holmes, Booth & Hodges of Richmond. At Second Bull Run, Byers was wounded in the hand. He was wounded again at Gettysburg and was subsequently captured. Byers was paroled in November 1863 and furloughed to Mississippi until he could be exchanged. He rejoined his company in the summer of 1864.

On October 19, 1864, Federal troops smashed Early's Corps at Cedar Creek. After the battle, Capt. Jesse C. Wright of Co. H sent a letter to Byers' father informing him that his son was dead. He wrote:

> He was shot through the heart and died instantly. I don't suppose he ever spoke after he was shot. There was no one of the company near him at the time but found him a short time afterwards.

Wright added that Byers "was a friend that I highly prized."[34]

With the Shenandoah Valley secured, Grant could concentrate all his forces against Lee's dwindling army. *Photo courtesy of Gettysburg National Military Park; original owned by Frances Maginnis*

JOHN ALEMETH BYERS
ambrotype

FREDERICK J. V. LECAND
copy print

Frederick LeCand was born in Natchez in 1841. At the age of twenty, he joined the Natchez Fencibles, which became Co. B, 12th Mississippi Infantry. LeCand served with the 12th Mississippi without incident until May 3, 1863, when he was wounded at the Battle of Chancellorsville. LeCand was moved to the hospital in Richmond and did not return to his regiment until after the Battle of Gettysburg. On April 18, 1864, LeCand became sergeant of his company.

By late March 1865, Grant's relentless pressure had so weakened the Confederates that they were near the breaking point. A massive attack on the morning of April 2, 1865, shattered the Rebel lines, and the Confederate forces around Richmond were in danger of being captured. Around noon Union columns began probing Fort Gregg, a Rebel stronghold whose garrison of 500 men included Sergeant LeCand. Lee needed time to evacuate his broken army, and the defenders of Fort Gregg gave it to him. The garrison, facing overwhelming odds, repulsed three Union attacks. They were overrun on the fourth assault, but the defenders still fought hand-to-hand for almost thirty minutes. LeCand and almost 160 other men were captured, but their spirited defense gave Lee time to evacuate his troops. *Photo courtesy of Beauvoir, The Jefferson Davis Shrine*

Pvt. James D. Malone, a farmer from Holly Springs, was single and only eighteen when he joined Co. G, 17th Mississippi Infantry, on May 27, 1861. Before the long retreat from Richmond began, his company had served with the Army of Northern Virginia in such bloody fights as First Bull Run, the Peninsular battles, Antietam, Fredericksburg, Chancellorsville, Gettysburg, the Wilderness, Spotsylvania Courthouse, Cold Harbor, Cedar Creek, and Petersburg. On March 1, 1865, Malone was still with his company, but only 67 of the original muster of 150 soldiers remained in the ranks.

Lee began retreating on April 2, 1865, with approximately 49,000 men; when his ragged army reached Appomattox Court House six days later, only 26,000 soldiers remained in the ranks. The rest had either deserted or been killed or captured. The next day, the Army of Northern Virginia surrendered. On April 12, 1865, Federal troops watched as the remnants of the Confederate regiments furled their battle flags and stacked arms for the last time. Private Malone surrendered with his regiment, which had been reduced to a mere 40 men. Out of the more than 16,000 Mississippians that had served in Virginia, only 698 soldiers remained in the ranks at Appomattox. The rest, if they had not deserted or been discharged or transferred, were either disabled, captured, or dead.[35]

Photo courtesy of the Museum of the Confederacy, Richmond; original owned by John M. Vick

JAMES D. MALONE
copy print

Chapter 4

Mississippians in the Western Armies

On May 8, 1865, 1st Sgt. William Pitt Chambers of Co. B, 46th Mississippi Infantry, walked into a tent at Cuba Station, Alabama, and politely asked the officer where his troops should surrender their arms. The Federal soldier smiled and pointed to the spot where the men could stack their weapons.

Chambers' company had numbered 123 soldiers when it mustered into service in the winter of 1862, but it was down to only 17 men when he conducted the unit's last muster on February 28, 1865. Since then the company had lost several more men at Fort Blakely, Alabama, and it is doubtful if Chambers actually surrendered more than a handful of soldiers to Federal authorities.[1] Throughout the previous two weeks the remains of as many as seventy-one other Mississippi commands were surrendering in theaters as far away as North Carolina. These units, which included at least thirty-one regiments, ten infantry battalions, nineteen cavalry formations, a dozen

artillery batteries, and scores of miscellaneous commands, represented more than half of all the organizations that the state of Mississippi raised during the war. These soldiers had spent most of their military careers serving in various armies that fought outside the states of either Mississippi or Virginia.

By the winter of 1862 at least sixteen Mississippi infantry regiments that were destined to spend most of their time fighting with the Western armies had already been raised. Twelve of these units were part of Gen. Albert Sidney Johnston's long defensive line that ran from Columbus, Kentucky, to the Cumberland Gap in Tennessee. Johnston had far too few troops to protect such an extended line. His position was shattered on February 16, 1862, when a Union army under Brig. Gen. Ulysses S. Grant captured 11,500 Confederates at Fort Donelson on the Cumberland River. Among the prisoners were perhaps as many as 3,000 Mississippians from six regiments.[2] By the fall of 1862, most of these men would be exchanged and returned to duty, but for now they were unavailable to Johnston.

After the loss of Fort Donelson, Johnston began falling back, eventually concentrating all his available forces at Corinth, Mississippi. By early April 1862, Johnston had 40,000 men there. The command, which was now called the Army of Mississippi, contained eight Mississippi infantry commands. The 5th, 7th, 9th, and 10th Infantry regiments were part of Brig. Gen. James R. Chalmers' "High Pressure" Brigade. The 6th Infantry served under Brig. Gen. Patrick R. Cleburne, and the 3rd Battalion was in Brig. Gen. S. A. M. Wood's command. Two additional units, the 15th and 22nd regiments, were part of Col. W. S. Statham's brigade.[3]

Johnston was determined to take the offensive against Grant's army, which was encamped twenty miles away near Shiloh Church. On April 6, 1862, Johnston surprised Grant and rolled the Federals back toward the Tennessee River. On that Sunday morning the 6th Mississippi Infantry passed through the nearly deserted camp of the 53rd Ohio Infantry and moved up a small hill toward the waiting Ohioans. "Again and again the Sixth Mississippi, unaided, charged the enemy's line," wrote Cleburne, "and it was only when the regiment had lost 300 officers and men killed and wounded, out of an aggregate of 425, that it yielded and retreated in disorder over its own dead and dying."[4] During the rest of the Civil War only three Confederate regiments suffered more casualties in a single battle.[5] That evening Federal reinforcements arrived, and the next day the Rebels were driven from the field. Chalmers' 1,739-man brigade lost 445 men in the two-day fight, and the remaining three Mississippi commands sustained moderate casualties. In two days of the most bitter fighting yet seen in the West, the Confederacy had lost almost 11,000

men; Gen. Albert Sidney Johnston was dead; and the beaten Rebel army was headed back to Corinth.

The Union forces had been badly shaken themselves and made only a feeble effort to pursue the retreating Confederates. The Western Theater remained quiet for the next six weeks. The new commander at Corinth, Gen. P. G. T. Beauregard, used this respite to strengthen the fortifications surrounding the city and to reinforce his army. By late May 1862, eleven more Mississippi regiments had joined the Confederate army at Corinth, and Beauregard's total strength was now 66,000 men. Even with these substantial reinforcements Beaureguard knew that there was no hope of defending the town against the Federal forces which numbered 110,000 men. On the evening of May 29, 1862, he began withdrawing southward toward Tupelo, Mississippi.

Shortly after the evacuation of Corinth, Beauregard went on sick leave without the permission of President Jefferson Davis. The president, who did not like Beauregard anyway and was disappointed with the recent campaign, used the unauthorized absence as a reason to remove him. On June 17, 1862, one of Davis's favorite generals, Braxton Bragg, assumed command of the Army of Mississippi.

Bragg, a West Point graduate and Mexican War veteran, had always had a reputation as a strict disciplinarian and a stickler for regulations. As an army commander, Bragg soon demonstrated a flair for strategic thinking, but he also proved to be an irresolute battlefield leader who refused to listen to sound advice from his subordinates. However, Davis trusted him implicitly. Bragg would remain in command of the army until after the Battle of Chattanooga, when the demoralized condition of his men and the near mutiny of his subordinates forced him to resign.

At Tupelo, Bragg reshuffled his new command. The 6th, 15th, 22nd, and 31st Mississippi regiments were transferred to the District of Mississippi. These four units served briefly in Louisiana before returning to Mississippi, where they remained for most of 1863. In 1864 the four regiments rejoined their fellow Mississippians who were then stationed in Georgia. Fourteen Mississippi infantry units remained with Bragg's army. Many of these men were in Chalmers' brigade, which now contained the 7th, 9th, 10th, 29th, and 44th regiments, and the 9th Battalion of Sharpshooters. The eight other infantry commands were scattered among various brigades in the Army of Mississippi.

Bragg hoped to draw the Union forces out of northern Mississippi and middle Tennessee by launching an invasion into central Kentucky. He planned to begin the offensive from Chattanooga, Tennessee, because he wanted to coordinate his advance with Maj. Gen. E. Kirby Smith's Army of Kentucky, which was in the vicinity of Knoxville.

Bragg's thirty-thousand-man army began its advance from Chattanooga on August 28, 1862. The first heavy fighting in the campaign occurred on September 14, 1862, when Chalmers' brigade suffered 288 casualties in an unsuccessful assault against the fortified town of Munfordville, Kentucky. Three days later, the garrison surrendered to overwhelming Confederate forces, and Bragg continued his march northward. On October 8, 1862, elements of Bragg's and Smith's armies suddenly found themselves facing heavy odds at Perryville, Kentucky. Several Mississippi regiments were engaged in the fighting, but Bragg failed to concentrate more than half of his available forces for the battle. Thousands of nearby troops, including Chalmers' Mississippians, took no part in the fight. When the battle ended at dark, Bragg's Kentucky invasion had been decisively checked, and he had no choice except to withdraw.

By late November 1862, Bragg's command, which was now officially known as the Army of Tennessee, was in camp at Murfreesboro, Tennessee. Twenty-seven miles away at Nashville were forty-seven thousand soldiers under the command of Maj. Gen. William S. Rosecrans. On the day after Christmas, Rosecrans began moving his army toward Murfreesboro. By December 30, 1862, the Federal troops were in front of Bragg's soldiers, who were deployed two miles northwest of the town.

Most of the Mississippians in Bragg's army were in Chalmers' and Brig. Gen. Patton Anderson's brigades. Chalmers still commanded the same regiments that had served together in the Kentucky Campaign. Anderson's brigade contained the 24th, 27th, 29th, and 30th Infantry regiments. Both brigades were attached to Maj. Gen. Jones M. Wither's Division of Lt. Gen. Leonidas Polk's Corps. Four other Mississippi infantry units were assigned to brigades in Lt. Gen. William J. Hardee's Corps.

Both commanders planned to attack on December 31, 1862, but Bragg managed to get his assault underway first. By 8 A.M. the Confederate left wing was heavily engaged, and soon Polk's Corps in the center joined the attack. Throughout the day the Confederate left and center drove the Federals back, but the Union line still held at nightfall. Desultory fighting continued the next day, but neither commander seemed eager to renew the combat. On the morning of January 2, 1863, Bragg made one more attempt to dislodge Rosecrans, but the assault failed. That evening Rosecrans launched a counterattack against the Confederate center and gained some ground, forcing Bragg to withdraw.

Bragg had lost 10,000 men, and he again failed to seize the initiative when the opportunity presented itself. The Battle of Stones River had cost the Mississippi infantry more than 1,513 killed, wounded, and missing men. Two units, the 29th and 30th infantries of Wither's Division, had lost 236 and 209 men, respectively. Only one other Rebel regiment had endured more losses than the 29th and 30th infantries.[6]

By the spring of 1863, Vicksburg was receiving priority for reinforcements, and Bragg had little choice except to remain on the defensive. His principal aim was to protect Chattanooga, which was both a strategic rail junction and the gateway to Georgia. In mid-June, Rosecrans, after much prodding from Washington, finally took the offensive. During the next few months, Rosecrans outmaneuvered Bragg and forced him to abandon Chattanooga. On September 9, 1863, the Army of Tennessee withdrew into the mountains south of the city.

Bragg had lost Chattanooga, but now Rosecrans had become overconfident. As the Federal commander pursued Bragg, he allowed his army to get badly strung out in the mountains (south of the city). Meanwhile, Confederate reinforcements from east Tennessee, Mississippi, and Virginia were being dispatched to reinforce Bragg. When Rosecrans realized the danger, he began concentrating his forces near Chickamauga Creek.

With the recent arrival of elements of Lt. Gen. James Longstreet's Corps from the Army of Northern Virginia, Bragg now had at least sixty thousand men under his command. Among Bragg's troops were fourteen regiments and three battalions of Mississippi infantry. Anderson's old brigade, now commanded by Brig. Gen. Edward Walthall, contained the 24th, 27th, 29th, 30th, and 34th Mississippi infantries. Walthall's brigade was assigned to Maj. Gen. W. H. T. Walker's Division. Anderson then commanded Chalmers' old brigade, which contained the 7th, 9th, 10th, 41st, and 44th regiments and the 9th Battalion of Sharpshooters. Anderson's men were assigned to the division of Maj. Gen. Thomas C.

Hindman. Most of the men of the two Mississippi brigades had now been fighting together for almost a year. Six other Mississippi infantry units were also in brigades of the Army of Tennessee.[7]

On the morning of September 19, 1863, Bragg attacked Rosecrans along Chickamauga Creek. All day the two armies slugged away at each other, but there was no clear winner. That evening the remainder of Longstreet's Corps arrived on the battlefield. Among the fresh units was Brig. Gen. Benjamin Humphreys' brigade, which included the 13th, 17th, 18th, and 21st Mississippi regiments. Bragg resumed the offensive on September 20. Shortly after 11:30 A.M. Longstreet's men, including Humphreys' brigade, began pouring through a hole in the Union lines that fortuitously appeared just as the Confederates launched a major attack. The Union right cracked. Before the day ended, Bragg was on the verge of destroying the Union army, but he lacked the resolution to continue the grinding offensive. That evening the battered Federals withdrew toward Chattanooga.

Casualty returns for the twenty-one Mississippi infantry units are incomplete, but the brigades of Walthall, Anderson, and Humphreys lost a total of 1,508 men. On September 19, the 5th and 8th Mississippi regiments, which were attached to Brig. Gen. John K. Jackson's brigade, mustered 656 men. When the battle ended 26 percent of the soldiers in the two Mississippi units were listed as killed, wounded, or missing. Combined losses among the Mississippi infantry probably exceeded 1,900 men.[8] Chickamauga was the bloodiest battle fought in the West, costing the Confederates over 18,000 casualties. For the Mississippians, it was the deadliest battle of the Civil War, surpassing even the Seven Days' Campaign and Gettysburg.

Bragg fully expected Rosecrans to evacuate Chattanooga. However, the Union commander had the Tennessee River at his back, and he feared that the army might be destroyed if it left the safety of the city. Therefore, Rosecrans began to dig in and wait for relief. Meanwhile, Bragg positioned his troops along Missionary Ridge and attempted to prevent any aid from reaching the beleaguered Federals. On October 17, 1863, Grant, who now commanded the newly created Military Division of the Mississippi, relieved Rosecrans of his command. Grant arrived in Chattanooga on October 23, 1863, and within the week he had opened a more reliable supply line into Chattanooga. By mid-November 1863, the Chattanooga garrison had risen to fifty-seven thousand men.

While the Union army grew in strength and confidence, the Army of Tennessee deteriorated. Recriminations over Bragg's handling of the Chickamauga Campaign divided his subordinates into feuding camps. Officers who objected to Bragg's lackluster performance were transferred to other commands. Simultaneously, the army's strength declined because Longstreet's Corps was ordered to march to Knoxville to invest Maj. Gen. Ambrose E. Burnside's forces.[9] The Army of Tennessee, now reduced to forty thousand men, waited passively in front of Chattanooga, while Grant prepared to take the offensive.

The majority of the Mississippians were now in Lt. Gen. William Hardee's Corps. He had recently replaced Polk, whom Bragg had removed from command. The corps contained the two Mississippi brigades of Walthall and Anderson. Brig. Gen. John K. Jackson's brigade, which included the 5th and 8th Mississippi regiments, was also in Hardee's Corps. Three other Mississippi regiments, the 32nd and 45th (consolidated) and the 15th Mississippi, were now commanded by a fellow Mississippian, Brig. Gen. Mark Lowrey. The brigade was part of Cleburne's Division of Maj. Gen. John C. Breckinridge's Corps.

On November 24 and 25, 1863, Grant's men drove the Army of Tennessee from the heights overlooking Chattanooga. Many of the demoralized Confederate regiments behaved badly in the two days' fighting. However, on the first day, Walthall's men fought hard in the famous battle for Lookout Mountain. His brigade lost 972 men. The next day, Lowrey's brigade played a prominent part in Cleburne's stubborn defense at Tunnel Hill. The action prevented the Union army from cutting off Bragg's line of retreat. On November 27, 1863, Cleburne again rescued the army when his small division held Ringgold Gap until the Rebels could escape to Dalton, Georgia. The Chattanooga Campaign cost Bragg 6,667 casualties; at least two-thirds of the losses occurred on Missionary Ridge, where Grant smashed the entire front of the Army of Tennessee and took almost 4,000 prisoners.

Bragg could not survive the disaster at Chattanooga, for he now commanded a thoroughly demoralized army, and many of his senior commanders were in near rebellion against his continued presence. On November 30, 1863, he left the Army of Tennessee, and on December 27, 1863, Gen. Joseph E. Johnston assumed command of the once-formidable force.

Johnston seemed satisfied with the present organization of the Mississippi infantry, and he left the units with their respective brigades. The only significant change in command occurred when Anderson was promoted to major general. Brig. Gen. William F. Tucker assumed control of Anderson's old unit.

No major activity occurred on Johnston's front until early in May 1864, when the Union armies, now under the command of Maj. Gen. William T. Sherman, began advancing against Johnston.[10] On May 12, 1864, Johnston evacuated Dalton and retreated to Resaca, Georgia, where he was reinforced by elements of Lieutenant General Polk's troops, which had been serving in Mississippi. Polk eventually brought three Mississippi brigades with him. Brig. Gen. Winfield S. Featherston, a veteran of the Army of Northern Virginia, commanded the 3rd, 22nd, 31st, 33rd, and 40th regiments as well as the 1st Mississippi Battalion of Sharpshooters. Brig. Gen. John Adams of Tennessee led the 6th, 14th, 15th, 20th, 23rd, and 43rd Mississippi regiments. Brig. Gen. Claudius Wistar Sears, a Massachusetts native who had settled in Mississippi, commanded the 4th, 35th, 36th, 39th, and 46th regiments and the 7th Mississippi Battalion. At least thirty-three Mississippi infantry organizations were now attached to Johnston. This represented the largest concentration of Mississippi commands ever assembled in one army. However, three years of war had decimated their ranks, and it is unlikely that the aggregate numbers exceeded those present with the twenty-one Mississippi units that fought at Chickamauga.

For the next three months, Sherman conducted a series of sophisticated flanking movements that Johnston parried by falling back on prepared positions. During the campaign many of the Mississippi regiments saw action at places such as Resaca, New Hope Church, Moore's Mill, and Kennesaw Mountain, but Johnston could not stop Sherman's remorseless advance on Atlanta. By the middle of July, the Federals were nearing the environs of the city, and Davis, who had never liked Johnston, decided to remove him from command.

On July 17, 1864, another of Bragg's favorites, Gen. John Bell Hood, assumed command of the Army of Tennessee. Earlier, Hood had served in the Army of Northern Virginia. He had earned a reputation as a hard fighter, but he also had a tendency toward rashness that would soon contribute to the final destruction of the Army of Tennessee.

On July 20, 1864, Hood threw his army against Sherman's forces along Peachtree Creek. The unsuccessful attack cost him almost 4,800 men; Featherston's 1,230-man brigade suffered 616 casualties. Two days later, Hood again tried to drive Sherman away from Atlanta. In this assault Lowrey's understrength brigade, which had earlier fought at Peachtree Creek, lost 276 men. On July 28, 1864, Hood attacked Union forces near Ezra Church, but he was again defeated. Walthall's old brigade, now commanded by Col. William Brantley, and Brig. Gen. William Tucker's brigade, under Brig. Gen. Jacob Hunter Sharp, lost a total of 340 men.[11] Hood's attacks cost him thousands of casualties that he could not afford and did nothing to relieve the pressure on Atlanta.

Sherman remained in front of Atlanta until August 25, 1864, when he sent his forces on a westward flanking march to cut the railroad lines below Atlanta. On August 31, 1864, Hood made a final attempt to block Sherman near Jonesborough. The brigades of Lowrey, Brantley, and Sharp were engaged in the fighting, along with most of Hardee's Corps, but they failed to drive the Federals away. The next day the Federals broke through Hardee's thin lines. Hood now had no choice except to evacuate Atlanta.

The summer's fighting had cost the Army of Tennessee more than 27,000 casualties. Returns for the Mississippi regiments are incomplete, but attrition due to illness, desertion, and death had clearly thinned their numbers. Walthall's old brigade, for example, contained five regiments that originally should have mustered approximately 5,000 men. However, at the Battle of Resaca the entire brigade contained only 1,158 men of which 169 soldiers were either killed or wounded in that fight. Indeed, the constant drain of manpower had so reduced the strength of several Mississippi regiments that they had to be consolidated. Mississippi had already been stripped of its infantry for the Atlanta Campaign, and replacements were almost nonexistent. Therefore, the regiments would have to continue to rely on the troops that still remained in the ranks.

Most of the remaining soldiers lacked proper accoutrements, food, and clothing. "I am glad to hear that you are sending me some clothes," wrote Pvt. Mathew Dunn of the 23rd Mississippi Infantry, "as I am barefooted & naked."[12] Most of the Mississippians were in the same condition as Dunn, and after the loss of Atlanta, their morale was dangerously low. Many of the men blamed Davis because, as another Mississippian wrote, "to a large extent he is held responsible for the reverses the Army of Tennessee has sustained since Johnston's removal."[13]

Despite the reduced numbers, poor morale, and chronic shortages of almost everything, the Army of Tennessee was the only instrument left to try to force Sherman out of Georgia. Throughout most of September 1864, the Rebel army kept well away from Sherman's forces around Atlanta and operated against the Union line of communications. Hood hoped that this strategy would draw Sherman back into Tennessee, but it ultimately failed. On November 16, 1864, Sherman left Atlanta in smoking ruins and headed eastward to join the bulk of his army, which was already marching toward Savannah, Georgia. He left behind Maj. Gen. George Thomas in Nashville, with instructions to use the remaining Federal forces to stop any possible invasion of Tennessee by Hood.

On November 21, 1864, Hood began moving his 40,000 men out of Florence, Alabama. His ultimate objective was Nashville. Serving with the Army of Tennessee were five Mississippi brigades that contained the remnants of twenty-six regiments and three battalions. Five additional regiments marched in other brigades. On the evening of November 30, 1864, Hood recklessly threw almost 16,000 infantrymen against fortified Federal positions at Franklin, Tennessee. By the end of the day over 1,750 Confederates

lay dead, and another 4,500 were wounded. The five Mississippi brigades were decimated in the assault, losing a total of at least 1,277 men. The futility of the attack did not stop at least 160 Mississippians from Sears' brigade from penetrating the Federal entrenchments. The Battle of Franklin proved that the Army of Tennessee would still fight, but the senseless attack destroyed what remained of both the strength and the morale of the Confederate infantry.

Hood, despite the losses at Franklin, continued his advance on Nashville. He arrived on the outskirts of the city on December 2, 1864. His army, which now numbered less than 24,000 men, was not large enough to surround Nashville, so he began digging in south of the town. Lt. Gen. Alexander F. Stewart's Corps, which contained only 4,761 effectives, held Hood's right flank. In the corps were three Mississippi brigades. The largest brigade, now commanded by Col. Robert Lowry, contained 1,047 men present for duty. Featherston's brigade was reduced to only 781 soldiers, and Sears' brigade had only 210 Mississippians left in the ranks. Sharp's and Brantley's brigades were part of Lt. Gen. Stephen D. Lee's Corps, which held the center of Hood's line. The exact strength of the two units is not known, but their four-brigade division contained only 3,100 soldiers. The Mississippi commands in Lee's Corps probably contained less than a thousand men each.

For almost two weeks the Confederates suffered from fierce winter weather. Conditions were at their worst on December 10, 1864, when an ice storm blanketed the area. Five days later Thomas, with almost fifty-five thousand men, attacked the overextended Confederate lines. Within hours the entire left wing of the Army of Tennessee had been shattered. Hood withdrew several miles and tried to make a stand the next day, but he was again routed. The Army of Tennessee now practically ceased to exist as an organized fighting force. During the long retreat, the ragged soldiers suffered horribly. "My shoes fell from my feet between Franklin and Columbia," wrote Lt. R. N. Rea of the 46th Mississippi, "and I was forced to march . . . a distance of three hundred miles barefooted, in constant snowstorm and sleet. . . ."[14]

The survivors of the campaign, some 13,000 troops, eventually straggled into Tupelo, Mississippi. There, as one Mississippian noted, "great numbers are going home every day" and "nine-tenths of the men and line officers are barefooted."[15] At first Hood refused to admit that his army had been practically annihilated. Finally, on January 13, 1865, he accepted the truth and requested to be relieved of command.

Despite the pitiful conditions, some men still stayed with their units. About 5,000 infantrymen eventually joined Gen. Joseph Johnston in the Carolinas. Among these troops were four Mississippi brigades which finally surrendered near Durham Station on April 26, 1865. A fifth brigade was sent to Alabama where they surrendered on May 4, 1865. The remaining Mississippi units that had served in the Army of Tennessee were scattered throughout Alabama, Mississippi, and the Carolinas when the war ended.

On May 12, 1865, Sgt. William Chambers of the 46th Mississippi Infantry received his parole. Like thousands of other Mississippians, he headed for home. After an uneventful trip, Chambers arrived in Fertile Glade, Mississippi. He asked himself what it had all been for, but he had no answer. Chambers' heart was "sick and sore," and he believed that as a people Americans had proved that they could not govern themselves. All Chambers could do was prepare himself to face the day-to-day problems of living in a state that had been practically destroyed by the war.[16]

The vast majority of Mississippians who fought in the Western armies served in commands from Mississippi, but unusual circumstances sometimes drew men into units raised in other states. Alfred Jefferson Vaughan, Jr., an 1851 graduate of the Virginia Military Institute, was farming in Marshall County, Mississippi, when the war began. Vaughan tried to raise a local company for service in the Confederate army, but he was unable to secure either arms or support from the state of Mississippi. Vaughan, who was frustrated with the lack of interest shown by the Mississippi authorities, took most of his volunteers and traveled five miles across the border to Moscow, Tennessee. There, his men organized the Dixie Rifles and elected Vaughan their captain. The company became part of the 13th Tennessee Infantry, and by November 1861, Vaughan was colonel of the regiment. Vaughan went on to fight at Belmont (Missouri), Shiloh, Richmond (Kentucky), Murfreesboro, and Chickamauga. On November 18, 1863, Vaughan was commissioned brigadier general, and he was at Dalton, Georgia, when the Atlanta Campaign began. In three years of fighting, eight horses had been shot from under Vaughan, but he had yet to be injured. His luck ended on July 4, 1864, when a shell tore off his leg while he was leading his brigade in a small action at Vining's Station, Georgia. The wound ended his military career, and Vaughan returned to his farm in Mississippi. *Photo courtesy of U.S.A.M.H.I., MOLLUS, Mass., Collection*

ALFRED JEFFERSON VAUGHAN, JR.
albumen print

JAMES O'NEIL
carte de visite
Anderson Photographic Gallery, New Orleans

Occasionally, Mississippians who lived in counties bordering Louisiana joined units from the Crescent State. On April 18, 1862, James O'Neil of Natchez, Adams County, Mississippi, entered the service as the first lieutenant of Co. G, Miles Legion. Most of the 137 men who eventually joined the company were also from Adams County, but the muster rolls contained a number of Louisiana surnames such as Arceneaux, De Meaux, and Le Blanc. The commander of the unit was a Mississippian, Col. William R. Miles, who had business interests in New Orleans.

Early in the war the Confederate Congress approved the formation of ten "legions" with companies of infantry, cavalry, and artillery. These hybrid outfits assumed the name of the famous Roman legions and were designed to bring all three combat arms together under one tactical command. Such small-unit coordination never worked well, and prior to the Civil War they had already declined in popularity.

Miles, nevertheless, received permission to organize such a unit. His regiment, like most of the Confederate legions, seldom operated as a tactical unit. O'Neil and his infantry company served briefly in Mississippi in the summer of 1862, but by mid-August they were part of the Port Hudson garrison. O'Neil, who was promoted to captain in the winter of 1863, surrendered with the garrison on July 8, 1863. He remained in prison until the end of the war.[17] *Photo courtesy of the L.L.M.V.C., L.S.U., Civil War Album*

Some Mississippians served first in commands from Mississippi then later joined units from other states. Joseph W. Cunningham was a gin maker in Holly Springs when he enlisted in the Jefferson Davis Rifles on April 17, 1861. The unit became Co. D, 9th Mississippi Infantry, and Cunningham served until his enlistment ended in May 1862. He and almost one hundred other Mississippians then decided to join a regiment of cavalry that was being raised by John Hunt Morgan of Kentucky. Morgan already had five Kentucky companies under his command, but his fame attracted Alabama, Texas, and Mississippi soldiers who were eager to serve under him. On May 14, 1862, Private Cunningham and his friends mustered into the service as Co. F, 2nd Kentucky Cavalry. For the next fifteen months the Mississippians rode with Morgan on a series of daring raids against Union forces.

On July 2, 1863, Morgan began his greatest exploit of the war. In a twenty-five-day raid through Ohio, his men rode over seven hundred miles, captured six thousand prisoners, demolished thirty-four bridges, and destroyed thousands of dollars' worth of property. On July 26, 1863, Union forces finally captured the raiders. Cunningham was sent to Camp Douglas, Illinois, where this photograph was taken. He was paroled near the end of the war. Morgan was confined in the Ohio Penitentiary as a common criminal. On November 28, 1863, he escaped from prison and was later killed in a skirmish at Greeneville, Tennessee, on September 3, 1864.[18] *Photo courtesy of Ernest and Cathy Cunningham*

JOSEPH W. CUNNINGHAM
carte de visite

FELIX HUGHES
copy print

Most Mississippi units that served in the West were attached to the Army of Tennessee. However, a number of Mississippians did serve in Louisiana during the first two years of the war.

Felix Hughes was thirty-two years old when he joined the Sarsfield Southrons at Vicksburg on June 20, 1861. He was elected captain of the company that mustered into the service as Co. C, 22nd Mississippi Infantry. Between July 27 and November 1, 1861, Hughes was on detached duty carrying dispatches to Richmond, Virginia. After completing his assignment, Hughes rejoined his regiment, which was now stationed in Kentucky. Hughes later led his company at the Battle of Shiloh on April 6 and 7, 1862.

On July 29, 1862, Hughes' regiment left Vicksburg and joined the Confederate forces at Camp Moore, Louisiana, that were about to attack Baton Rouge. On August 5, 1862, elements of the 15th, 22nd, 31st, and 39th Mississippi Infantry regiments participated in the assault on the Louisiana state capital. Fever and the hard march from Camp Moore to Baton Rouge had reduced the 22nd Mississippi to no more than a few hundred men, and Captain Hughes was in temporary command of the regiment. Shortly before 10 A.M. Hughes was at the head of his troops when he was mortally wounded by enemy gunfire. His regiment had thirteen men killed and another thirty-four wounded in the battle. *Photo courtesy of the Old Court House Museum, Vicksburg*

FREDERICK Y. DABNEY (*seated right*),
JAMES P. PARKER (*seated center*),
UNKNOWN (*seated left*);
W. B. SEAWELL (*standing right*),
A. J. LEWIS (*standing left*)
carte de visite

Most of the Mississippi units that served in Louisiana after the Battle of Baton Rouge eventually became part of the Port Hudson garrison.

Capt. A. J. Lewis enlisted in the army at Port Gibson, Mississippi, on June 6, 1862, and he led the Claiborne Light Infantry in the unsuccessful attack at Baton Rouge. His command numbered only thirty-eight men and was not attached to any regiment. After the battle, Lewis fell back to Port Hudson with the defeated Confederates.

James P. Parker of Jackson, Mississippi, joined the 1st Mississippi Light Artillery in the spring of 1862, and on June 30, he was elected lieutenant colonel of the unit. Parker joined the Port Hudson garrison in the fall of 1862, and he commanded four of the regiment's batteries during the siege. Lewis and Parker surrendered with the garrison on July 8, 1863, as did the soldiers from the 1st and 39th Mississippi infantries.

First Lt. Frederick Y. Dabney was chief engineer at Port Hudson, and Capt. A. B. Seawell, an Alabamian, commanded one of the heavy batteries that guarded the river. The five men were prisoners of war in New Orleans when this image was made. *Photo courtesy of L.L.M.V.C., L.S.U., Civil War Album*

THOMAS P. GOOCH
copy print

Thomas P. Gooch was nineteen years old when he enlisted at Carrollton, Mississippi, on June 20, 1861. His unit, the Carroll Guards, became Co. C of the 20th Mississippi Infantry.

In September 1861, the regiment joined Brig. Gen. John B. Floyd's command in western Virginia and campaigned there until the middle of December. The brigade then received orders to join Gen. Albert Sidney Johnston in Kentucky. After the fall of Fort Henry on February 6, 1862, it was clear that Grant planned to attack Fort Donelson on the Cumberland River. Johnston ordered Floyd to move with reinforcements to Fort Donelson and assume command of the garrison. Gooch and the 20th Mississippi arrived at Fort Donelson at daylight on February 13, 1862. The next day Floyd's artillerists drove back a Union flotilla that tried to reduce the fort. The victory did nothing to inspire Floyd, who was now convinced he could not hold his position, and he decided to break out of the trap. On February 15, 1862, the Confederates attacked the surprised Federals. By noon Floyd had opened an escape route, but courage failed him and he ordered the troops to return to their entrenchments. Gooch was not injured in the fighting, but in Floyd's bungled attempt to escape, the 20th Mississippi suffered seventy-eight casualties out of a total of five hundred men.[19] *Photo courtesy of the Museum of the Confederacy, Richmond*

106

Thomas's brother, Pvt. Alphonso S. Gooch, was also in Co. C, 20th Mississippi. On the evening of February 15, 1862, Gooch's commander, Maj. William N. Brown, received information from Floyd that he planned to take his old brigade across the river to safety. In fact, Floyd had decided to flee because, as secretary of war under President James Buchanan, he had done little to protect Federal military property during the secession crisis, and he feared that he might be tried for treason. He detailed Brown's men to guard the steamboat landing and turned the Fort Donelson garrison over to Brig. Gen. Gideon J. Pillow, another antebellum politician, who also thought that he might be charged with treason. Pillow immediately relinquished command to Brig. Gen. Simon B. Buckner and began plotting his own escape. As news of the planned surrender spread, panic-stricken soldiers flocked to the river to escape. The 20th Mississippi stood in a semicircle around the wharf and held the panicky soldiers in check until Floyd and his Virginia regiments steamed away.[20] Alphonso Gooch, his brother, and 453 other members of the 20th Mississippi remained behind to fend for themselves. Pillow managed to escape in a rowboat. On February 16, 1862, Buckner surrendered unconditionally. General Johnston had lost 11,000 men; his defensive line was shattered; and he could do nothing but withdraw southward with the rest of his army. *Photo courtesy of the Museum of the Confederacy, Richmond*

Alphonso S. Gooch
copy print

TOLIVER V. LINDSEY
ninth-plate ambrotype

By late March 1862, Johnston had been reinforced. He now had 40,000 troops at Corinth, Mississippi, and he was determined to attack Grant's army, which was bivouacked twenty miles away near Shiloh Church. Early on Sunday morning, April 6, 1862, Toliver F. Lindsey was one of 425 men of the 6th Mississippi Infantry who waited for the orders to advance against Grant's unsuspecting troops.

On August 24, 1861, Lindsey mustered into the service as first lieutenant of the Crystal Springs Guards. The Guards became Co. F in the 6th Mississippi, and Lindsey was promoted to captain after the company's commander had resigned.

Shortly before the Battle of Shiloh began, Lindsey heeded the advice of his lieutenant and realigned the company so that the older men were in the first attacking line. Perhaps the two officers hoped to spare the lives of their younger soldiers, but no one could be protected from what was about to happen. Between 7:45 A.M. and 8 A.M. the 6th Mississippi was decimated, primarily by gunfire from the 53rd Ohio Infantry. When the brief fight ended, 61 soldiers from the 6th Mississippi had been either killed or mortally wounded. Another 269 men, including Captain Lindsey, had been wounded. During the entire Civil War only three Confederate regiments, the 1st Texas, the 21st Georgia, and the 26th North Carolina, suffered higher percentages of casualties in one battle.[21] *Photo courtesy of Dale Snair*

James Ronald Chalmers was born in Halifax County, Virginia, in 1831 and later graduated from South Carolina College. He subsequently moved to Holly Springs, Mississippi, where he practiced law until his election to the state secession convention in January 1861. Three months after the convention, Chalmers became colonel of the 9th Mississippi Infantry, and on February 12, 1862, he was promoted to brigadier general. A month before the Battle of Shiloh, Chalmers assumed command of six regiments which his commander, Braxton Bragg, christened the "High Pressure Brigade." Among the six units were the 5th, 7th, 9th, and 10th Mississippi Infantry regiments. At the beginning of the Battle of Shiloh, Chalmers commanded 1,739 men.

Gen. Albert Sidney Johnston's attack surprised Grant and threw his men into confusion. However, Brig. Gen. Benjamin Prentiss managed to rally several thousand Federals in a sunken road. For more than three hours, Prentiss held up the Rebel advance in a fierce fight that became known as the Hornets' Nest. Chalmers' brigade participated in the attack that finally forced Prentiss to surrender, and Chalmers' men drove forward until they were stopped by Grant's massed artillery. By the end of the day the High Pressure Brigade had been involved in six major assaults against the Federals. Chalmers had 82 men killed and another 343 wounded, but his brigade had taken over 1,600 Federal prisoners. *Photo courtesy of the Arkansas History Commission*

On April 6, 1862, Johnston almost succeeded in driving Grant's army into the Tennessee River. However, by the end of the day the Rebel fury was spent, and Johnston was dead. That evening Federal reinforcements arrived on the field, and the next morning Grant took the offensive.

Capt. Robert McNair commanded the McNair Rifles of the 3rd Mississippi Battalion when the Union attack began on April 7, 1862. In the fall of 1861 McNair had raised the company from Pike County men; the soldiers elected McNair their captain and named the company after him. In the first day's fighting at Shiloh, the battalion lost 47 men of its 280 soldiers. By April 7, straggling had reduced the unit to no more than one hundred muskets. Early that morning, the battalion seized a Union battery that had strayed too far from its infantry support. Forty yards away, the Confederates could see what appeared to be a friendly battle line. When the advancing troops unfurled their Union battle flags, the Rebels realized their mistake and opened fire. McNair, standing "exposed, cheering his men to stand bravely and fire coolly," fell mortally wounded. The advance on McNair's battalion was temporarily halted, but elsewhere the Federal attack was irresistible. Late that afternoon the Confederate army, after losing over 10,000 men in two days, began retreating toward Corinth.[22]

Less than a month after Mississippi seceded from the Union, Robert Smith was at Jackson, mustering into state service as captain of the Mississippi Rifles. The company's first official duty was to escort Jefferson Davis to Grand Junction, Tennessee. From there, Davis traveled by rail to Montgomery, Alabama, where he was sworn in as president of the new Confederacy. Smith's company then went to Pensacola, Florida. After twenty Mississippi companies had arrived, Maj. Gen. Braxton Bragg organized them into the 9th and 10th regiments. These were the first units from Mississippi to be accepted into the Confederate service. When the colonel of the 10th died suddenly, the men elected Smith as his replacement. The new colonel was only twenty-five. The 10th Mississippi Infantry first fought at Shiloh with Chalmers' High Pressure Brigade, and the young colonel was favorably mentioned in the general's official report of the battle.

Smith was with his regiment when Bragg invaded Kentucky in the fall of 1862. On September 14, Chalmers launched an unsupported attack against 4,000 entrenched Federals at Munfordville, Kentucky. Smith fell mortally wounded at the foot of the Federal entrenchments.[23] His regiment suffered 108 casualties in the premature assault. The garrison surrendered three days later, and Bragg continued his advance.

JOHN T. TRIMBLE (*right*)
AND WILL A. TRIMBLE
copy print

On April 3, 1861, several hundred men from Jefferson County mustered into service as the Jefferson Troop of Cavalry. Almost immediately, state authorities converted them into a battery which they designated the Jefferson Flying Artillery. John Trimble and his brother, Will, apparently joined the battery in February 1862. The Trimble brothers fought at Shiloh and were with the battery during the Kentucky Campaign.

On October 8, 1862, the Jefferson Artillery was present at the Battle of Perryville, providing fire support for the infantry on the left wing of Bragg's army. By the end of the day, the two divisions that fought on the left wing had driven the Federal infantry back more than a mile, but the Rebels had lost over seventeen hundred men. The Jefferson Artillery continued shelling the enemy until darkness and a shortage of ammunition forced them to cease firing. Only two men from the battery were wounded in the battle.

Bragg had made headway against the Federals, but at least thirty-five thousand Union soldiers were in the vicinity of the battlefield. Bragg, who had failed to concentrate all his available forces, was now down to fewer than twelve thousand troops. Therefore, he had no choice except to withdraw. That evening the beaten Confederates began retreating toward Tennessee. *Photo courtesy of the Grand Gulf Military Monument Park*

JAMES PATTON ANDERSON
copy print

Bragg's army next fought at Stones River on December 31, 1862. That morning Brig. Gen. James Patton Anderson's brigade was deployed near the center of the Confederate battle line. Among his six infantry units were the 24th, 27th, 29th, and 30th Mississippi regiments.

Anderson, a Pennsylvania native, graduated from Jefferson College in 1842, then moved to Frankfort, Kentucky, where he studied law. In 1842 Anderson settled in Hernando, Mississippi, and was practicing law when the Mexican War began in 1846. In the summer of 1847, Anderson became lieutenant colonel of a battalion of Mississippi riflemen, but the war was already over when his men reached Mexico. He returned home and was elected to the Mississippi General Assembly in 1850. Anderson resigned his seat in 1853 to accept an appointment as U.S. Marshal in the Washington Territory. He later served one term as the territorial delegate to Congress, before moving to Florida in 1857. Anderson was in the Provisional Congress of the Confederate States prior to being appointed colonel of the 1st Florida Infantry on April 5, 1861. On February 10, 1862, Anderson was promoted to brigadier general and subsequently fought at Shiloh and Perryville.

Soon after daylight on December 31, 1862, Anderson heard "the thick roll of musketry" and knew that Bragg had begun his assault. When the Confederate offensive died down at sunset, Anderson had lost 766 men.[24] *Photo courtesy of U.S.A.M.H.I., MOLLUS, Mass., Collection*

113

GEORGE W. HOPE
copy print from Thomas P. Buford, comp.,
Lamar Rifles, a History of Company G,
Eleventh Mississippi Regiment, C.S.A.

Third Lt. George W. Hope of the 30th Mississippi Infantry was with his company at Stones River when Anderson's brigade began advancing. In 1861 Hope was a twenty-year-old student at the University of Mississippi. He had originally mustered into the 11th Mississippi Infantry as a private and later served with the unit in Virginia. On December 30, 1861, Hope was discharged from the regiment because of an accidental puncture wound through his left wrist. On February 10, 1862, he received a commission in the "True Mississippians," which was now Co. B of the 30th Mississippi Infantry.

Early on the morning of December 31, 1862, Hope's regiment was moving across an open field when it was decimated at short range with "grape, canister, and shrapnel." The regiment had 62 men killed and another 139 wounded on less than an acre of ground.[25] Hope was killed in the first day's fighting at Stones River; it is likely that he died in the brief but furious artillery barrage.

Pvt. Samuel E. McNulty joined the service at Natchez, Mississippi, on November 11, 1861. He was twenty-nine at the time of his enlistment. McNulty was eventually assigned to Co. E, 45th Mississippi Infantry.

On December 31, 1862, McNulty's regiment was part of Cleburne's Division when it began advancing against the right wing of the Union army. At first the regiment met little resistance, but soon random artillery shots began to spread confusion among the men. McNulty's commander and an officer from another regiment finally got the men re-formed. The 45th Mississippi then charged the enemy, but they were repulsed. The regiment withdrew to resupply its dwindling ammunition and later returned to the battle. The 45th Mississippi then charged a group of Federals posted behind a stone pile; this time the soldiers carried the position and captured about seventy men. By 4 P.M. the Federal right had been driven back almost three miles, but their lines still held. On New Year's Day sporadic fighting continued, and the 45th Mississippi took a few casualties when it drove some Federal soldiers away from a cotton gin.[26] McNulty had survived the first day's fighting, only to be captured in the small action around the gin. When Bragg withdrew from the battlefield on January 2, 1863, he had suffered more than 10,000 casualties. Cleburne's Division, which originally numbered 6,045 men, had lost one-third of its numbers, including 118 men from the 45th Mississippi. *Photo courtesy of the Confederate Memorial Hall, New Orleans*

SAMUEL E. MCNULTY
sixth-plate ambrotype

JOHN SPELL
copy print

Twenty-nine-year-old John Spell was a farm laborer when he enrolled at Raleigh, Mississippi, on June 1, 1861, as a private in the True Confederates, most of whom were from Smith County. Early in October 1861, the unit became Co. C of the 8th Mississippi Infantry.

Spell's regiment came under artillery fire at Fort Pickens, Florida, in November 1861, but it saw no serious fighting until Stones River, where it suffered 133 casualties. Spell apparently was sick in the hospital during the battle and did not return to his regiment until January 1863. After Stones River, the 8th Mississippi was detached from the Army of Tennessee and sent to Bridgeport, Alabama. From there, Spell's regiment hunted bushwhackers and deserters in the pro-Union counties in North Alabama. Sometime in August 1863, the 8th Mississippi rejoined the Army of Tennessee at Chattanooga. On August 27, a Federal artillery shell killed three men and wounded another soldier in Spell's regiment. On September 9, 1863, Bragg abandoned Chattanooga and withdrew into Georgia. Rosecrans' troops entered the city the same day. Two other Union columns moved southwest of Chattanooga and tried to cut off what appeared to be a full scale retreat by the Army of Tennessee. However, thousands of reinforcements were being rushed to Bragg. On September 19, 1863, his command, which now numbered at least 60,000 men, struck the Union army along Chickamauga Creek. *Photo courtesy of Nelda Spell Mitchell*

Capt. Henry Luse Foules commanded Maj. Gen. Alexander Stewart's cavalry escort during the Chickamauga Campaign. Foules had originally mustered into the troop at Washington, Mississippi, on July 24, 1862, as a first lieutenant. In April 1863, he was promoted to captain and given command of the cavalry company. The next month Foules' company was assigned to escort Stewart. Foules' primary duty was to protect the commanding general, but he also helped to ensure that Stewart's orders were efficiently dispatched to the commander's subordinates.

On September 19, 1863, Stewart's Division was in the center of Bragg's line near Chickamauga Creek. There was heavy fighting all day, and Stewart's brigades "suffered severely both in officers and men." By nightfall the Federals had lost some ground but the results were inconclusive. Stewart's Division went back into action the next day. When the battle ended he had lost 2,140 men, though Foules' cavalry company of thirty-five men suffered only two casualties. Foules performed his duties well, and Stewart acknowledged this in a dispatch following the battle: "My thanks are due to Capt. H. L. Foules commanding my escort, and who acted as an aide, and to the officers and men of his admirable company, for their intelligence, activity, and zeal. I have never required a service from the company, nor from any member of it, that was not performed to my entire satisfaction."[27] *Photo courtesy of Eugene R. Groves*

HENRY LUSE FOULES
copy print

BENJAMIN G. HUMPHREYS
copy print

At 2 A.M. on September 20, 1863, Brig. Gen. Benjamin Grubb Humphreys arrived on the battlefield at the head of the 13th, 17th, 18th, and 21st Mississippi Infantry regiments. His men were part of Lt. Gen. James Longstreet's Corps that had been detached from the Army of Northern Virginia to reinforce Bragg.

Humphreys, a native of Claiborne County, Mississippi, had entered West Point in 1825, but was later dismissed for participating in a cadet riot on Christmas Eve, 1826. Humphreys returned to Mississippi where he read law, became a successful planter, and served in the state legislature. On September 11, 1861, Humphreys became colonel of the 21st Mississippi Infantry and later led his men through many battles in Virginia. Humphreys was promoted to brigadier general on August 12, 1863, but he actually assumed command of the Mississippi brigade immediately after the death of Brig. Gen. William Barksdale at Gettysburg.

Shortly after 11 A.M. on September 20, 1863, Longstreet's men poured through a gap in the Union lines that appeared when a Union division was mistakenly shifted to the left. The attacking Confederates shattered the Union right, which then began streaming back toward Chattanooga. Humphreys' brigade surged forward, capturing five stands of colors, four hundred prisoners, and twelve hundred small arms.[28] Rosecrans himself was also swept away in the rout, and the remainder of his army was in danger of being destroyed. *Photo courtesy of the Library of Congress, no. USZ62-83384*

118

George Eisele of Adams County, Mississippi, joined the Natchez Southrons on March 8, 1862. The new unit became Co. B, 10th Mississippi Infantry. Eisele's regiment subsequently fought at Shiloh, Munfordville, and Stones River.

On the morning of September 20, 1863, Private Eisele waited to go into action on the Chickamauga battlefield. His regiment was part of Patton Anderson's brigade which mustered a total of 1,865 soldiers. The 10th Mississippi came into contact with Union infantry shortly after 11:30 A.M. when they advanced to support a Confederate brigade that had been shattered by enemy fire. The men helped drive the Federals back and pursued the retreating soldiers for over a mile until a Union counterattack almost surrounded the regiment and forced the men to retreat. Late in the day the regiment's ammunition was exhausted and most of the men's rifles were so choked with burned powder that the soldiers could not drive their ramrods down the barrels. The 10th went into reserve; the rest of Anderson's brigade advanced on Snodgrass Hill where the remnant of the Union army was making a stand. Repeated attacks failed to dislodge the stubborn Federals, who subsequently withdrew toward Chattanooga. Chickamauga was a major Confederate victory, but it had cost Bragg more than 18,000 men. Anderson's brigade suffered 558 casualties. Eisele had not been hurt, and he was cited for "conspicuous bravery" by his commander.[29] *Photo courtesy of M.D.A.H.*

GEORGE THOMAS EISELE
copy print

119

EDWARD C. WALTHALL
carte de visite

A few days after the Battle of Chickamauga, most of Bragg's army was positioned on the heights overlooking Chattanooga. Meanwhile, reinforcements were being rushed to the Federal army, and Grant arrived to take command of the forces in the city. Brig. Gen. Edward Walthall, a Holly Springs lawyer and ex-district attorney, commanded five Mississippi regiments that were deployed atop Lookout Mountain on the left of Bragg's line.

Walthall had begun his career as a lieutenant in the Yalobusha Rifles of the 15th Mississippi Infantry. On April 11, 1862, Walthall became colonel of the 29th Mississippi; eight months later he was promoted to brigadier general. At Chickamauga, Walthall's 1,827-man brigade had lost 705 soldiers. Because of these losses the brigade was so small that four of his regiments had been temporarily combined into two commands.

Early on the morning of November 24, 1863, a Union column attacked the Confederate forces on the mountain. The ensuing struggle, which took place almost 1,100 feet above the Tennessee River in a heavy fog and mist, became known as the "Battle above the Clouds." By nightfall the Rebels had been driven off the mountain and had retreated to Missionary Ridge. The next day Grant's men smashed the Confederate positions on the ridge. Walthall was shot through the foot during the fight, but he remained in command of his brigade until they were safely off Missionary Ridge.[30]
Photo courtesy of the Marshall County Museum

On November 25, 1863, Brig. Gen. Mark Perrin Lowrey, a Baptist minister and Mexican War veteran from Tishomingo County, Mississippi, commanded a brigade in Maj. Gen. Patrick Cleburne's Division. Cleburne's brigades held the extreme right of Bragg's line near Tunnel Hill.

Lowrey had little formal education and had seen no action in the Mexican War, but he was nevertheless given command of the 4th Regiment of sixty-day troops when the Civil War began. At the end of their enlistment, many of the men decided to stay with Lowrey, who was then raising a regiment for service in the Confederate army. In April 1862, Lowrey became the colonel of his new command, the 32nd Mississippi Infantry. Lowrey later led the 32nd at Perryville, Stones River, and Chickamauga. On October 4, 1863, Lowrey, who had proven to be an excellent commander, was promoted to brigadier general.

By the evening of November 25, 1863, most of Bragg's army had been crushed, but Cleburne's men covered its disorderly retreat. Two days later, the division, including Lowrey's 1,330-man brigade, saved the beaten army from destruction by defending Ringgold Gap, Georgia, against a Federal corps. Cleburne, who was an outstanding divisional commander, praised his brigadiers, writing that "four better officers are not in the service of the Confederacy." On November 27, 1863, Cleburne's men received the official thanks of Congress for their action at Ringgold Gap.[31]

MARK PERRIN LOWREY
copy print from Ezra Warner, *Generals in Grey*

WILLIAM F. TUCKER
albumen print

The first major engagement in the campaign to capture Atlanta began at Resaca, Georgia, on May 14, 1864. Brig. Gen. William F. Tucker led one of four Mississippi brigades that fought there.

Tucker, a Virginia native, moved to Mississippi shortly after he graduated from Emory and Henry College. In 1855 Tucker was elected probate judge of Chickasaw County. After serving one term, he studied law and was admitted to the bar, and when the Civil War began he was practicing in Houston, Mississippi. In May 1861, Tucker entered the service as a captain in the 11th Mississippi Infantry. After First Bull Run, Tucker's company was transferred to the West and incorporated into the 41st Mississippi Infantry. On May 8, 1862, Tucker became colonel of the regiment and commanded the unit until his promotion to brigadier general on March 1, 1864.

Tucker's brigade, which contained six Mississippi infantry units, was in reserve at Resaca on May 14, 1864. Early in the battle, his men were sheltered in a ravine, but they nevertheless came under heavy artillery fire. Tucker was eager to learn about the progress of the battle and rode to the front to visit with Edward Walthall, who also commanded a Mississippi brigade. There, Tucker was severely wounded while watching the enemy's advance.[32] His wound disabled him from active duty until the war was almost over. *Photo courtesy of U.S.A.M.H.I., MOLLUS, Mass., Collection*

Capt. Jerome H. Bowen commanded Co. I, 34th Mississippi, when his regiment fought at Resaca. His unit was part of Walthall's brigade, which had 49 men killed and another 119 wounded in two days of fighting.

Bowen was born near Tyro, Mississippi, and was farming when the war began. He helped to organize a local militia company which was known as the Bowen Rebels; the unit mustered into Confederate service on March 22, 1862, as Co. I, 34th Mississippi Infantry. Bowen saw his first action on May 9, 1862, in the engagement at Farmington, Tennessee; he later fought at Perryville and Chickamauga.

On May 15, 1864, Bowen's company was deployed behind a rock wall in an orchard when they came under sustained fire from the Federals. Bowen, hoping to inspire his men, leapt onto the wall and was seriously wounded by enemy fire. He died the next day as Johnston's army withdrew southward to new defensive positions. His commander, Col. Samuel Benton, later wrote that Bowen "had done his duty during the action and gave his life to his country."[33] *Photo courtesy of the U.A.L.R. Archives, J. N. Heiskell Collection*

FRANK A. MONTGOMERY
copy print from Frank L. Montgomery,
Reminiscences of a Mississippian in Peace and War

Johnston established another defensive line about twenty-five miles northeast of Atlanta around New Hope Church and waited for Sherman to attack. Lt. Col. Frank A. Montgomery's regiment, the 1st Mississippi Cavalry, had recently joined Johnston's army and was deployed as infantry on the left of the Confederate positions.

Montgomery was born on January 7, 1830, in Adams County near the little village of Selsertown on the Natchez Trace. He later moved to Bolivar County, became active in local politics, and was serving as president of the Board of Police when the Civil War began. On March 20, 1861, he mustered into service as captain of the Bolivar Troop, which became Co. H, 1st Mississippi Cavalry. Montgomery became lieutenant colonel of the regiment in May 1862.

Since May 25, 1864, there had been heavy skirmishing in front of Montgomery's regiment and "minie balls, shot and shell" often flew over his camp. On May 28, 1864, his regiment scaled their works and advanced toward the enemy, only to be thrown back with the loss of twenty men. Several days later the regiment occupied the now-deserted Federal lines. They found many of their comrades buried in shallow graves; Montgomery's men reinterred the men in deeper plots "so that their bones might lie undisturbed till they had all crumbled into dust."[34] On June 4, 1864, Johnston began shifting his army toward prepared positions that were a few miles closer to Atlanta.

ISOM D. HERRINGTON
copy print

Sherman's flanking movements and Johnston's decision to withdraw rather than engage in a major fight against a numerically superior foe set the tone for the next several weeks. Each commander was content to avoid a pitched battle in favor of maneuvering against his adversary.

Pvt. Isom D. Herrington had enlisted in the Confederate service at Westville, Mississippi, on April 5, 1862. His unit, the Simpson Greys, became Co. A, 39th Mississippi Infantry. The regiment, after fighting at Corinth on October 3 and 4, 1862, had been transferred to Port Hudson, Louisiana, where Isom surrendered with the garrison on July 8, 1863. After his exchange, Isom returned to the 39th Mississippi Infantry, but he deserted at Enterprise, Alabama, in November 1863. Isom later rejoined his unit on April 24, 1864, and was part of the reinforcements that had arrived earlier at Resaca.

By June 18, 1864, Johnston's forces had fallen back to Kennesaw Mountain. The next day, heavy skirmishing occurred between the two armies, and Isom was captured. By the end of the Atlanta Campaign, the 39th Mississippi had fought in six major battles; its losses totaled fifteen killed, sixty-seven wounded and twenty-seven missing. *Photo courtesy of McCain Library, University of Southern Mississippi; original owned by Sandra E. Boyd and Mrs. L. E. Brooks*

WILLIAM SPELL
copy print

Sherman had grown impatient with a war of maneuver and decided to throw sixteen thousand troops against the Confederate defenses at Kennesaw Mountain. Pvt. William Spell was among the seventeen thousand Confederates who fought there.

Spell had joined the Confederate service on the same day as his brother, John (see page 116), and he too was in Co. C, 8th Mississippi Infantry. Prior to the Battle of Kennesaw Mountain, Spell had seen action at Stones River, Chickamauga, and Chattanooga.

On June 27, 1863, his regiment was attached to Lowrey's brigade, which was at least a mile from the immediate point of the Federal attack. Early in the fight Lowrey received orders from his divisional commander, Patrick Cleburne, to reinforce the line. Lowrey quickly marched his men to the front. By 10 A.M. the attack had failed, and Sherman had suffered three thousand casualties. Cleburne's 4,683-man division had 85 men killed and another 363 wounded in the brief but bloody fight.[35] Spell had been shot just below the left kneecap. On July 8, 1864, he was admitted to the Ocmulgee Hospital in Macon, Georgia, for treatment of the infected wound. *Photo courtesy of Nelda Spell Mitchell*

After the Battle of Kennesaw Mountain, Sherman returned to his campaign of maneuver. By July 8, he had forced Johnston to withdraw to the south bank of the Chattahoochee River. Sherman then crossed this last natural barrier in front of Atlanta; his forces were a scant seven miles from the city. Jefferson Davis had now seen enough of Johnston's delaying tactics, and on July 17, 1864, he gave the command of the Army of Tennessee to Gen. John B. Hood. On July 20, 1864, Hood ordered twenty thousand men to attack the Union forces along Peachtree Creek. Claudius Davis was with the soldiers who fought in that battle.

Davis was born in Liberty, Mississippi, on June 23, 1843. On April 29, 1861, he mustered into the Confederate service as a private in the Liberty Guards. Davis's regiment finally completed its organization at Memphis, Tennessee, and the Liberty Guards became Co. E, 22nd Mississippi Infantry. Davis then served with the regiment at Shiloh and Corinth; he was wounded in both battles.

On July 20, 1864, Davis was a lieutenant and the adjutant of his regiment, which was part of Featherston's Mississippi brigade. During the advance Davis seized the 22nd Mississippi's flag after three color bearers had been shot down. Shortly afterward, Davis himself was killed while carrying the flag and urging his men forward. Featherston's 1,230-man brigade lost 616 soldiers in the failed attack along Peachtree Creek.[36] *Photo courtesy of Beauvoir; The Jefferson Davis Shrine*

CLAUDIUS VIRGINIUS HUGHES DAVIS
copy print

127

Col. Samuel Benton, a nephew of Senator Thomas Hart Benton, was born in Tennessee on October 18, 1820, and moved to Holly Springs, Mississippi, as a young man. There he practiced law and entered politics. Benton first served in the Mississippi General Assembly and was later elected to the 1861 Secession Convention. Early in 1862, Benton became colonel of the 34th Mississippi Infantry. Benton, as the senior officer among the 24th, 29th, 30th, and 34th Mississippi regiments, commanded the brigade when it reached the outskirts of Atlanta.

On July 22, 1864, Hood ordered a second assault against Sherman's army, which also failed to drive the Federals away. During the fighting, a shell struck Benton in the chest and also mangled his foot, which doctors amputated. On July 26, 1864, Benton was promoted to brigadier general. Two days later he died of his wounds. *Photo courtesy of Beauvoir, The Jefferson Davis Shrine*

Hood's two assaults had not seriously weakened Sherman, but the Federal commander still had no desire to attack the strong Rebel positions north of Atlanta. Instead, Sherman planned to cut Confederate communications south of the city, and he began moving around Hood's left flank. On July 28, 1864, elements of two Confederate corps struck the advancing Federals west of Atlanta at Ezra Church. Capt. Thomas P. Hodges commanded Co. A of the 41st Mississippi Infantry when the fighting began there.

Hodges was the son of a prominent Mississippi planter who owned over three hundred slaves. When the war began Hodges was in Chapel Hill, North Carolina, but he returned to his home state to join the service. On October 12, 1861, Hodges mustered into the army at Tallibonela, Mississippi, as first lieutenant of Co. A, 41st Mississippi Infantry. On January 14, 1862, he was promoted to captain and later led his company at Stones River, Chickamauga, and Missionary Ridge.

At Ezra Church, Hodge's regiment was part of Brig. Gen. Jacob Sharp's 1,020-man brigade of Mississippians. The twenty-eight-year-old captain was leading his company when he was hit in the chest by a Federal Minié ball. Within minutes Hodges was dead. Confederate casualties exceeded 5,000 men, including 214 from Sharp's brigade. In eight days Hood had lost almost 18,000 men in three furious but unsuccessful attacks.

THOMAS P. HODGES
copy print from *Confederate Veteran*,
Vol. XIX (January 1911)

WILLIAM L. SPINKS
copy print from Nan Fairly, *Paths to the Past*

William L. Spinks was thirty-one years old when he joined the Meridian Invincibles on May 1, 1861. Within three weeks his unit and forty-nine other companies were ordered to report immediately to Corinth, where they would be organized into regiments. On June 8, 1861, Spinks mustered into the service as the first lieutenant of Co. H, 14th Mississippi Infantry. On February 16, 1862, Spinks surrendered with his regiment at Fort Donelson. Spinks and the 14th Mississippi were exchanged in October 1862; they later fought at the Siege of Jackson, Resaca, Kennesaw Mountain, and Ezra Church in front of Atlanta.

Throughout most of August 1864, Confederate and Union soldiers fought behind fieldworks to the north and east of Atlanta. In places the two lines were no more than sixty yards apart; both sides suffered casualties from sharpshooters and artillery fire. On August 25, 1864, Spinks was struck and killed by an enemy projectile. That night Sherman began withdrawing the bulk of his infantry from the trenches in preparation for a movement around Hood's left flank. At first Hood believed that Sherman was retreating, and he began planning a victory ball. On August 28, 1864, he learned that Sherman's forces, rather than retreating, were marching against his rail communications south of the city.

Pvt. George A. Grammer's battery, the Warren Light Artillery, was among the troops that Hood deployed to meet Sherman's advance. On August 31, 1864, the last rail line to the city, the Macon & Western Railroad, fell into Union hands. When Hood failed to dislodge the Federal forces at Jonesborough, he had no choice except to abandon Atlanta. During the engagement at Jonesborough, Federal infantry charged through Grammer's battery, capturing two guns, the colors, and sixteen soldiers. Five men died in the fight, and another fourteen were wounded. Grammer, who had served in the Warren Light Artillery throughout the Atlanta Campaign, was not injured.

The Atlanta Campaign practically destroyed the Warren Light Artillery. From Dalton to the Chattahoochee River the battery had thrown up fourteen different breastworks, fired 1,708 rounds, and suffered thirty-one casualties. Between July 21 and August 16, 1864, the battery lost another sixteen men.[37] Total losses during the campaign were thirteen dead, fifty-three wounded, and sixteen captured.

The casualty records for the Mississippi units that fought in the Atlanta Campaign are incomplete, but they undoubtedly suffered losses comparable to those of the Warren Light Artillery. The Army of Tennessee had lost over twenty-seven thousand men, and it had been fatally weakened during the campaign. *Photo courtesy of M.D.A.H.*

GEORGE A. GRAMMER
copy print

JAMES (*left*) AND THOMAS SHULER
copy print from F. M. Glass,
Long Creek Rifles, a Brief History

After Atlanta fell, Hood contented himself with harassing Sherman's lines of communications with Nashville. The tactic annoyed Sherman, but it failed to force the Federal commander to evacuate the city. On November 15, 1864, Sherman began his march to the sea; six days later Hood led forty thousand soldiers northward on the Confederacy's last Western offensive. Among the men who marched with Hood was 2nd Lt. James Shuler.

James and his older brother, Thomas, joined the Long Creek Rifles on May 27, 1861. The unit became Co. A, 15th Mississippi Infantry. On January 19, 1862, the brothers fought at Mill Springs, Kentucky; their regiment suffered 197 casualties, including Thomas, who died in the battle.

On the morning of November 30, 1864, the 15th Infantry was with Adams's Mississippi brigade as it followed the retreating Federals toward Franklin, Tennessee. James arrived in front of the formidable entrenchments that protected Franklin after mid-day. His men rested and waited for the remaining Rebel infantry to arrive. At 4 P.M. the first line of almost 16,000 attacking Confederate infantry moved forward.[38] Adams and his horse died astride the breastworks. Shuler, one of twenty-one officers who advanced with the regiment, fell wounded. Twelve of his fellow officers were either killed or injured, and four different color bearers died. When the battered regiment withdrew, its battle flag remained in the trenches.

Samuel Gibbs French, a New Jersey native, graduated from West Point in 1843 and later served with distinction in the Mexican War. After the conflict, French married into a wealthy Mississippi family. In 1856 he gave up a promising military career and moved to Mississippi to manage one of the family's plantations.

When the Civil War began, French first served as chief of ordnance for the state of Mississippi and then received a commission as brigadier general in the Confederate army. French was stationed in Virginia and North Carolina during the first two years of the war; he saw little action but was promoted to major general on October 22, 1862. In July 1863, French was transferred to the Western Theater and given a division, which he subsequently led through the Atlanta Campaign.

On November 30, 1864, French's Division was in the vanguard of Hood's army when it arrived in front of Franklin. French rested throughout most of the afternoon, but he felt anxious as he waited for the impending assault. Across the fields he could see the Union entrenchments that his men would soon be ordered to assault. Near sundown the signal came to advance, and French felt relieved to finally go into action. The attack had hardly begun when French's men came under heavy fire, but they crushed the advance line of Federals and headed toward the main entrenchments.[39] *Photo courtesy of U.S.A.M.H.I., MOLLUS, Mass., Collection*

SAMUEL GIBBS FRENCH
albumen print

133

134

JOHN D. JONES
sixth-plate tintype

John D. Jones enlisted as a private in the Confederate army at Dry Creek, Mississippi, on May 1, 1862. His company, the Burt Rangers, became Co. I, 39th Mississippi Infantry. Jones later fought at Corinth and subsequently surrendered with the 39th at Port Hudson, on July 8, 1863. Jones was paroled and then joined the 20th Mississippi on August 1, 1864. Shortly afterward, he transferred back to his old company in the 39th Mississippi.

On November 30, 1864, Jones' regiment was part of Sears' Mississippi brigade, of French's Division. The sun was sinking when Jones began advancing. Smoke obscured the whole field, but the soldiers could still see "an incessant sheet of flame"; when the haze cleared they saw wounded and dead everywhere. Sears' brigade drove back the first Union line and then charged the main entrenchments. Jones and forty-one other soldiers of the 39th Mississippi reached the ditch in front of the parapet, but they could go no further. That evening the men from the 39th Mississippi withdrew from the ditch.[40] Jones and six other dead soldiers were left behind. The total losses in Sears' brigade numbered 652 men. The Army of Tennessee once more proved that it had the heart to fight, but it had been decimated, suffering over six thousand losses in the most costly charge of the Civil War. *Photo courtesy of George Esker*

ROBERT A. JARMAN
copy print

Robert A. Jarman had been a private in Co. K, 27th Mississippi Infantry, since he joined the service at Aberdeen, Mississippi, on September 27, 1861. Jarman was twenty-one when he enlisted. At Franklin, Jarman and a fellow soldier had survived a shooting match with two Federal soldiers who were only eight paces away.

Hood, undeterred by the stinging defeat at Franklin, led his tattered army forward toward Nashville. He arrived there on December 2, 1864, but with only thirty-one thousand effectives he had no hope of taking the city. For the next few days Jarman helped construct breastworks. In camp he pounded corn into meal and occasionally "made a raid on a neighboring hog pen for meat." Jarman was in the line on December 15, 1864, when the Union army delivered a crushing blow against Hood's small army. Hood re-formed his battered line about a mile south of its original position, only to be routed by the Federals the next day.

On the evening of December 16, 1864, Jarman's company was down to only four men; the rest were either prisoners, casualties, deserters, or stragglers. For the next twelve days Jarman struggled southward with the retreating army. By December 24, 1864, more than four inches of snow covered the ground, and Jarman was living off what food he could scrounge. Three days later the remains of the Army of Tennessee went into winter quarters near Tupelo, Mississippi.[41]
Photo courtesy of Frances Evans

On April 26, 1865, Gen. Joseph E. Johnston surrendered all Confederate troops under his command, including about twenty thousand soldiers of the Army of Tennessee. The surrendered army contained the remnants of twenty-seven Mississippi regiments, two infantry battalions, and one artillery battery —a total of perhaps three thousand men. Brig. Gen. Winfield Scott Featherston was one of the parolees, and his varied service was typical of that of many Mississippians who had soldiered for the Confederacy.

Featherston, a prominent Mississippi attorney and former U.S. Congressman, joined the Confederacy in 1861 as colonel of the 17th Mississippi Infantry. He first served in Virginia and saw action at First Bull Run, Ball's Bluff, Second Bull Run, and Fredericksburg. In February 1863, Featherston, who was now a brigadier general, transferred to Mississippi and fought in the Vicksburg Campaign.

In May 1864, his brigade joined the Army of Tennessee. Featherston led his men through the Atlanta Campaign and on Hood's 1864 invasion of Tennessee. Between March 19 and 21, 1865, Featherston and many of the Mississippi regiments in the Army of Tennessee fought their last battle at Bentonville, North Carolina. During the war, he had served with three Rebel armies, marched in six states, fought in at least eleven major battles, and been wounded once. Now the war was over, and he could go home. *Photo courtesy of M.D.A.H.*

WINFIELD SCOTT FEATHERSTON
copy print

Chapter 5

The Struggle for
Northeast Mississippi

In early 1861 the little northeast Mississippi town of Corinth bustled with activity as thousands of Confederate troops arrived there. Most were Mississippians who were being mustered into service, hastily trained, and then quickly dispatched to other theaters of operations.

The town itself was barely seven years old when the Civil War began, but it already was a prosperous community of about twelve hundred people. Inside the city limits were five churches, a college, three hotels, and several small businesses.[1] Corinth's prosperity and its growing strategic value were inextricably tied to the two railroads that intersected on the town's western edge. The older of the lines was the Memphis and Charleston Railroad. The railroad began in Memphis and ran almost due eastward through Corinth, Burnsville, and Iuka, Mississippi, to Chattanooga, Tennessee. There it connected with two other lines. The first ran eastward to Knoxville, Tennessee, and eventually terminated at Richmond, Virginia. A second line ran south-ward to Atlanta, Georgia, and from there other lines connected to Savannah and Charleston. The second line that passed by Corinth, the Mobile & Ohio Railroad, had opened only a few weeks before Mississippi seceded from the Union. It began at Columbus, Kentucky, and ran almost due south through Corinth and Meridian, Mississippi, before reaching Mobile.

The juncture of these two railroads made Corinth the most important railhead west of Chattanooga and thus served as a mobilization point for Confederate troops in Mississippi. The railroads that ran through Corinth also gave the Confederates the potential to move large numbers of troops to threatened points in Tennessee and western Kentucky.

Union strategists were very much aware of the value of Corinth to the Confederacy; in the spring of 1862 a Federal army under Maj. Gen. Ulysses S. Grant moved to the banks of the Tennessee River near Shiloh Church, a scant twenty miles from Corinth. The Confederates, anticipating such a move against the city, had already concentrated troops there; they were determined to attack Grant before he could begin his advance. On April 6 and 7, 1862, more than one hundred thousand men clashed in the small fields, dense woods, and deep ravines that surrounded Shiloh Church. On the afternoon of the second day's fighting, the Confederates, who had suffered almost eleven thousand casualties, retreated toward Corinth.

It was raining in Corinth four days after the Battle of Shiloh when Kate Cumming arrived there to help nurse the wounded soldiers. Until then she had never seen a large army or an injured man; she was nervous about what lay ahead. Traveling into town she saw a sea of muddy slop and tents "as far as the eye could reach." At the depot the crowd of soldiers was so great that she had trouble getting downtown, but she finally managed to reach the Tishomingo Hotel. The hotel, along with every other major building in town, flew the yellow flag of a hospital. Inside she found "Gray-haired men—men in the pride of manhood—beardless boys—Federals and all, mutilated in every imaginable way, lying on the floor, just as they were taken from the battlefield." Kate, despite her inexperience, stayed up all night tending the wounded and continued to work in the hospitals until she left Corinth.[2]

While Kate and others helped the wounded and sick, Maj. Gen. Henry W. Halleck arrived at Shiloh to take personal command of the advance on Corinth. On April 29, 1862, Halleck, with ninety thousand men, began moving toward his objective. In Corinth, Gen. P. G. T. Beauregard had strengthened his defenses by constructing a ten-mile-long series of trenches along the ridges to the east and north of town. Furthermore, the Rebel losses at Shiloh had been more than replaced by the arrival of at least thirty thousand troops that had been scraped together from throughout the western Confederacy.

Halleck's advance toward Corinth was painfully slow, because he entrenched at the end of each day's march. By May 25, 1862, Halleck had the bulk of his forces, which now numbered 110,000 men, within two miles of Corinth; he had wasted the better part of a month in getting there. Inside the fortifications Beauregard had decided that he could not hold his position against such odds. He was already sending large quantities of stores out of the city in preparation for its evacuation.

Kate Cumming left Corinth for Okolona, Mississippi, on May 27, 1862. Two days later Beauregard's army began pulling out of the town at night, but Halleck remained ignorant of the large scale movement that was taking place almost within shouting distance of his troops. The next day Halleck's troops cautiously entered the nearly deserted railhead; they found that the Rebels and most of their supplies were gone.

After the capture of Corinth, Halleck decided to disperse his huge army.[3] Approximately fifty-five thousand Union troops under the command of Maj. Gen. Don Carlos Buell moved eastward along the Memphis and Charleston Railroad toward Chattanooga. Grant, with the balance of Halleck's troops, spread his sixty-five thousand soldiers among at least seven garrisons to protect the strategic railroad network in northeast Mississippi and west Tennessee. In northeast Mississippi Grant left nine thousand troops under Brig. Gen. William S. Rosecrans at Corinth; another eight thousand soldiers under Maj. Gen. E. O. C. Ord were stationed a few miles to the east at Burnsville. Several thousand other Union troops were scattered along the Mississippi sections of the Memphis and Charleston Railroad.

Confederate authorities responded to Halleck's strategic deployment by dividing their forces. Gen. Braxton Bragg, with thirty-five thousand men, moved toward Chattanooga. From there he planned to draw Buell away from the city by launching an offensive into Kentucky. A second force, the Army of the West, commanded by Maj. Gen. Sterling Price, concentrated fifty miles south of Corinth at Tupelo. His seventeen thousand troops were there to block any Federal advance into central Mississippi. A third Rebel force, under Maj. Gen. Earl Van Dorn, guarded the Mississippi River in scattered garrisons between Vicksburg and Port Hudson, Louisiana. His command numbered about sixteen thousand troops.

On September 1, 1862, Price received orders from Braxton Bragg, who had just begun his Kentucky Campaign, to prevent the Union forces in northeast Mississippi from reinforcing Buell's army. Price knew that he needed to act immediately to pin down the Federals; he decided to see if Van Dorn might be willing to cooperate with him in an offensive aimed at cutting the Memphis & Charleston Railroad east of Corinth.

Instead, Van Dorn urged Price to swing his army westward toward Holly Springs, Mississippi. This plan, Van Dorn argued, would simultaneously deter Rosecrans from reinforcing Buell and open up the possibility of invading west Tennessee. Price demurred because Bragg had given him explicit orders to prevent reinforcements from reaching Buell, and because recent Federal activities around Iuka on the Memphis & Charleston Railroad had convinced him that Federal troops were preparing to move northward. He began advancing toward Iuka to carry out Bragg's orders. Meanwhile, Van Dorn, who still favored threatening west Tennessee, was trying to assemble a force for such an operation.

On September 14, 1862, Price's men drove a small garrison out of Iuka and occupied the town. Grant reacted to Price's advance by ordering a two-pronged attack against Iuka, which he hoped would trap the Confederates between converging forces. Ord's troops at Burnsville were to move directly toward Price; a second column of nine thousand men under Rosecrans was to

march southward to Rienzi and then turn eastward through Jacinto to cut off Price's line of retreat. By September 18, Price was becoming convinced that Grant was not moving to reinforce Buell, and that evening he learned that Ord was marching toward him with a large force. During the evening Price also received another urgent request from Van Dorn to bring the Army of the West to Ripley so the two forces could unite. Price, faced with Ord's advance and now convinced that Grant was not trying to reinforce Buell, decided to comply with Van Dorn's request; he issued orders for the army to be prepared to move at dawn along the road to Jacinto.[4]

On the afternoon of September 19, 1862, the leading elements of Price's retreating column suddenly made contact with Rosecrans' troops coming up Jacinto Road. Both sides began deploying for battle. To the northwest, Ord, who was under orders to attack when he heard the sound of Rosecrans' guns, sat quietly throughout the ensuing battle.[5] Around 4 P.M. Rosecrans launched a major attack against Price's army and pushed the Confederates toward Iuka. However, Price's men rallied and drove the Federals back. When the fighting stopped that evening, the bulk of Price's infantry was in front of Rosecrans, but only a thin screen remained behind to cover Ord. Price wanted to renew the fighting on the next day, but his subordinates convinced him that Ord's uncommitted troops would likely pounce on the rear of the Army of the West. Price reluctantly decided to continue the withdrawal.[6] Iuka cost the Confederates slightly more than fifteen hundred casualties, and the Federals lost almost eight hundred men. Ten days later Price and Van Dorn united at Ripley, Mississippi.

Van Dorn now had 22,000 men, and he still planned to liberate west Tennessee. However, he could not undertake such an offensive as long as Rosecrans' garrison at Corinth threatened his lines of communications. Therefore, the Federals in Corinth had to be dealt with first. Rather than take a direct approach to Corinth, Van Dorn planned to first move northward and place his army astride the Mobile & Ohio Railroad. From there he would be in a position to threaten not only Corinth but also the Union garrison at Bolivar, Tennessee. He hoped that such a strategy would confuse the Union forces and keep them from reinforcing Corinth. Meanwhile, Rosecrans, who was unsure of Confederate intentions, ordered his scattered troops to concentrate at Corinth. By late September 1862, he had 23,000 Federal troops available for his defenses.

On October 1, 1862, Van Dorn sent out his cavalry and began moving west and north of Corinth. Behind the screen were three infantry divisions. On the evening of October 2, the army bivouacked along the railroad line at Pocahontas, Tennessee, about fifteen miles west of Corinth. At dawn on October 3, part of Van Dorn's cavalry headed north toward Bolivar to pin down that Union garrison, while his infantry marched southward toward Corinth.

Van Dorn's elaborate plans had not deceived the alert Rosecrans. On October 2, his cavalry scouts confirmed the location of Van Dorn's infantry, and that evening he issued orders for Col. John Oliver's brigade of Brig. Gen. Thomas McKean's Division to march at dawn toward Van Dorn. Oliver was to test the strength of the Confederate advance and then conduct a fighting retreat back to Corinth. Rosecrans had already constructed a strong series of positions to the north and west of Corinth. On the morning of October 3, 1862, he deployed three divisions in the old Confederate entrenchments 400 yards in front of his more recent fortifications. On the extreme right Hamilton's Division guarded Purdy Road. In the Union center, Brig. Gen. Thomas Davies' Division protected the Mobile & Ohio Railroad while McKean's men held the Union left flank. Brig. Gen. David Stanley's

Division remained in reserve near Battery Robinett, which anchored the center of the new Union fortifications protecting Corinth.[7]

Shortly after daylight, Van Dorn's vanguard began skirmishing with Oliver's brigade, which withdrew slowly toward Corinth as instructed. About three miles from the town Van Dorn deployed his infantry for battle. He placed Brig. Gen. Louis Hebert's Division on the left and Brig. Gen. Dabney H. Maury's Division in the center. Both units were under the tactical control of Price. Maj. Gen. Mansfield Lovell's Division went into line on the Confederate right.

In front of the advancing Rebels were hundreds of felled trees that Beauregard's Confederates had cut the previous spring. The line of trees, known as an abatis, was designed to impede the progress of advancing infantry. Van Dorn's men would have to fight their way through the tangled timbers that originally had been cut to block a Federal advance that had never occurred.

Inside the Federal entrenchments, William W. Cluett and his regiment, the 57th Illinois Infantry, had just arrived at the double quick. As soon as he got into position, the firing commenced, and Cluett saw "the angry legions of the south moving towards our front in terrible array." Price's two divisions rushed forward, screaming as they ran. Cluett watched as the charging infantry was thrown back, only to rally and move forward again, still shouting "that cold-blooded yell which has to be heard to be appreciated."[8] Federal rifle fire turned back the attack a second time, but the Confederates re-formed their ranks for another attack. This time they broke through; Cluett and the rest of the Federal infantry began withdrawing toward their second line of defenses.

By sunset the Federals had been driven into their interior defenses. However, Price's men had been unable to overwhelm those positions, and Lovell had yet to aggressively commit his troops to the assault. Inside the defenses Cluett was exhausted, and like most of the Union troops he got little rest during the night. Price's men were equally tired, having marched and fought in ninety-degree temperatures with almost no water to relieve their thirst.[9] Under such conditions Van Dorn acceded to Price's opposition to further action until the men had been rested. He would take up the battle at dawn the next day.

During the night Van Dorn placed three artillery batteries on the high ground west of town to support the next morning's attack. At 3 A.M. the guns opened fire. Cluett thought that the heavens seemed ablaze as the Rebel shells burst in the air. At dawn the Union siege guns, now able to see their targets, opened fire and quickly suppressed the Rebel artillery.[10]

Van Dorn hoped to attack at first light with a simultaneous advance by all three of his divisions, but Lovell and Hebert seemed unable to get their troops moving. Indeed, before the advance began Hebert reported in sick and turned his command over to Brig. Gen. Martin Green, who wasted valuable time issuing new instructions to his subordinates. Lovell, on the Confederate right, seemed content to do little more than throw out skirmishers and await developments. In the Confederate center Maury had orders not to advance until he heard the fire of Green's men on his left. Finally, at 10:30 A.M., an exasperated Van Dorn gave the orders for Maury to move forward anyway. As Maury advanced he finally heard the roll of musketry from Green's troops on his left. The two divisions were cut down as they attacked. Cluett, who was near Battery Robinett, could feel the ground tremble from the concussions caused by the battery's heavy guns.[11]

Despite heavy casualties, several regiments from the two divisions broke into Corinth. However, without the supporting fire of Lovell's Division, they were unable to hold their gains.

By noon the Confederates had withdrawn, after suffering almost twenty-five hundred losses. Rosecrans' army had also been badly mauled, suffering an equal number of casualties in the two days of bloody fighting.

Van Dorn's force was further reduced by stragglers as it limped into Chewalla, Tennessee, some eight miles from Corinth. There the Confederates bivouacked for the night. At sunrise the next morning Van Dorn continued his retreat toward the Hatchie River Bridge. Van Dorn's advance guard crossed the stream, but was suddenly thrown back by Union infantry. The Federals were part of a five-thousand-man column under Ord that Grant had earlier sent to reinforce Rosecrans. Ord now appeared to have the Confederates trapped between his men and Rosecrans' forces, which were just then skirmishing with the Rebel rear guard near the Tuscumbia River Bridge. However, quick action by the Rebels held Ord's column back until the weary Confederates found another crossing six miles upstream at Crum's Mill. There Confederate troops converted a small dam into a makeshift bridge; by evening the last of Van Dorn's men were safely across the Hatchie River. They continued unmolested until the rain-soaked army reached Ripley on October 6, 1862.

Van Dorn's defeat at Corinth ended his hopes for regaining control of west Tennessee and cast a shadow over his military career. He was soon superseded by Lt. Gen. John C. Pemberton and became commander of the new general's cavalry. The victor at Corinth, William Rosecrans, replaced Buell as commander of the Army of the Cumberland; he, too, would later be removed from command after his crushing defeat at Chickamauga, Georgia.

Northeast Mississippi was now firmly under Union control; neither occasional Confederate cavalry raids nor the ubiquitous guerrillas seriously threatened the Federal presence there.

Indeed, the war had now passed by Corinth, and the rail junction that had meant so much in 1862 lost its strategic importance after the Federals occupied Chattanooga in the fall of 1863. On January 25, 1864, before withdrawing, the Federal garrison in Corinth burned all the buildings that might have been used for military purposes. In the waning weeks of 1864 Maj. Gen. Nathan Bedford Forrest briefly occupied the nearly destroyed town, but after Hood's defeat at Nashville it was again abandoned.

Pvt. Elisha Stockwell of the 14th Wisconsin Infantry had fought at Corinth in October 1862, and in the last months of the war he returned to the city in pursuit of retreating Rebels. "Corinth is all burned down," he wrote his mother, "the country as far as we went is completely destroyed it dont look like the same place that it did 2 years ago."[12] The war in northeast Mississippi had not only wrecked Corinth and its railroads, but it had also devastated the countryside and left thousands of dead Americans in its path.

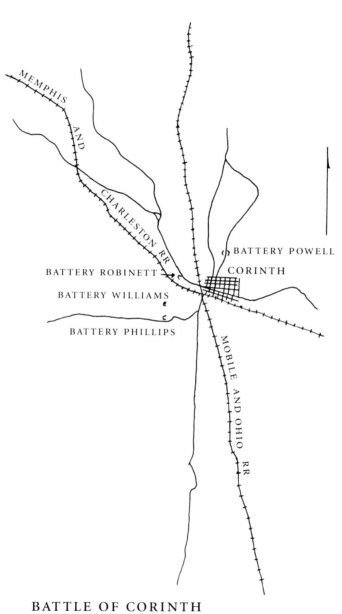

BATTLE OF CORINTH

Northeast Mississippi was a vitally important strategic area because two major railroads crossed over its rolling hills. The older of the two lines, the Memphis & Charleston Railroad, carried passengers and freight from the Mississippi River to Chattanooga, Tennessee. From there, other lines connected to Southern cities such as Nashville, Atlanta, Savannah, Charleston, and Richmond. The second and newer line, the Mobile & Ohio Railroad, began in Columbus, Kentucky. It then traveled southward through western Tennessee and eastern Mississippi until it reached its terminus at Mobile, Alabama. The junction of the two lines was Corinth, Mississippi, a community of twelve hundred inhabitants who depended largely on the railroads for their living. Until Corinth fell, no Federal force operating either along the Mississippi River or in west-central Tennessee could be safe from a rapid concentration of Rebel troops by rail.

In 1861, the Tishomingo Hotel, which faced the Memphis & Charleston Railroad, was the largest of three buildings that provided accommodations for travelers. Immediately after the Battle of Shiloh the hotel was converted into a Confederate hospital. When Kate Cumming arrived there on April 11, 1862, the wounded soldiers were so closely packed together that she could hardly walk without stepping on them.[13] *Photo courtesy of the Chicago Historical Society, no. ICHi - 07781*

TISHOMINGO HOTEL AND
THE MEMPHIS & CHARLESTON RAILROAD
AT CORINTH, MISSISSIPPI
carte de visite

HENRY WAGER HALLECK
glass negative

On April 11, 1862, forty-seven-year-old Maj. Gen. Henry Wager Halleck arrived at Shiloh. The commander of the Department of the Tennessee had come to personally lead the Union troops who had fought at Shiloh against Corinth.

Halleck, a Phi Beta Kappa from Union College and an 1839 graduate of West Point, enjoyed scholarly pursuits and bureaucratic details. Two of his books, *Elements of Military Art and Science* and his translation of Henri Jomini's *Vie Politique et Militaire de Napoleon*, were widely read by soldiers and established Halleck as America's leading scholar-officer. Halleck had always been a capable administrator, and during the previous year his subordinates had enjoyed an almost unbroken string of battlefield victories. However, Halleck had never commanded an army in the field.

On April 29, 1862, "Old Brains," as Halleck was sometimes called, ordered his 90,000-man army to advance on Corinth, which was only twenty miles away. Halleck soon proved to be overly cautious and consumed with administrative details. His army moved at a snail's pace. On May 25, 1862, Halleck finally had his army, which now numbered 110,000 men, before his objective. That evening he telegraphed Secretary of War Edwin Stanton that he had every confidence "that we shall succeed, but dislike to run any risk, and therefore have waited to ascertain if any more troops can be hoped for."[14] *Photo courtesy of the U.S. National Archives, no. 111-BA-681*

Gen. P. G. T. Beauregard, the hero of Fort Sumter, was not a scholar, but he had commanded troops in battle. Since mid-April the energetic Creole had been strengthening Corinth's defenses in anticipation of Halleck's advance. His primary line of entrenchments began about two miles northwest of Corinth on a high ridge near the Memphis & Charleston Railroad. From there a series of fortifications meandered along the ridge in a huge arc that hooked around the northern and eastern approaches to Corinth before terminating south of the town. On paper Beauregard had eighty thousand men under his command, but, in fact, eighteen thousand soldiers were already sick, and many of the others were weakened by poor sanitary conditions in the camps. On May 26, 1862, Beauregard, not wishing to further weaken his army in a siege that he would surely lose, decided to evacuate Corinth. He immediately started moving the sick and his military stores down the Mobile & Ohio Railroad. His infantry began leaving on the evening of May 29; to confuse Halleck, Beauregard ordered the retreating troops to cheer as if they were being reinforced, when in actuality their trains were departing. The ruse worked. "The enemy are reenforcing heavily . . ." declared one of Halleck's subordinates, "The cars are running constantly, and the cheering is immense every time they unload . . ." When the Union troops entered the city next morning, they found only a few stragglers.[15] *Photo courtesy of the U.S. National Archives, no. 111-B-5176*

149

THORNTON HARDIE BOWMAN
copy print from Thornton Hardie Bowman,
Reminiscences of an Ex-Confederate

Pvt. Thornton Bowman, a native of Louisiana, was attending college in Alabama when the Civil War began. He immediately returned home and joined the Tensas Cavalry. On October 15, 1861, the unit became Co. A of Col. Wirt Adams' Mississippi cavalry.

During Halleck's advance on Corinth, Bowman's company surprised a Union cavalry patrol, capturing about 40 prisoners. After the fall of the town the Confederates did not have enough infantry to take the offensive, but they did conduct a series of cavalry operations against the railroads in the region. In late August 1862, Col. Frank Armstrong left Holly Springs, Mississippi, with 2,700 cavalrymen to raid the railroad lines in western Tennessee. Private Bowman was with Armstrong's cavalry when they captured 71 prisoners in front of Bolivar, Tennessee. Armstrong then moved north of the city and destroyed the bridges between there and Jackson, Tennessee. On his return Armstrong inflicted 75 casualties and captured another 213 prisoners at Britton's Lane, Tennessee. During the fighting, Bowman fell beneath his horse and was captured.[16] Cavalry raids such as these did not force the Union to abandon western Tennessee and northeast Mississippi, but they did pose major problems for Federal communication lines in the region

Prior to the Civil War, Maj. Gen. Sterling Price was an influential Missouri politician who had served in the state legislature and the U.S. Congress before being elected governor. He was also a Mexican War veteran and ex-military governor of New Mexico. In March 1861, Price served as president of the Missouri Secession Convention. He was ambivalent about leaving the Union, but after the attack on Fort Sumter, he joined the secessionists and accepted command of the Missouri State Guard. He later led his men at Wilson's Creek, Missouri, and Pea Ridge, Arkansas.

After the fall of Corinth, Price remained behind at Tupelo with 17,000 men to watch the Union forces in northeast Mississippi. When Bragg began his fall invasion of Kentucky, Price received orders to prevent Union troops in the area from reinforcing Buell's army in central Tennessee. In early September 1862, Union activity fifty miles north of Tupelo, at Iuka, Mississippi, convinced Price that such a move was underway. On September 11, Price began advancing toward Iuka; three days later his infantry marched into town unopposed. Since the Federals had retreated westward it was clear that they were not moving to reinforce Buell. Price notified Van Dorn of these developments and started preparing to evacuate the town. On the morning of September 19, 1862, his troops began withdrawing, but Price left a weak force to watch a Union column advancing toward Iuka from the northwest. *Photo courtesy of the Arkansas History Commission*

STERLING PRICE
carte de visite

EDWARD OTHO CRESAP ORD
albumen print

The column approaching Iuka was commanded by Maj. Gen. E. O. C. Ord, a West Point graduate and Indian fighter who had been in the United States Army since 1839. About 5 P.M. on September 17, 1862, Ord received orders from Grant to press forward toward Iuka. Grant also ordered Rosecrans to take a second column of nine thousand men from Corinth and move southward to Jacinto. Rosecrans' column was then to turn northeast toward Iuka. Grant planned to catch Price between these converging columns and then launch a coordinated attack against him. On the evening of September 18, 1862, Grant thought he had everything in place, when he received a dispatch from Rosecrans informing him that some of his troops had gotten lost during the march. It would be at least 1 P.M. the next day before all of Rosecrans' troops could be in position. Grant immediately notified Ord of the situation and ordered him to begin skirmishing but not to advance until he heard the sound of Rosecrans' guns south of Iuka. At 10 A.M. the next morning Grant cautioned Ord, "Do not be too rapid with your advance this morning, unless it should be found that the enemy are evacuating."[17] Throughout the Battle of Iuka, Ord, operating under Grant's strictures and unable to hear the gunfire because of a phenomenon known as "acoustical shadow," remained inactive. Nothing lay between him and Rosecrans but a small Rebel force that Ord could easily have brushed aside. *Photo courtesy of U.S.A.M.H.I., MOLLUS, Mass., Collection*

Around 2 P.M. on September 19, 1862, Confederate scouts stumbled onto Union skirmishers south of Iuka. Until then Price had been unaware of the existence of Rosecrans' column. The newly discovered Federals were from Brig. Gen. Charles S. Hamilton's Division, which was trying to close the trap on the Rebel army.

Hamilton, a West Point graduate and Mexican War veteran, had resigned from the army in 1853 to go into business. When the Civil War began he was operating a flour mill in Wisconsin. On May 11, 1861, Hamilton reentered the service as colonel of the 3rd Wisconsin Infantry. Six days later he was promoted to brigadier general. Hamilton's military career almost ended shortly after the Siege of Yorktown, when Maj. Gen. George B. McClellan relieved him from command. Hamilton was saved by his old classmate from West Point, Ulysses S. Grant, who agreed to give him command of a division in the West.

By 4 P.M. on September 19, 1862, Hamilton had deployed about 2,800 soldiers, and they were quickly engaged in a bloody infantry battle. Hamilton later remarked that he "never saw a hotter or more destructive engagement."[18] When the fighting ended that evening, Hamilton had lost 679 men. After the battle Grant commended Hamilton to President Lincoln, who responded by promoting him to major general to rank from the day of the Battle of Iuka. *Photo courtesy of U.S.A.M.H.I., MOLLUS, Mass., Collection*

CHARLES SMITH HAMILTON
albumen print

WILLIAM H. TUNNARD
copy print

Twenty-three-year-old Commissary Sgt. Will H. Tunnard of Baton Rouge was with the 3rd Louisiana Infantry as it hurried forward to meet the new threat posed by Hamilton's Division. Earlier that morning the men had not suspected that they would be attacked, and the news took many by surprise. Prior to the Battle of Iuka, the regiment, which originally numbered 1,037 men, had taken heavy casualties at Wilson's Creek and Pea Ridge. On September 19, 1862, it numbered only 238 men, including Sergeant Tunnard. At Iuka the men of the 3rd Louisiana fought against the 5th Iowa Infantry, which was protecting the right flank of the 11th Ohio Light Artillery. During the battle the two regiments poured "destructive volleys into each other's ranks." The brief battle cost the Louisianans 115 casualties.[19]

On December 2, 1911, Tunnard sent a copy of this photo in a letter to a friend. He wrote:

I am sending herewith my picture as I came from the war, with my original knapsack with blanket, my correspondent cylinder in which I carried pencils and paper for my correspondence with journals, my tin cup and plate and combination knife, fork and spoon, carried during the war. The shirt I wore was part of the velvet cover of the piano in the ladies cabin of the steamer *Hodges* made by the owner, Mrs. Ellen Sleade, a handsome young widow, and presented to me with a similar one for my brother Fred.[20]

Photo courtesy of L.L.M.V.C., L.S.U., William H. Tunnard Papers

GEORGE WORK
carte de visite

George Work was twenty-two years old when he volunteered for military service on June 24, 1861. On September 19, 1862, he was a fourth corporal in Co. B, 5th Iowa Infantry, when it fought against the 3rd Louisiana at Iuka. Work's commander, Col. Charles Matthies, had barely gotten his men in place along the crest of a hill when he saw the better part of two brigades moving toward the Federal line. The Confederates "came up in front and poured a terrible fire of musketry" into the 5th Iowa. Matthies' soldiers returned the fire. The battle raged for the next fifteen minutes, when Matthies found that he was being flanked. He promptly attacked and drove the Rebels down the hill, where they re-formed and charged again, "cheering as they came." Matthies again repulsed the attackers, but his own regiment was shattered. Before the battle ended, the 5th Iowa received orders to retire from the field. The regiment had lost 217 men, more than a fourth of all the casualties that the Federals suffered at Iuka. Corporal Work was among 176 soldiers of the 5th Iowa who were wounded in the fight.[21] *Photo courtesy of Roger Davis*

156

LEWIS HENRY LITTLE
copy print

One of Price's best friends and trusted sub-ordinates was Brig. Gen. Lewis Little. In 1839 Little received a direct commission in the army and was posted to the infantry. In the Mexican War he was brevetted for gallantry and remained in the army until joining the Confederacy on May 7, 1861. Little was first attached to Price's staff, but the Missourian quickly promoted him to brigadier general. Little assumed command of a Missouri brigade, which he led at Pea Ridge.

Little had been chronically ill since his arrival in Mississippi, but he still commanded one of Price's Divisions in September 1862. He was not well when the Iuka Campaign began; on the march northward he could barely ride and often traveled in an ambulance. Little was also plagued by fleas, and conditions did not improve in Iuka. "Nearly devoured by fleas last night," he wrote on September 16. For the next three days Little's duties and his nagging illness kept him from getting much rest. When he awoke on September 19, 1862, he felt "unrefreshed." Even though Little was ill, he was able to command his division at Iuka. That after-noon Little was talking with Price when he was shot above the left eye and killed instantly. His stunned commander could only mutter "My Little, my Little; I've lost my Little."[22] *Photo courtesy of the Chicago Historical Society, no.ICHI-11550*

RUFUS KING CLAYTON
copy print

Capt. Rufus King Clayton of Jasper County commanded Co. A of the 40th Mississippi Infantry, which was deployed near the 3rd Louisiana. Clayton's regiment had been organized on May 14, 1862, and presently numbered 314 men. It had never been in combat.

Much of the fighting at Iuka centered on Confederate attacks against the 11th Ohio Light Artillery and its supporting infantry. The 40th Mississippi, along with at least five other Confederate regiments, eventually succeeded in capturing the six-gun battery, forcing the Federals to withdraw for a short distance. The 40th Mississippi suffered seventy casualties, including Captain Clayton, who was wounded in his right arm.

At the end of the day the Confederates held much of the battlefield, and they had inflicted almost eight hundred casualties on the Federals. Price wanted to resume the battle the next day. However, he had already lost fifteen hundred men, and Ord's fresh troops to the north of Iuka were still uncommitted. Price reluctantly heeded the advice of his subordinates and decided to continue the retreat the next morning.

Price left several hundred wounded soldiers behind. On September 20, 1862, Clayton was taken prisoner. He was paroled on October 14, 1862, but his wound had become infected. On November 15, 1862, the twenty-six-year-old captain died from the infection.[23] *Photo courtesy of Beauvoir, The Jefferson Davis Shrine*

Maj. Gen. William S. Rosecrans had a reputation as a man who liked to drink and
swear. However, he also took care of his
men's needs and was already becoming
affectionately known among the ordinary
soldiers as "Old Rosey." As a boy growing up
in rural Ohio, Rosecrans was an avid reader
who worked hard to educate himself. At the
age of fourteen he secured an appointment
to the U.S. Military Academy and graduated
in 1842. Rosecrans resigned from the army in
1854 after an unexceptional career, and none
of his subsequent civilian pursuits were successful. When the Civil War began he joined
the Federal army; since May 1862, he had
been serving in Mississippi.

Rosecrans handled his troops well at
Iuka, and Price's escape had largely occurred
because of circumstances beyond the Federal
commander's control. After the battle,
Rosecrans returned to Corinth where he
began concentrating his infantry and working to finish the city's defenses. By October
2, 1862, Rosecrans had repaired the old
Confederate entrenchments that had been
abandoned that summer, and he had completed an interior series of stronger fortifications along the northern and western edges
of town. He now had twenty-three thousand
men under his command, and his cavalry
patrols were fanned out northwest of
Corinth looking for Van Dorn's infantry.[24]
Rosecrans had no intention of being surprised in his fortifications that protected
Corinth. *Photo courtesy of U.S.A.M.H.I.,
MOLLUS, Mass., Collection*

159

Rosecrans believed that one of the best avenues for a Confederate attack lay along the line of the Memphis & Charleston Railroad. Near the outskirts of town, the tracks passed through a cut in a low ridge that appears on the left-center section of this image. Rosecrans had been worried about this particular sector of the Union fortifications since August 1862, and he occasionally prodded Grant to strengthen the position. Grant finally agreed with Rosecrans and gave orders to correct the weakness. By the time of the Battle of Corinth, Grant's engi-neers had constructed batteries Williams and Robinett to protect the railroad cut. Battery Williams is on the left of this image; the edge of Battery Robinett is just above the Union tents on the extreme right. Sometime after September 26, 1862, Rosecrans ordered his engineers to connect the two batteries with the line of breastworks seen in the center of this image.[25] The bloodiest fighting in the struggle for Corinth occurred near these two batteries and their supporting entrench-ments. *Photo courtesy of Dale Snair*

Rail line cut for the Memphis & Charleston Railroad at Corinth
carte de visite

On September 28, 1862, Price and Van Dorn joined forces at Ripley, Mississippi. Van Dorn brought with him a seven-thousand-man infantry division under the command of Maj. Gen. Mansfield Lovell. Van Dorn's subordinate had fallen from favor with the authorities in Richmond because of his recent loss of New Orleans.

In 1842, Lovell had graduated ninth in his class at West Point. His fellow cadet, William Rosecrans, finished fifth in the same class. Lovell later served with distinction in the Mexican War, while Rosecrans remained in the states with the Engineers Corps. Both men resigned from the army in 1854 to pursue private interests. In the fall of 1861 Lovell left his position as deputy street commissioner of New York City to accept an appointment as major general in the Confederate army.

Before Van Dorn invaded western Tennessee he had to destroy the garrison at Corinth. He planned to confuse Rosecrans by first moving north of the city to feint an advance along the Memphis and Ohio Railroad. He then would turn southeastward and surprise the Federals in Corinth. At daybreak on October 3, 1862, Lovell's Division was advancing toward Corinth from the northwest as Van Dorn had planned. His men suddenly encountered Rosecrans' cavalry patrols, which were being reinforced by Union infantry. Lovell's men pushed forward. By 10 A.M. his division was in front of Rosecrans' first line of defenses; the other Confederate divisions were coming to his support. *Photo courtesy of U.S.A.M.H.I., MOLLUS, Mass., Collection*

MANSFIELD LOVELL
albumen print

ELISHA STOCKWELL, JR.
copy print from Byron R. Abernathy, ed.,
Private Elisha Stockwell, Jr., Sees the Civil War

Sixteen-year-old Pvt. Elisha Stockwell, Jr., enlisted in Co. I, 14th Wisconsin Infantry, on February 8, 1862. Less than two months later he was slightly wounded at the Battle of Shiloh. The 14th Wisconsin arrived in Corinth in August 1862, and Stockwell drew a new pair of badly needed shoes. Unfortunately, the pegged soles on the cowhide footwear quickly rubbed a blister on his left foot. Stockwell was barefooted when his regiment received orders to move to Iuka. Stockwell went to his captain's tent to explain his condition, only to be curtly told to get back in ranks. Stockwell was standing in line ready to march when his lieutenant, who was actually under arrest for striking another officer, asked where Stockwell thought he was going. "I don't know," Stockwell replied, "I am going with the company as long as I can stand it." "Get out of there and take off that knapsack," shouted the lieutenant. Stockwell countered by explaining that the captain would not excuse him. "I don't give a damn what the captain says," the lieutenant snapped, "you get out."

Stockwell missed the Iuka Campaign, but on the morning of October 3, 1862, he was with the 14th Wisconsin a few miles northwest of Corinth. His regiment, fighting a delaying action, slowly withdrew until it reached the old Confederate entrenchments. In the distance Stockwell could see the Rebel infantry deploying for battle.[26]

In 1842 Dabney H. Maury graduated from the University of Virginia and began reading law. He wanted to pursue a military career, however, and he obtained an appointment to West Point, where he graduated thirty-seventh in the class of 1846. Maury was assigned to the cavalry and left almost immediately for the Mexican War. During the war, Maury was brevetted twice for meritorious service. He remained in the army until June 25, 1861, when he was dismissed for expressing "treasonable designs" against the Union. Maury joined the Confederate army as Van Dorn's chief of staff. He was promoted to brigadier general on March 18, 1862, and later assumed command of a division.

On October 3, 1862, Maury's four thousand men deployed on Lovell's left. The right wing of Maury's line rested on the Memphis & Charleston Railroad. By 10 A.M. Van Dorn had his infantry in place and ordered a general advance. Maury's line pushed into the defenses that Beauregard had constructed earlier that spring. His infantry drove the Union defenders back, but the men met determined opposition as they began crossing the fields toward Rosecrans' main line.[27] On Maury's left Brig. Gen. Louis Hebert's Division also drove through Rosecrans' initial defensive line, but they too were encountering increased resistance as they neared the principal Union fortifications. Lovell's attack on Maury's right was less aggressive, but he too drove the Federals back toward their main line. *Photo courtesy of U.S.A.M.H.I., MOLLUS, Mass., Collection*

DABNEY H. MAURY
albumen print

164

DAVID B. WILSON
albumen print

RICHARD J. OGLESBY
albumen print

Richard "Uncle Dick" Oglesby was born into a slaveholding Kentucky family on July 25, 1824, and he was orphaned at the age of nine. Later in his life, he stated that the shock of seeing the family slaves sold to clear the family's estate converted him to abolitionism. Young Oglesby moved to Illinois to live with his uncle. There he held a number of menial jobs while he educated himself and saved enough money to study law. Shortly after being admitted to the bar, he volunteered for the Mexican War. Oglesby returned to Illinois after the war and began practicing law, but he was soon lured away by the California gold rush. Oglesby eventually returned to Illinois and became active in the fledgling Republican party. After an unsuccessful congressional race in 1858, Oglesby was elected to the state senate in 1860. The next year he resigned his seat to accept a commission as colonel of the 8th Illinois Infantry, and on March 22, 1862, he was promoted to brigadier general.[28]

On the afternoon of October 3, 1862, Oglesby's brigade was deployed in the sector where Maury's Division attacked. Oglesby's four regiments held their ground until the left wing of his line started to waver. Oglesby tried to rally his shaken men, but he was seriously wounded by a Rebel bullet. The temporarily leaderless and hard-pressed brigade fell back in disorder. *Photo courtesy of U.S.A.M.H.I., MOLLUS, Mass., Collection*

First Lt. David B. Wilson of Co. E, 2nd Iowa Infantry, was with his regiment as it deployed on the right of Oglesby's brigade. Wilson's commander, Col. James Baker, had 246 men in line when the Rebel attack began that afternoon. The regiment helped repulse the first Confederate attack, but Baker was mortally wounded. The 2nd Iowa held their position until Oglesby's brigade collapsed. By then the regiment's brigade commander, Brig. Gen. Pleasant Hackleman, had already died trying to rally Oglesby's men. Col. Thomas Sweeney of the 52nd Illinois Infantry then assumed command of the brigade and withdrew it in good order.

The 2nd Iowa suffered forty-two casualties in the first day's fighting at Corinth. On October 4, the regiment lost another sixty-five men. Wilson was not harmed; he and eleven other lieutenants in the regiment were cited for bravery in the "protracted and deadly engagement."[29] *Photo courtesy of U.S.A.M.H.I., Ted Alexander Collection*

L. YATES
carte de visite

Eighteen-year-old Pvt. L. Yates of Co. B, 18th Arkansas, mustered into the Confederate service on March 12, 1862, and he saw his first fighting at Iuka. Between September 29 and October 3, 1862, the 18th Arkansas marched more than fifty miles as Van Dorn tried to fool Rosecrans about his intentions.

On October 3, 1862, the 18th Arkansas was with Maury's reserves when the attack against Corinth began. Around 4 P.M. the 18th and two other Arkansas units received their orders to reinforce Brig. Gen. Charles W. Phifer's brigade of Maury's Division. Phifer's brigade had already driven the Federals on their front to within eight hundred yards of the main line of Union entrenchments. However, his men were "exhausted with heat and dust" and could go no further.[30] The three Arkansas units relieved Phifer's men and began skirmishing with the enemy. At nightfall the Federals withdrew most of their infantry into the main line of fortifications. Yates and the rest of the Confederates moved forward as close as they dared. That evening Van Dorn rested his troops. He would continue the attack at daybreak.

Yates' regiment participated in the general assault on October 4, 1862. The two-day Battle of Corinth cost the regiment 128 casualties, but Yates was not hurt. *Photo courtesy of L.L.M.V.C., L.S.U., Civil War Album*

166

During the night Van Dorn rested his tired infantry and issued orders for the advance on the 4th. Hebert's Division on the left received orders to begin the attack promptly at daylight. Maury and Lovell's divisions were to attack when they heard the firing of Hebert's infantry. However, daylight came and there was no attack by Hebert. Van Dorn promptly dispatched a courier to learn why the attack had not begun, but he was unable to find Hebert. About 7 A.M. Hebert came to Van Dorn's tent and reported that he was sick. Van Dorn then ordered Brig. Gen. Martin Edwin Green to assume command and attack.

At the beginning of the Civil War, Green was operating a sawmill in Lewis County, Missouri. In the summer of 1861, he organized a regiment of cavalry, but by September he was an infantry commander in the Missouri State Guard. Green saw his first action at Pea Ridge, Arkansas, and after the transfer of Price's command to Mississippi, he was promoted to brigadier general. Green's brigade had been present at Iuka, but it had seen almost no action.

Thus Green, who had no formal military training and precious little practical battlefield experience, now commanded the spearhead of Van Dorn's assault. Green was apparently ignorant of the plan of attack and wasted valuable time realigning his troops. His delay helped destroy any lingering hope of a coordinated assault. *Photo courtesy of the Library of Congress, no. LC B816-2985*

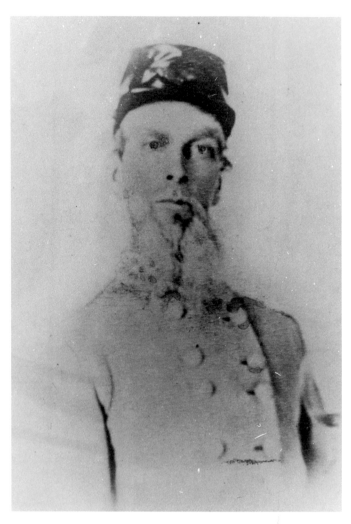

MARTIN EDWIN GREEN
albumen print

WILLIAM DENSON EVANS
ninth-plate ambrotype

In December 1861, William Denson Evans of Jasper County met with a group of friends at a schoolhouse near Stringer, Mississippi. There the young men formed a volunteer company and selected L. B. Pardue as their captain. The company appears to have fought as an independent command at Shiloh, but on May 2, 1862, it became Co. A, 7th Mississippi Battalion. Evans was carried on the rolls as a private.

On October 4, 1862, Evans was with the battalion at the Battle of Corinth. The 7th Mississippi, attacking with Green's old brigade, charged an eight-gun battery supported by infantry. During the attack six men were killed and another twenty-three were wounded. Evans lost his left eye and was slightly wounded in the arm during the charge. His commander, Lt. Col. James S. Terral, was mortally wounded.

Sixty-one years after the battle, Evans wrote his brother a letter about the Battle of Corinth and Terral's death. Evans remembered that he was nearby when the lieutenant colonel fell from his horse. "He was shot all to peaces," he wrote, "boath leges were broke[,] boath arms was broke[,] and 4 or five bullits were shot in his boddy." Evans recalled Terral hollering "knock them off of there guns boys for I caint do any more." Evans added that "we done what he told us to do and spiked the big guns . . ." Evans later helped carry his stricken commander to the rear, staying with him until he died.[31] *Photo courtesy of Mary Johnson*

168

THOMAS ISAAC DUVAL (*left*)
AND WILLIAM RUSSEL DUVAL
copy print

Thomas, William, and Henderson Duval
(see p. 239) had all joined the 3rd Missouri
Infantry as privates in Co. C. The men
apparently enrolled in the unit late in 1861.
The regiment then fought at Pea Ridge
before being transferred to Mississippi. On
May 8, 1862, William was elected second
lieutenant of Co. C; his two brothers
remained in the ranks as privates.

On the morning of October 4, 1862, the
3rd Missouri was part of Col. Elijah Gates'
brigade of Green's Division. The brigade was
deployed in front of the Mobile & Ohio
Railroad. Green finally got his men moving
about 10 A.M. Gates' men, advancing under a
"hurricane and torrent of fire," charged forward. Officers and men scrambled over logs,
brush, and fallen timber as they advanced on
the Federal positions. Lt. William Duval was
carrying the 3rd Missouri's colors when he
was killed in front of the Union breastworks.[32] His two brothers were not hurt in
the fighting, which cost the 3rd Missouri
ninety-three casualties. *Photo courtesy of Tom
Sweeney*

LORENZO SWAGERTY
carte de visite

Capt. Lorenzo Swagerty joined the Confederate army at Clarksville, Arkansas, on September 12, 1861. Swagerty was twenty-seven at the time of his enlistment. His unit then traveled to Fayetteville, Arkansas, where the men mustered into the service as Co. A, 16th Arkansas Infantry. Swagerty was elected captain of the company, and subsequently led his command at Pea Ridge.

On the morning of October 4, 1862, his regiment was also part of Gates' brigade. Gates' men swept into the Union entrenchments and the defenders fled toward Corinth. The brigade now held a large section of the Union line, and they had captured at least forty artillery pieces. However, his men were exhausted and short of ammunition. Within a few minutes the Federals counterattacked, and Gates called for reinforcements. Swagerty was not injured in the fighting, but his regiment lost fifty-five men. *Photo courtesy of Dale Snair*

Col. Henry P. Johnson, a merchant from Washington, Arkansas, organized the McCulloch Avengers and mustered into service as its captain on March 1, 1862. The McCulloch Avengers became Co. B, 20th Arkansas Infantry, and Johnson had been its commander since May 13, 1862.

On October 4, 1862, Johnson's regiment was part of William Lewis Cabell's brigade, which was temporarily assigned to Green's command. Cabell's men had been under artillery fire for more than an hour when they received orders from Green to reinforce Gates. The men were so relieved to get away from the artillery fire that they cheered when they learned that they were about to be committed to battle. Cabell quickly got his men moving. When Cabell neared the Federal entrenchments he expected to see elements of Gates' brigade, but by then Gates had been driven back; Cabell's infantry, led by the 20th Arkansas, suddenly faced a line of Union infantry about three hundred yards in front of the recently recaptured breastworks. Cabell gave the command to advance, and his men moved forward, cheering as they went. The Federal line fell back, and Cabell's men continued forward until they reached the crest of the Federal entrenchments. There they were met by a withering infantry fire. Part of the 20th Arkansas managed to fight their way into the entrenchments, but Cabell's men could not retake the position. Johnson died in front of the entrenchments, and his regiment lost ninety-two men. *Photo courtesy of Old Washington State Park*

HENRY P. JOHNSON
copy print

WILLIAM H. FULLWOOD
copy print

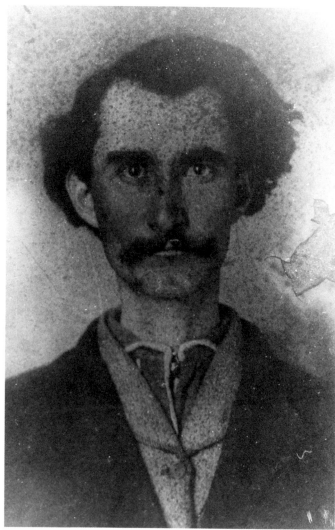

While Green's men were fighting for control of the Federal entrenchments, 1st Sgt. William H. Fullwood was advancing toward the Federal positions on the west side of the Mobile & Ohio Railroad. His regiment was part of Phifer's brigade.

William's father, Samuel M. Fullwood, owned a farm near Shiloh, Tennessee; on two occasions during March of 1862 Federal quartermasters took cattle and feed from the Fullwoods. According to family legend, young William, who was no doubt incensed by the incidents, took his father's shotgun and went to Corinth, Mississippi, to join the Confederate army. On April 29, 1862, he mustered into Co. E of the 3rd Arkansas Cavalry.[33]

On October 4, 1862, Fullwood's unit fought as dismounted cavalry. As soon as Phifer's men left the timberline they were exposed to heavy fire, and hundreds fell before they swarmed over the Federal entrenchments. Phifer's brigade and Fullwood actually fought their way into Corinth; a few soldiers managed to reach the railroad junction before they were finally stopped. Fullwood survived both days' battles, but his regiment lost 107 men. *Photo courtesy of Dr. Ronnie Fullwood*

First Lt. Laurens Wolcott of Co. D, 52nd Illinois Infantry, participated in the counterattack that drove the Rebels out of the recently captured Union entrenchments. Years after the battle, Wolcott wrote that the Federal regiments that had retreated only minutes before in total disorder "suddenly stopped, faced about and with but a moment of delay charged their pursuers with a vim that nothing could withstand." During the confusion of the sudden counterattack, several distant Union artillery batteries and infantry regiments mistook the advancing infantry for Confederates and fired into their comrades' ranks. A number of Union soldiers died from the misdirected firing; Wolcott himself was standing next to a Federal soldier who was shot in the back by his own men. Wolcott's regiment had begun the Battle of Corinth with 380 men; they had lost one-fourth of their number by the time the fighting ended.[34] *Photo courtesy of U.S.A.M.H.I., Richard Tibbals Collection*

LAURENS W. WOLCOTT
copy print

The most famous attack at Corinth occurred around Battery Robinett, which was located on the right of Phifer's advancing brigade. The earthen and log fortification sat on a ridge near the Memphis & Charleston Railroad and mounted three 20-pounder Parrott guns. Four Union infantry regiments were stationed nearby to protect the artillerists.

On the morning of October 4, 1862, Brig. Gen. John Creed Moore sent almost 1,900 soldiers to attack the battery and its supporting infantry. Col. William P. Rogers commanded the 2nd Texas Infantry when it attacked Battery Robinett. Rogers, sitting astride his horse, led the 2nd Texas forward with relatively light casualties until they emerged onto the open ground about one hundred yards in front of the lunette. There

the men recoiled from the intensity of the combined infantry and artillery fire, but they rallied and moved forward. Rogers' horse was shot from under him near the base of the battery, but he jumped to his feet and led scores of his soldiers onto the parapet. Rogers died atop the wall. Two hundred and seventy-two other men from Moore's brigade were either killed or wounded. Another 985 soldiers were reported missing after the battle; most were stragglers who later returned to their commands.

After the battle, Union soldiers found Rogers' body near the base of the rampart and apparently propped him up for this photo. Colonel Rogers is the bearded corpse near the left corner of this image. *Photo courtesy of the Library of Congress, no. LC B8184-10072*

BATTERY ROBINETT
copy print

174

ALONZO COURTNEY
copy print

Alonzo Courtney of Ohio was the eleventh
of fourteen children. In August 1861, the
twenty-six-year-old farmer joined Co. A,
63rd Ohio Infantry, at Marietta, Ohio.

The 275 men of the 63rd Ohio had seen
no action during the first day at Corinth,
and on the morning of October 4, it was one
of the four regiments assigned to protect
Battery Robinett. At about 10 A.M. Courtney
saw Rebel infantry moving onto the open
ground in front of his regiment. The colonel
of the 63rd Ohio kept his men lying down
until the battle line was only fifty yards
away; then he ordered his soldiers to stand
and fire. The 63rd Ohio, Courtney wrote
shortly after the battle, "fought like tigers."
At times the struggle was hand to hand. "My
God!" he added, "it was awful to behold the
slaughter. The dead lay in piles where our
artillery had mowed them down by hundreds." Courtney saw Rogers climb the rampart only to be shot dead. He added that

"The Rebel flag was planted on our breastworks
and the scene that ensued in that terrible hour I
cannot describe . . . It was a death struggle and
both sides fought with desperation. The ground
was covered with blood and for more than a mile
in length there was a continual belching forth of
lead and fire and smoke."

The next day Courtney walked over the
ground and "there was hardly a spot on a
hundred acres but what there lay the dead
Secesh."[35] Courtney escaped injury, but the
63rd Ohio lost 132 men in the second day's
struggle at Corinth. *Photo courtesy of
Northeast Mississippi Museum Association*

ALBERT O. McCOLLOM
copy print from Walter J. Lemke, ed.,
The War-Time Letters of Albert O. McCollom

Van Dorn began retreating from Corinth on the afternoon of October 4, 1862. His army was completely wrecked; forty-eight hundred soldiers were either killed, wounded, captured, or straggling. Many of the stragglers eventually returned to their ranks, but actual losses totaled at least twenty-five hundred men—11 percent of those on the field of battle. Van Dorn's best avenue of escape lay across the Hatchie River Bridge about twelve miles west of Corinth.

Albert O. McCollom was twenty years old when he walked into Fayetteville, Arkansas, on October 9, 1861, and mustered into the Davis Light Horse Cavalry. The unit became Co. E of a mounted battalion of sharpshooters. McCollom's battalion fought at Corinth as dismounted cavalry under the command of Col. E. I. "Ras" Stirman; it lost ninety-six men in the battle.

On the morning of October 5, 1862, McCollom was in the vanguard of Van Dorn's army when scouts reported that a Union column was moving toward the Hatchie Bridge. The weary infantry then advanced first at quick time and finally at double time. When McCollom arrived at the bridge he was "tolerably run down, after the two days fight at Corinth, doing on short rations and the fatigue of the retreat." He nevertheless crossed the bridge under fire. His brigade was attacked before it could deploy. Many of the men got back across the bridge, but McCollom was captured.[36]

Twenty-three-year-old Sinclair Carter was farming near French Camp, Attala County, Mississippi, when he joined the Choctaw Guards on May 29, 1861. The Choctaw Guards became Co. I, 15th Mississippi Infantry; prior to Corinth, the Guards had fought at Mill Springs, Shiloh, and Baton Rouge.

At Corinth, the 15th Mississippi was part of Lovell's Division, which sat idly on the right wing of Van Dorn's army while their comrades were slaughtered on the rest of the field. By the end of the battle, a total of almost 2,200 men had been either killed or wounded in Maury's and Green's divisions. Lovell had lost only 352 men.

On October 5, 1862, Lovell's relatively fresh division was covering the Confederate retreat when the head of the army was surprised at Hatchie Bridge. At that time Lovell's men were skirmishing with Rosecrans' pursuing infantry near the Tuscumbia River Bridge. Van Dorn was caught between two converging Union columns and was in danger of losing his entire army. He immediately ordered one of Lovell's brigades to reinforce the Confederates at Hatchie Bridge. Carter and the 15th Mississippi remained behind with Brig. Gen. John Bowen's brigade to defend the Tuscumbia River Bridge. The 15th Mississippi was one of the last regiments to cross the bridge, which was promptly burned by Bowen. Lovell later wrote that "the Fifteenth Mississippi distinguished itself particularly" in the defense of the Tuscumbia River Bridge.[37] *Photo courtesy of John H. Luckey*

SINCLAIR B. CARTER
copy print

First Lt. John Waldock of Co. D, 15th Illinois Infantry, was part of Ord's column that had been ordered to intercept the retreating Rebels at Hatchie Bridge. His regiment arrived near the bridge about the time that the Rebel infantry was deploying to protect the crossing.

Waldock was an Englishman who had served in the Crimean War before moving to America in 1856. In England he had been a brewer, and when the Civil War began, he owned a bakery in Belvidere, Illinois. Waldock mustered into the service as a second lieutenant, and when his immediate superior resigned he should have been in line for promotion to first lieutenant. However, because of his "John Bull proclivitie," the men of his company elected their first sergeant to the vacant position. The authorities ignored the men's wishes and promoted Waldock to first lieutenant to rank from September 3, 1862.

Ord's men threw the Rebels back across the bridge and then had to cross the same structure under Confederate fire. Waldock led his company across, "trailing arms and at the double quick." Not a man was lost.[38] Federal and Rebel troops clashed on the east bank of the Hatchie River for most of the afternoon. Ord's Division suffered 570 casualties in the fight. Waldock's regiment lost six men. *Photo courtesy of U.S.A.M.H.I., Don Wisnoski Collection*

ALEXANDER J. GERRARD
carte de visite
Anderson & Blessing, New Orleans

First Lt. Alexander J. Gerrard joined Co. F, 39th Mississippi Infantry, in April 1862. When he enlisted, the six-foot-tall Gerrard was twenty-eight years old and living in Georgetown, Mississippi.

On October 5, 1862, the 39th Mississippi was part of Brig. Gen. John Villepique's brigade, which Lovell sent to reinforce Van Dorn's troops at Hatchie Bridge. Gerrard's regiment arrived at Hatchie Bridge just as the Union infantry was deploying on the east bank of the river. They had to help hold the Federals until Van Dorn found another place to cross the Hatchie River. Van Dorn's men found a suitable crossing about eight miles south of Hatchie Bridge at Crum's Mill. There his men hastily laid planks across an old dam that spanned the stream. Late that afternoon the 39th Mississippi withdrew from Hatchie Bridge and Gerrard crossed the river at Crum's Mill. The Confederates lost 452 men at Hatchie Bridge, but they had been lucky to escape capture.

On October 6, 1862, Van Dorn's ragged force slogged through the rain until they reached Ripley, Mississippi. There they rested for the night. The Confederate offensive to regain northeast Mississippi and western Tennessee had failed. In less than a month the Federals would begin the first of many attempts to take Vicksburg. *Photo courtesy of L.L.M.V.C., L.S.U., Civil War Album*

Chapter 6

From Court House Dome VBurg Miss

Stalemate at Vicksburg

Eons before the United States fought its bloody Civil War the forces of nature had already created the conditions that would make the future city of Vicksburg the center of a mighty struggle between the Southern and Northern armies. Vicksburg is located on an escarpment that begins in Kentucky near the mouth of the Ohio River and then winds its way southward until it disappears into the Gulf Coastal Plain in the vicinity of Baton Rouge, Louisiana. Long before man set foot in North America, winds deposited millions of tons of sediment called loess on this uplift. This rich dirt eventually became covered with hundreds of varieties of lush vegetation. In places the depth of the loess exceeds one hundred feet, but it erodes easily, producing nearly vertical slopes. As a result, the terrain is frequently gouged with deep, irregular ravines that limit the uplift's value as farmland and make travel difficult.

A few miles north of Vicksburg, the bluffs give way to the bottom lands formed by the confluence of the Mississippi and Yazoo rivers. This area, which is drained primarily by the Yazoo River, encompasses about seven thousand square miles of delta land. For thousands of years, periodic flooding of the two rivers left behind both rich deposits of alluvial sediment and extensive marshy areas. The delta, which averages about sixty miles in width, is bordered on the east by the same bluffs which slowly curl westward to Vicksburg. Across the river from Vicksburg, the Louisiana Delta is similar in character to the Yazoo bottom lands.

East of Vicksburg the loess surface extends about ten miles before it meets the flood plain of the Big Black River. Here the loess-covered escarpment is also slashed by deep ravines. The Big Black River eventually cuts its way through the bluffs and empties into the Mississippi River about twenty-two miles below Vicksburg near the village of Grand Gulf. East of the alluvial river bottom, firm rolling farmland slowly replaces the softer soil. South of Vicksburg, the bluffs follow the general meandering of the Mississippi River until they merge with the Gulf Coastal Plain. These bluffs, like those in the vicinity of Vicksburg, are heavily wooded and scarred with steep ravines.

This rugged geography makes the region the strongest natural defensive position on the Mississippi River. Any force approaching the city through the vast bottoms had to cross an almost trackless flood plain cut by innumerable bayous, swamps, and oxbow lakes, all of which were clogged with cypress, tupelo, cottonwood, and gum trees. The high ground to the east and south of the city offered better footing for an invading army, but the heavy foliage and steep ravines clearly favored the defenders. Finally, the tall bluffs along the river would place any naval force under the punishing fire of heavy artillery situated there. Any person with an eye for military terrain would have easily seen the defensive advantages of the bluffs below the Yazoo River. However, when Newet Vick and his family arrived in the region sometime around 1814, they came only in search of good farmland.

By the time of Vick's death in 1819 he had acquired farmland in the interior, and he also owned land along the high bluffs. These bluff properties, which Vick left in his estate to be parceled out to form a town, became part of the original site for the city that bears his name. Six years after Vick's death, his town was incorporated. By 1835 Vicksburg had a population of twenty-five hundred people and was the commercial center of the immediate region. There local cotton growers brought their crops to brokers, purchased the articles they needed to conduct farming operations, and spent some of their profits on the amenities that made life on the frontier more tolerable.[1]

By 1860 Vicksburg was a major transportation hub that catered to both steamboats and railroads. Packets arrived and departed daily from the city, providing connections to most of the major river towns in the Mississippi River Valley. Rail service on the west bank of the river linked Vicksburg with Monroe, Louisiana, and the line's owners planned to lay track all the way to Texas. On the other side of the river the Southern Railroad of Mississippi connected Vicksburg with the capital city of Jackson, forty miles to the east. From there, lines led to Meridian, Mississippi, Memphis, and New Orleans. On the eve of the Civil War, cotton and transportation interests had turned the town into a thriving community of forty-six hundred persons.

In the waning months of 1860 many of the people of Vicksburg and the surrounding county of Warren were lukewarm toward the growing movement of Southern independence; the city itself chose a block of pro-Union candidates to attend the upcoming Secession Convention in Jackson. However, once Mississippi voted to leave the Union, the citizens began raising military companies and preparing for war. On January 11, 1861, a four-gun battery sitting on the tall bluffs of the city fired the first shots of the war in Mississippi. Their target was an innocent steamer that was unlucky enough to be flying the Union flag when it rounded the great bend in the river.[2] During the next two years the sounds of thousands of shells would be heard booming across the river as rival armies clashed to control the citadel of Vicksburg.

By the beginning of 1862 Federal forces were in position to begin a two-pronged advance to liberate the Mississippi River from Rebel control. South of Vicksburg, Adm. David Farragut's ships and supporting troops were assembled to attack New Orleans. North of Vicksburg several Federal armies backed by a fleet of gunboats were starting to push down the Mississippi River and its tributaries.

During the early months of 1862 the Confederate defensive positions in the Mississippi River Valley began to collapse rapidly. North of

Vicksburg, Federal victories at Forts Henry and Donelson, Island No. 10, and Shiloh cleared Confederate power from the valley as far south as Memphis. Meanwhile, Farragut fought his way past the forts that protected New Orleans and captured the Crescent City. Within weeks, Baton Rouge, Louisiana, and Natchez, Mississippi, easily fell into his hands. On May 18, 1862, the vanguard of Farragut's fleet arrived before Vicksburg and demanded its surrender. The garrison commander, Brig. Gen. Martin Luther Smith, laconically replied that "Having been ordered to hold these defenses, it is my intention to do so as long as it is in my power."[3]

North of Vicksburg, the last feeble Confederate flotilla on the Mississippi River was destroyed in front of Memphis on June 6, 1862. The way was now clear for Union gunboats to advance on Vicksburg. In six months, Confederate control of the Mississippi River had been compressed to nothing more than the tall bluffs at Vicksburg; it was there, at the strongest natural point along the river, that the final struggle for control of the Mississippi had to be fought.

By mid-June 1862, the full weight of Union naval power had converged on Vicksburg. Farragut, standing aboard the quarterdeck of the USS *Hartford,* could see the city's church spires, but he had no hope of taking Vicksburg without cooperating infantry to seal the land approaches to the garrison. The closest available troops, approximately 110,000 men under the command of Maj. Gen. Henry W. Halleck, were in northeast Mississippi. If Halleck had kept that formidable force united and moved immediately toward Vicksburg, there would have been little that the Rebel forces in the region could have done to stop him. However, Halleck was fixated on capturing the rail center at Chattanooga, Tennessee. He therefore decided to send half his force toward that objective while the rest of his men remained behind to protect the territory that he had already

won. It was a fateful decision; the soldiers that Farragut desperately needed were being frittered away by Halleck's strategy. With this reprieve, the Confederates had time to rush reinforcements to Vicksburg and to begin building extensive defensive works around the city.

Thus, between May 18, 1862, when Farragut's vessels first demanded the surrender of Vicksburg, and July 25, 1862, when the admiral took his vessels back to New Orleans, operations against the city were left almost entirely to the navy. On June 28, 1862, Farragut did run part of his fleet past the Vicksburg batteries and join the gunboats that had earlier cleared the upper tributaries of the Mississippi River. However, without supporting infantry, he could do little more than harass the citadel.

From time to time the big guns from Farragut's ships and his mortar boats lobbed shells toward Vicksburg. These attacks did little discernible damage to the city's defenses, but they were a nuisance that unnerved soldiers and citizens alike. Increasingly, the townspeople responded to the attacks by digging caves for immediate protection, while the soldiers prepared ever more elaborate entrenchments and bombproofs.

The Federal blockade of Vicksburg from the river approaches received a major setback on July 15, 1862, when the CSS *Arkansas* drove three Union gunboats from the Yazoo River. The Rebel ironclad then boldly steamed through the surprised Union fleet and arrived at a safe anchorage under the guns of Vicksburg. Farragut was mortified by the *Arkansas's* successful exploit, and that evening his ships steamed downriver in an unsuccessful attempt to sink the vessel. For the next several days, Farragut, with the cooperation of the gunboats that remained upriver, tried without success to destroy the boat.

The unsuccessful attacks against the *Arkansas* coincided with the end of the naval operations against Vicksburg. For weeks Farragut had feared that his fleet might be trapped by the rapidly falling water, and on July 20, 1862, he finally received permission to steam to New Orleans. Five days later his fleet headed downstream. North of Vicksburg, Flag Officer William H. Davis, now without Farragut's support, felt that he too had no choice except to break off operations against the city.

By August 1862, the Confederates had regained nominal control of the Mississippi River in the vicinity of Vicksburg. Within the month they would establish the southern anchor of their new defensive positions at Port Hudson, Louisiana. Through this 130-mile-long gap supplies from the western Confederacy, Mexico, and Europe were again flowing to the Rebel armies. The naval campaign against Vicksburg had failed, and a land effort would not get under way until that fall.

On October 16, 1862, Maj. Gen. Ulysses S. Grant assumed command of the Department of the Tennessee and began developing his plan of attack. In late November Grant moved southward from Tennessee, following roughly the line of the Mississippi Central Railroad. The route kept Grant's army on firm ground. However, the rail lines to his rear were Grant's only source of logistical support, and they were vulnerable to marauding Rebel cavalry. By early December 1862, Grant had pushed as far south as Oxford, but his advance began to stall.

Meanwhile, Maj. Gen. John A. McClernand, a powerful Illinois Democrat whom Abraham Lincoln could ill afford to ignore, had, with the president's permission, been busily raising a second army to operate against Vicksburg via the Mississippi River. When Grant learned of McClernand's plans, he used his authority as theater commander to send Maj. Gen. William T. Sherman back to Memphis to assume control of the operation before McClernand arrived.

Grant's overland campaign against Vicksburg came to a sudden end on December 20, 1862, when twenty-five hundred cavalrymen under Maj. Gen. Earl Van Dorn destroyed the Federal army's major supply base at Holly Springs, Mississippi. Grant immediately saw that he could not maintain a secure line of rail communications in central Mississippi, and he prudently withdrew his forces.

When Grant's men began moving northward toward LaGrange, Tennessee, the Confederate troops that had been contesting his advance rushed southward to counter Sherman's offensive. On December 26, 1862, Sherman's thirty-two thousand infantry accompanied by Acting Rear Adm. David D. Porter's gunboats ascended the Yazoo River, and three days later the Federals launched a major assault against the hastily reinforced Confederate positions along Chickasaw Bluffs. The assault was unsuccessful. Four days later Sherman began withdrawing his forces.

Even though the Chickasaw Bluff Expedition had failed, Grant was convinced that the meandering waterways around Vicksburg were the best avenues along which to advance. In the winter of 1863 Grant first tried to penetrate the region by working a small flotilla through a series of bayous, lakes, and streams until they reached high ground northeast of Vicksburg. When Confederates blocked the Yazoo Pass Expedition at Greenwood, Mississippi, Grant made a second and equally unsuccessful attempt through Steele's Bayou.

While these campaigns unfolded, other soldiers labored on various projects on the west bank of the Mississippi River. There Grant hoped to link together various bayous, swamps, and lakes into a continuous waterway that would allow him to reach the high ground south of Vicksburg without having to pass by the city's guns. For months his men worked digging canals and removing obstructions from the waterways. Despite their best efforts, Grant's soldiers failed to create an alternative route around Vicksburg.[4]

The watery terrain thwarted every attempt that Grant made either to reach the high ground northeast of Vicksburg or to find a waterborne path that led to the dry land below the city. By the end of March 1863, the mighty river and the watery lands that it had created had done what the Rebel army could never have accomplished: They had stopped Grant and had saved Vicksburg for the Confederacy.

Passengers standing on the decks of the
numerous packet boats that plied the
Mississippi River in 1860 had the most dra-
matic view of Vicksburg when they were
going downstream. The travelers, after
rounding a huge bend in the meandering
river, suddenly saw a sprawling river town
that ran for almost a mile along the bluffs
on the east side of the river. In the center of
this image is the newly constructed Warren
County Courthouse, which sat on one of the
tallest hills in Vicksburg. The structure was
perhaps the most impressive public building
in Mississippi, and its four-faced clock dominated the city's skyline.[5] *Photo courtesy of
Gary Hendershott*

VIEW OF VICKSBURG AS SEEN FROM
THE MISSISSIPPI RIVER
carte de visite

Along the waterfront, steamboats unloaded goods from around the world into Vicksburg's wharves and warehouses. After the fall harvest, the buildings in the warehouse district held thousands of cotton bales that awaited shipment to busy textile mills in Europe and the North.

A few blocks above the waterfront were the commercial buildings which housed the enterprises that thrived on the cotton trade. The largest concerns supplied the diverse needs of cotton producers, but there were also dozens of smaller shops that provided more specialized services to the populace.[6]

The tall tower and steeple on St. Paul's Catholic Church rose above the southern skyline of Vicksburg, and was almost as impressive as the Warren County Courthouse to the north. The fortress-like facade of the Catholic church is near the left of this photograph. It may well have caused an uninformed observer to mistake it for a citadel rather than a place of worship. *Photo courtesy of Gary Hendershott*

VICKSBURG WATERFRONT
carte de visite

187

Hundreds of residences were scattered around the city. Many of the larger homes were located away from the river and were often landscaped with trees, hedges, and fences. The more modest middle-class dwellings and the rough shacks of laborers could usually be found perched along the city's steep hills and in the deeper gorges in the town.

During the antebellum years, economic opportunity lured farmers, land speculators, businessmen, artisans, and unskilled laborers to Vicksburg. In 1860 the majority of its townspeople were Southerners, but Yankees and Midwesterners also mingled among the populace. Furthermore, sizeable numbers of foreigners, a few free blacks, and hundreds of slaves lived in the booming city. Together they added a cultural diversity to life in Vicksburg that could not be found in any other Southern river town except New Orleans.[7] *Photo courtesy of Gary Hendershott*

VIEW OF VICKSBURG AS SEEN
FROM THE CUPOLA OF THE
WARREN COUNTY COURTHOUSE
carte de visite

The terminus of the Southern Railroad of Mississippi was near the southern section of the city. During the harvest season, cotton that had been produced in the interior of the state was moved to its depots for later shipment aboard steamers.

Trains leaving Vicksburg followed a track that looped around the southeastern edge of the city and then crossed a series of trestles and bridges that spanned the lowlands along the Big Black River bottoms. After crossing the flood plain, the trains traveled eastward through Jackson to Meridian, Mississippi. Both cities offered north-south rail connections for passengers and freight. Nineteen miles west of Jackson, a feeder line connected the main track of the Southern Railroad of Mississippi with the town of Raymond.

West of Vicksburg, a small line began at Monroe, Louisiana, and terminated on the banks of the Mississippi River. From there, passengers and freight either crossed the Mississippi River by ferry or moved by boat to their destination.

The railroad network tied Vicksburg by land to the entire United States; it was another reason for the city's growing prosperity and its strategic importance. *Photo courtesy of Kean Archives*

DEPOT OF THE SOUTHERN RAILROAD
OF MISSISSIPPI
copy print

In the first weeks of May 1862, Capt. Harrison Soule of Co. I, 6th Michigan Infantry, was aboard the old steamboat *Laurel Hill* as it traveled northward with the rest of the Union flotilla. New Orleans had already fallen, and Soule's transport was one of dozens of boats assigned to free the southern reaches of the Mississippi River from Rebel control. At night the gunboats anchored in mid-channel, while the unarmed troopships tied up at a nearby bank. Pickets were immediately thrown out, and soon the cooks were ashore preparing supper for the infantry. Often the men slept on land if the "numerous varieties of bugs and musquitoes [sic]" did not make them too uncomfort-able. Early the next morning the flotilla would reassemble and resume its journey upstream. Along the way the vessels halted "at little cities and villages" to put a patrol ashore to raise the Union flag. The towns-people expressed no Unionist sentiment, but the troops encountered no resistance. "Thus day by day we passed upstream," wrote Soule. At dusk on May 20, 1862, Soule caught his first sight of "the bluffs of Vicksburg with her frowning batteries . . ."[8] He quickly learned that Vicksburg, unlike the other river towns that had capitulated without a fight, had already declined to surrender. *Photo courtesy of the Bentley Historical Library, University of Michigan*

MARTIN LUTHER SMITH
glass negative

On May 12, 1862, Brig. Gen. Martin Luther Smith arrived in Vicksburg to take command of the troops that were being hastily assembled to protect the city. Smith, a New Yorker by birth, graduated from West Point in 1842 and married a Georgia girl four years later. He had spent most of his military career in Southern posts, and when the war began he joined the Confederacy. During the previous year Smith had spent much of his time as chief engineering officer for the defense of New Orleans.

When Smith arrived in Vicksburg he found only three artillery batteries ready to protect the river and no more than one thousand armed soldiers to guard the city's landward approaches. For the next six days Smith worked his men day and night to pre-pare their positions. By May 18, 1862, he had six batteries in place; Smith felt that he had at least a chance of holding his position. When the Federal fleet appeared that day and demanded the surrender of the city, Smith refused to comply. Meanwhile, Confederate troops continued to arrive, but with "batteries incomplete; guns not mounted; troops few, and, . . . not a regular officer to assist in organizing and commanding," Smith feared that a "vigorous attack" might still overwhelm his defenses. However, the Federals took no action until May 26, 1862; by then Smith knew that he could hold the city against even the most determined attacker.[9] *Photo courtesy of the Library of Congress, no. B813-1607*

192

NATHANIEL GREEN
carte de visite

DAVID GLASGOW FARRAGUT
albumen print

When Midshipman David G. Farragut first went to sea, he was only nine years old and the United States had yet to fight its second war with Great Britain. Now Flag Officer Farragut was nearly sixty-one; he had recently become a popular hero by first running his fleet past the forts on the lower Mississippi River and then capturing New Orleans.

Farragut arrived at Vicksburg on May 21, 1862, but he found little enthusiasm among his subordinates for attacking the city. Within days Farragut, who disliked risking his deep draft vessels in the treacherous river, decided to take the big ships and return to New Orleans. He had barely gotten downstream when he received explicit orders from the Navy Department to return to Vicksburg and open the Mississippi River. On June 25, 1862, Farragut and his warships rejoined the gunboats that he had left behind to watch the city. He was determined to carry out his orders to the letter and force his way past the Vicksburg batteries.

On the night of June 28, 1862, Farragut maneuvered eight of his ships past the Confederate batteries and united them with the fleet above the river. Farragut had again proven what he already knew: Steamships could run by static defenses with minimum losses. Beyond this, Farragut had accomplished very little, since he still needed at least fifteen thousand infantry to invest the city.[10] *Photo courtesy of U.S.A.M.H.I., MOLLUS, Mass., Collection*

The Union fleet could not capture Vicksburg without the help of the army, but it could use its superior mobility to harass the garrison. One such operation occurred on May 30, 1862. At 2:30 A.M. Lt. Nathaniel Green of the USS *Kathadin* loaded the ship's cutter with twelve armed sailors and joined another boat from the USS *Iroquois*. The two crews rowed to one of the wharfboats at Vicksburg and set fire to the boat. The flames soon spread to a few buildings along the riverbank. The sailors also managed to burn about 250 bales of cotton and to return with a single slave.[11] Such raids were a nuisance to the Confederates, but they did not stop the Rebels from continuing to methodically strengthen and expand their control of the river's east bank. *Photo courtesy of the Historic New Orleans Collection*

Before dawn on July 15, 1862, the crew of the big ironclad USS *Carondelet* got up steam and prepared to get underway. The vessel was one of seven boats that had been constructed by James B. Eads in less than sixty days. The "Eads" boats were the most formidable class of ironclads on the Western rivers. At 4:30 A.M. the *Carondelet* trailed two smaller Union gunboats into the Yazoo River. They were looking for the CSS *Arkansas.*

Prior to the Battle of Memphis, the partially completed Confederate ironclad had been towed to Yazoo City, and by July 1862 the vessel was operational. She was the only Confederate boat left in the West that was capable of fighting a vessel like the *Carondelet.*

At 6 A.M. on July 15, 1862, the flotilla saw the *Arkansas* coming downstream with a full head of steam. The Union crews immediately cleared for action. Shortly afterward, the Confederates opened fire, and the flotilla rounded to and headed downstream, firing as it went. The *Arkansas* immediately sought out the *Carondelet,* and for the next hour the two boats engaged in a running duel. The *Arkansas* had closed to within fifty yards when the *Carondelet* ran aground. The Rebel ironclad did not stop to destroy the crippled gunboat but continued pursuing the other two vessels. Once in the Mississippi River, the *Arkansas* steamed by the surprised Union fleet.

Aboard the *Carondelet* four men had died and another fifteen were wounded. When she finally rejoined the fleet her nemesis was safe under the guns of Vicksburg.[12] The next day Farragut took his ships downstream to attack the ironclad, but he failed to destroy the vessel. As long as the *Arkansas* existed, the Union fleet would never be completely safe.

Falling water levels forced Farragut to withdraw to New Orleans before he could destroy the *Arkansas.* Ironically, the *Arkansas,* which had defied the might of the entire Union fleet on the Mississippi, was later scuttled by her own crew when the ironclad's engines failed. *Photo courtesy of the U.S. Naval Historical Center, Washington, D.C.*

After the Federal fleet left, the Confederates had an opportunity to regain control of a considerable length of the Mississippi River. In early August 1862, they began building a second fortified position 130 miles south of Vicksburg at Port Hudson, Louisiana. Port Hudson, like Vicksburg, overlooked the river from high bluffs and was surrounded by difficult terrain on its landward sides.

Twenty-nine-year-old Isaac Whitaker was an overseer on a plantation in Claiborne County, Mississippi, when he joined Co. K, 1st Mississippi Light Artillery, on May 7, 1862. Artillerymen usually needed more training than any other branch of the combat arms. Therefore, Whitaker and his company remained near Jackson, Mississippi, until August 1862. They spent their time learning how to fire and maintain their fieldpieces.

Around October 25, 1862, Whitaker's battery joined the garrison at Port Hudson. Other Mississippi units sent there included the 1st and 39th Infantry regiments, Claiborne's Infantry Company, English's battery (without its artillery), batteries B and F of the First Light Artillery, and the Seven Stars Battery. By mid-January 1863, heavy guns protected the river, and entrenchments were being thrown up around the town. As long as the Rebels held Vicksburg and Port Hudson, the Confederacy could never be split along the Mississippi River. *Photo courtesy of the Old Court House Museum, Vicksburg*

ISAAC WHITAKER
copy print

USS CARONDELET
copy print

ULYSSES S. GRANT
glass negative

The withdrawal of the Union fleets from Vicksburg ended the naval campaign, and little activity occurred until Maj. Gen. Ulysses Simpson Grant assumed command of the Department of the Tennessee on October 16, 1862. By then Grant had a reputation as a fighting general, but nothing in his career before the Civil War indicated that he would ever be successful at anything.

As a boy in Illinois he had shown no interest in either books or hard work. Nevertheless, Grant's father used his influence to get his son appointed to West Point. There Grant showed little concern for his studies, preferring instead to read novels and practice his horsemanship. He graduated twenty-first in a class of thirty-nine. Grant demonstrated glimmerings of military talent in the Mexican War, but he was later assigned to several obscure Western posts. In 1854 he resigned from the army under a cloud. During the next six years he eked out a living and often survived only with the financial help of his family.

The outbreak of the Civil War saved Grant from obscurity; his subsequent successes at Fort Donelson and Shiloh brought him to the attention of a public hungry for victories. As commander of the Department of the Tennessee, he was about to embark on a campaign that would establish him as the Union's premier general. During the next nine months Grant's reputation for aggressiveness and tenaciousness would be severely tested, but in the end he would prevail.[13]
Photo courtesy of the U.S. National Archives, no.111-B-5901

JOHN C. PEMBERTON
carte de visite

The day before Grant received his command, Lt. Gen. John C. Pemberton assumed control of the Department of Mississippi and East Louisiana. The two commanders had been casual acquaintances during the Mexican War.

Pemberton entered West Point in 1833; like Grant, he was an average student, standing twenty-seventh in a class of fifty. Even though Pemberton was born in Philadelphia, Pennsylvania, he was captivated by the South and made many friends among the cadets from the slaveholding states. In 1848, Pemberton strengthened his Southern connections by marrying a Virginian. Prior to the secession crisis, Pemberton had spent his entire life in the United States Army, serving in the Seminole Wars, the Mexican War, and the 1857 expedition against the Mormons in Utah. On April 24, 1861, he resigned his commission and joined the Confederate army.

Pemberton held no important field command until President Jefferson Davis promoted him to lieutenant general and ordered him to assume command of the defense of Vicksburg. During the next nine months Pemberton proved to be a competent but uninspiring officer. Ultimately, he lacked the military resources to take the initiative away from Grant. Facing such circumstances only a brilliant commander or a lucky one was likely to stop Grant. Pemberton was neither; he could only react to conditions which were largely beyond his control.[14] *Photo courtesy of L.L.M.V.C., L.S.U., Civil War Album*

Grant's first campaign against Vicksburg began on November 2, 1862, when his army moved southward from Tennessee. He planned to advance along the track of the Mississippi Central Railroad, a route which bypassed much of the wetlands that dominated the northern approaches to Vicksburg. By December 4, Grant's infantry had reached Oxford, Mississippi, and a division of his cavalry was already scouting eighteen miles south of the city.

Pvt. Halmer Swift of Wayne County, Michigan, was one of the cavalrymen operating below Oxford. Swift was twenty-one years old when he joined Co. I, 3rd Michigan Cavalry, at Fentonville, Michigan, on September 12, 1861.

On December 5, 1862, the 3rd Michigan and elements of several other cavalry regiments were scouting near Coffeeville, Mississippi, when they encountered enemy skirmishers. At first the troopers thought they were only facing a force of dismounted cavalrymen, but it soon became clear that they had stumbled on a large force of Rebel infantry. The cavalrymen could not hold their ground against the infantry, and they retreated toward Oxford.[15]

The fight at Coffeeville and Grant's concern over his overextended supply lines forced him to halt the advance. Grant planned to continue the offensive after he established a new supply base at Oxford, but meanwhile the Federals had to rely on logistical support from Holly Springs, Mississippi, which was some thirty miles north of Oxford. *Photo courtesy of the Arkansas History Commission*

HALMER SWIFT
carte de visite

EARL VAN DORN
copy print

Pemberton knew that Grant could not maintain his position in north central Mississippi if the Holly Springs depot could be destroyed. It was the weak point in Grant's position, and Pemberton decided to send Maj. Gen. Earl Van Dorn's cavalry to raid the depot.

Van Dorn, a native of Mississippi, graduated from West Point in 1842 and was a major in the 2nd U.S. Cavalry when the Civil War began. He immediately resigned his commission and joined the Confederate army as an infantry officer. However, Van Dorn was a cavalryman at heart; the tactics that he subsequently used at Pea Ridge and Corinth were more reminiscent of cavalry charges than infantry assaults. After the defeat at Corinth, Van Dorn was relegated to commander of

Pemberton's cavalry. It was a demotion, but the position better suited his talents.

On the afternoon of December 17, 1862, Van Dorn's twenty-five hundred cavalrymen were issued three days of rations and ordered to move out. Around noon on the eighteenth, Federal cavalry sighted his men, but twenty-four hours passed before the news reached Grant. Late on the evening of December 19, Grant warned his garrison commanders about the column. Around 10 o'clock that evening Van Dorn's men halted about five miles from Holly Springs. Pickets were posted on every road. The night was bitterly cold, but no fires were allowed. Before dawn on December 20, his men quietly mounted their horses and moved toward Holly Springs.[16] *Photo courtesy of the Grand Gulf Military Monument Park*

200

Despite earlier warnings by Grant, the commander of the Holly Springs garrison, Col. Robert C. Murphy, did nothing to prepare for an attack. On the morning of December 20, 1862, the garrison, which numbered approximately eighteen hundred men, was spread out in three areas which were too far apart to give mutual support. Furthermore, Murphy failed to post additional pickets or even inform his subordinates of the possibility of an attack.

Six companies of the 2nd Illinois Cavalry, including Pvt. George H. Wilson of Co. H, were camped in the fairgrounds when Van Dorn's troopers swept into town. Wilson and the other troopers suddenly found themselves under attack from several different directions. Many of the men were captured in the initial assault, but Wilson and about 130 other men got mounted and cut their way out of the trap. During the melee 9 men from the 2nd Illinois died, 39 were wounded, and at least 100 were captured. Elsewhere, the Union infantry surrendered after only token resistance. Van Dorn's troopers then rounded up more than 1,500 prisoners and burned an estimated $1,500,000 worth of Federal supplies. In one swoop Van Dorn ended Grant's overland campaign against Vicksburg; within the week the Federals were moving northward. On January 8, 1863, Murphy was cashiered from the army for "his cowardly and disgraceful conduct" at Holly Springs.[17]
Photo courtesy of Richard F. Carlile

GEORGE H. WILSON
carte de visite

201

202

JOHN ALEXANDER MCCLERNAND
albumen print

In the late fall of 1862 there were rumors that a second campaign against Vicksburg was being planned. The person designated to lead the mysterious expedition was Maj. Gen. John A. McClernand, a powerful Illinois Democrat. McClernand had little military talent, but President Lincoln could not dismiss his ideas without running the risk of angering loyal Democratic politicians. When McClernand offered to raise a new army and lead it against Vicksburg, the president agreed to support him. By December 1862, McClernand was traveling through the Midwest, recruiting new regiments and forwarding them to Memphis.

When Grant got wind of McClernand's scheme, he decided to act because "Two commanders on the same field are always one too many." Grant immediately sent Maj. Gen. William T. Sherman to assume command of the troops in Memphis. He then wired Halleck, who approved of Grant's decision. McClernand, upon hearing the news, telegraphed Lincoln saying, "I believe I am superseded. Please advise me." Secretary of War Edwin Stanton, replying for Lincoln, informed the astonished general that Grant was the theater commander, but McClernand, as a subordinate, was to command the river expedition. However, when McClernand reached Memphis, he found that Sherman's troops had already left.[18]
Photo courtesy of U.S.A.M.H.I., MOLLUS, Mass., Collection

Sherman planned to take his troops up the Yazoo River and land them on the high ground northeast of Vicksburg. However, he first had to clear the stream of any mines that might have been laid by the Confederates. One of the boats assigned to that task was the USS *Cairo*, commanded by Lt. Com. Thomas O. Selfridge, Jr.

Selfridge, a native of Massachusetts, graduated from the Naval Academy in 1854 and was on active duty when the Civil War began. On March 8, 1862, he commanded the forward guns of the USS *Cumberland* when she was sunk by the CCS *Merrimac* at Hampton Roads, Virginia. The *Cumberland* was the first wooden ship to be destroyed by an ironclad.

On December 12, 1862, the USS *Cairo* was on the Yazoo River protecting a tinclad that was trying to clear mines from the stream. When the lighter boat came under heavy Rebel fire, Selfridge quickly moved his ironclad forward to protect the vessel. Suddenly, two rapid explosions almost lifted the *Cairo* out of the water. She went down in twelve minutes, leaving only her stacks showing above the water. All hands were rescued. Selfridge's boat, which was a sister ship to the *Carondelet*, was the first vessel to be sunk by a mine. Sixteen months later Selfridge was sunk a third time when his boat, the USS *Conestoga*, collided with another Union vessel.[19] *Photo courtesy of the U.S. Naval Historical Center, Washington, D.C.*

Thomas O. Selfridge, Jr.
copy print

The loss of the *Cairo* did not prevent the river from being cleared of mines. On December 26, 1862, Sherman began disembarking his troops four miles northeast of Vicksburg near Chickasaw Bayou. The lands immediately around the swampy bayou were almost impassable, but, about a mile and a half to the east, a narrow ridge rose above the flood plain. The ridge, which ran northeasterly from Vicksburg until it touched the Yazoo River ten miles above the city, was known as Walnut Hills. Chickasaw Bluffs was near the center of Walnut Hills, and it was there that Sherman hoped to break the Confederate defenses. If he succeeded, the Federals would have control of the high, firm ground that they needed to advance on Vicksburg. *Photo courtesy of U.S.A.M.H.I., MOLLUS, Mass., Collection*

CHICKASAW BLUFFS
albumen print

George W. Morgan
albumen print

Pennsylvania-born George W. Morgan was not a professional soldier, but he seemed to be drawn to military service. When Morgan was sixteen he left college to fight for Texas independence as a captain in Sam Houston's army. Morgan returned to the U.S. in 1839; two years later he entered West Point, but resigned in 1843 because of poor grades. Morgan then moved to Ohio where he studied law. In 1846 the twenty-six-year-old lawyer became colonel of the 2nd Ohio Volunteers and left for the Mexican War. On March 3, 1847, he was promoted to colonel in the regular army and given command of the 15th U.S. Infantry. Morgan led his regiment in Gen. Winfield Scott's campaign against Mexico City and was brevetted to brigadier general. After the war Morgan practiced law in Ohio until 1856, when he became a diplomat. At the outbreak of the Civil War Morgan was Minister to Portugal, but he returned home to accept an appointment as a brigadier general.

On December 28, 1862, Morgan's soldiers skirmished with isolated Confederate infantry units which were withdrawing to their main entrenchments on Chickasaw Bluffs. The next morning his seventy-five-hundred-man division led the main assault against the Confederate positions at Chickasaw Bluffs. About 11 A.M. Morgan's troops advanced with a wild shout. The assaulting columns, attacking on a narrow front, were jammed together. They moved forward, only to be "mowed down by a storm of shells, grape and canister, and minie-balls."[20] *Photo courtesy of U.S.A.M.H.I., MOLLUS, Mass., Collection*

On the morning of December 28, 1862, Lt. Col. Winchester Hall was in command of the 26th Louisiana Infantry. His men were in a series of rifle pits five hundred yards in front of the Confederates' primary fortifications along Chickasaw Bluffs. Their positions guarded a road which ran parallel to Chickasaw Bayou, the main track that Morgan's men had to follow to get to Chickasaw Bluffs. Hall's front was protected by the bayou, but behind him there were open fields which would be difficult to cross under fire. Hall's men held Morgan's skirmishers back until nightfall, and at 2 A.M. the 26th Louisiana noiselessly withdrew toward Chickasaw Bluffs. "It was a long weary day to us," wrote Hall. By the morning of December 29, the regiment was hastily dug in at the base of the bluffs. That day Morgan's men got within fifty yards of the 26th Louisiana, but the Union line wavered and broke. Other less-determined attacks followed, but they too were repulsed. After dark Hall sent his pickets forward where they found the ground littered with casualties. Many of the wounded were begging for water, and Hall's soldiers filled the injured men's canteens.

Later that night it began to rain, and Hall "crept into the surgeon's tent" to check on his wounded. There he enjoyed a bowl of custard that one of the ladies of Vicksburg had sent to the troops.[21]

WINCHESTER HALL
copy print from Winchester Hall,
The Story of the 26th Louisiana Infantry

In the summer of 1862 soldiers of the 13th Illinois posed for this photograph in Helena, Arkansas. Their unmilitary appearance was typical of many Federals who served in the Western armies.

On December 29, 1862, the 13th Illinois was part of Brig. Gen. Frank P. Blair's brigade of Brig. Gen. Frederick Steele's Division, which had been ordered to support Morgan's attack. It was the 13th Illinois's first fight. Before the 13th Illinois could reach the bluffs, the men had to struggle through a three-hundred-yard entanglement of felled cottonwood trees and then cross Chickasaw Bayou, which was about fifteen feet wide and three feet deep. The bank on the opposite side was steep and crowned by a line of Rebel rifle pits. Behind the bank was Chickasaw Bluffs, which was also covered with rifle pits. During the advance, the 13th Illinois came under heavy fire, but they managed to cross the bayou and drive the Rebels from the opposite bank. However, Confederate fire from Chickasaw Bluffs pinned the Federal columns down. By the end of the day the 13th Illinois had lost 173 men and Chickasaw Bluffs remained in Rebel hands.[22] *Photo courtesy of Skip Mayorga*

SOLDIERS OF THE 13TH ILLINOIS INFANTRY
albumen print

On May 13, 1862, Thomas O. Harris, a twenty-nine-year-old farmer, enlisted in the Confederate service at Monroe, Louisiana. Under the terms of enlistment he was to serve for "three years or the war" and be paid a fifty-dollar bounty. Private Thomas's unit, the Gladden Avengers, became Co. E, 31st Louisiana Infantry. The regiment remained in Louisiana until they were transferred to Jackson, Mississippi, in November 1862. From there they moved to Chickasaw Bluffs.

On December 28, 1862, Thomas's 320-man regiment held the ground in front of an Indian mound near the center of the Confederate lines at Chickasaw Bluffs. The regiment came under heavy fire that day, and "it was almost impossible for a man to show himself above the works without being instantly killed." On December 29, the Federals tried to storm the 31st Louisiana's position, but they were driven back. Thomas was not hurt; his regiment had nine men killed and seventeen wounded.

After the battle, one of Thomas's fellow soldiers in the 31st Louisiana wrote his sister, telling her that "wee have had a battel hear and whipt the Yankeeys." The Confederates had, indeed, "whipt the Yankeeys," since the combined losses for Sherman's Corps was 1,766 men. Total Confederate casualties were 187.[23] The Confederates had smashed the first major infantry assault against Vicksburg, and by sunrise on January 2, 1863, Sherman had withdrawn from Chickasaw Bluffs. *Photo courtesy of George Esker*

THOMAS O. HARRIS
sixth-plate ambrotype

Despite the failure at Chickasaw Bluffs, Grant still believed that he could find a water route to the high ground northeast of Vicksburg. Six miles below Helena, Arkansas, an earthen dam blocked an old channel that had once allowed steamers to reach Yazoo City, Mississippi. If that route were reopened, Grant could bypass the batteries that protected the Yazoo River above Chickasaw Bluffs and get in the rear of Vicksburg. On February 3, 1863, his engineers cut the dam. Four days later the USS *Rattler* and nine other boats entered the backwaters of the delta.

The *Rattler* was typical of military vessels called "tinclads." The name came from the thin skin of metal that the navy used to cover the frail superstructures of the boats.

The *Rattler*, like most of the tinclads, had originally been built to serve as a river packet, but the shallow draft design was well suited for military service.

For almost a month the men on the Yazoo Pass Expedition battled the obstructions that choked the waters. Sometimes the channel was blocked by natural timber rafts; in other places trees stretched across the streams. Often four-foot-thick cottonwood or sycamore logs, which weighed as much as thirty-five tons, had to be removed from the narrow channels. Overhead a canopy of vines and branches tore at the superstructure of the gunboats.[24] *Photo courtesy of the U.S. Naval Historical Center, Washington, D.C.*

USS *Rattler*
copy print

210

When Pemberton learned that the Union forces had entered the Yazoo Pass, he ordered Maj. Gen. William W. Loring to stop the expedition. Loring, who was then in Jackson, immediately sent his chief engineering officer, Maj. Minor Meriwether, to find a suitable location to block the expedition.

When the Civil War began Meriwether was a civil engineer in Memphis, Tennessee. For several years he had been chief engineer of the Mississippi River levees from the Tennessee line to the mouth of the Yazoo River. He was, therefore, thoroughly familiar with the countryside and had already speculated that the Union forces might try to open the old Yazoo Pass route. Meriwether thought that the best place to block the flotilla was near Greenwood, Mississippi, where the Tallahatchie and Yazoo rivers converge. Meriwether gathered together all the laborers and soldiers that he could find and hastily constructed a crude cotton-bale and earthen line between the two rivers. Behind the line were seven heavy guns that commanded the two rivers. Loring named the structure Fort Pemberton. On March 6, 1862, the Union fleet reached the Tallahatchie River; five days later the fleet appeared before Fort Pemberton.[25]

MINOR MERIWETHER
copy print from J. Harvey Mathes,
The Old Guard in Grey

211

THOMAS H. BRINGHURST
carte de visite

On the morning of March 11, 1863, Col. Thomas H. Bringhurst of the 46th Indiana Infantry disembarked his troops about three quarters of a mile from Fort Pemberton; his men were soon exchanging fire with Rebel skirmishers. Meanwhile, a Union ironclad steamed forward and began firing on the fort. After a few well-aimed artillery shells struck the boat, she withdrew out of range and then used her eleven-inch guns to bombard Fort Pemberton. Around 4 P.M. another ironclad took up the duel; neither vessel could do any significant damage to the cotton-bale and dirt fort. Two days later Bringhurst's regiment participated in an attack on Fort Pemberton, but the big guns inside the fortification held both the infantry and gunboats at bay. Another attack failed on March 16. Three days later, the expedition withdrew. However, on March 21, 1863, the withdrawing force met reinforcements coming downriver; the combined force returned to the old positions. Bringhurst and his men were safe from attack by the outnumbered Rebel infantry, but they were not immune from either accidents or artillery fire. On March 23, six men of the 46th Indiana died when a huge tree fell across a tent. On April 4, a twelve-pound shell smashed into Co. K, cutting one soldier in two and wounding another. On April 5, 1863, the 46th Indiana, along with the rest of the expedition, began withdrawing toward Helena.[26] *Photo courtesy of Indiana State Library*

While the Yazoo Pass Expedition floundered in front of Fort Pemberton, a second waterborne expedition got underway. On March 15, 1863, the USS *Pittsburg* and four other ironclads entered Steele's Bayou, which was about seven miles from the mouth of the Yazoo River. They hoped to move northward through several sluggish bayous and streams until they reached the Big Sunflower River. From there the boats could travel downstream and emerge just north of the batteries that protected the Yazoo River. If the route proved navigable, transports could then be brought up to land troops on the high ground above Vicksburg.

By March 21, 1863, the Union flotilla was becoming mired among the willows and other debris that covered the increasingly shallow water. Behind the ironclads, Rebel guerrillas were cutting trees into the water to block the boats' escape route. The situation was serious enough for the flotilla commander, Acting Rear Adm. David D. Porter, to issue orders to his captains explaining that "Every precaution must be taken to defend the vessels to the last, and when we can do no better we will blow them up."[27] That evening Federal infantry arrived. The next day they cleared the banks of Rebels, and Porter extracted his boats from their dangerously exposed position. The failure of the Yazoo Pass and Steele's Bayou expeditions ended Grant's campaign to take Vicksburg from the northeast, and he now turned his attention to the high ground south of the city.

USS *Pittsburg*
copy print from H. A. Gosnell,
Guns on the Western Waters

Chapter 7

The Fall of Vicksburg

Ulysses S. Grant was not a general who gave up easily, but he now doubted if Vicksburg could be taken from its northern approaches. There the wetlands conspired against him, and Pemberton had reacted effectively to every move he had made. Much of the Northern press, which was always hungry for victories and equally critical of generals who did not deliver them, was openly calling for Grant's dismissal. To add to the general's troubles, incessant rains and extensive flooding made it difficult for his tired troops to pitch their tents on dry ground. Conditions were miserable in the makeshift camps, and diseases disabled thousands of soldiers.[1] A lesser general might have given up, but Grant remained undeterred by such adversity.

Conversely, Pemberton had every reason to be satisfied. With numerically inferior forces he had thwarted the Federals at Holly Springs, Chickasaw Bluffs, Yazoo Pass, and Steele's Bayou. The reprieve had given Pemberton time to strengthen his defenses, and he had received a steady trickle of reinforcements throughout the last months of 1862. By March 31, 1863, Pemberton had fifty-seven thousand troops available for the defense of Vicksburg and Port Hudson.

Still, the odds against Pemberton were formidable; on that same date Grant had 105,000 men deployed in dozens of places stretching from Columbus, Kentucky, to Lake Providence, Louisiana. And Maj. Gen. Nathaniel Banks had another 35,000 soldiers in Louisiana. Although Banks was independent of Grant, he posed a serious threat to Port Hudson and therefore tied down thousands of troops that Pemberton needed to defend Vicksburg. But Grant's numerical superiority was useless if he could not find some way to deploy his troops on dry ground.

Throughout the early months of 1863, Grant had been contemplating moving his army to the high ground below Vicksburg, but he could not undertake such a maneuver until the flood waters receded. Once the land dried Grant planned to move south of the city by taking his army down the Louisiana side of the Mississippi River.[2] Meanwhile, Acting Rear Adm. David Porter would run his gunboats and transports past the Vicksburg batteries to rendezvous with Grant's troops. Once the two forces were united, Porter's boats could ferry Grant's soldiers to the high ground on the east bank of the river. It was a risky plan, because Grant had to place his army deep in enemy territory with no secure line of communications to its supply bases north of Vicksburg. It could only succeed if Grant first confused Pemberton about his intentions and then quickly seized the initiative before the Confederates could recover their balance.

On March 29, 1863, Grant set his plan in motion when the leading elements of his army began marching south from Milliken's Bend, Louisiana, toward Hard Times, Louisiana. Grant's soldiers would have to travel over almost fifty miles of soggy ground before reaching their objective, but the move would place them thirty-five miles below Vicksburg.

On the evening of April 16, 1863, Porter ran ten boats past the Vicksburg batteries so that he could cooperate with the Federal forces that were now concentrating at Hard Times.[3] The next day seventeen hundred troopers under Col. Benjamin Grierson left LaGrange, Tennessee, and began riding toward east-central Mississippi. His raid was undertaken both to confuse Pemberton about Grant's ultimate plans and to draw Rebel troops away from Vicksburg. Feint attacks on the Yazoo River at Hayne's and Drumgould's bluffs during the last two days of April further distracted Pemberton and pinned down more Confederate troops. During those crucial days Pemberton had lost the "eyes" of his command because most of his horsemen were chasing Grierson. Without adequate scouts he could not

unravel Grant's plan. He therefore had little choice except to keep his men dispersed in a vain attempt to guard all the points that might possibly be threatened.

On April 30, 1863, Grant began ferrying his men across the river to a landing near Bruinsburg, Mississippi. He met no opposition. By noon he had five divisions across the river, and more units were on the way. "When this was effected," Grant later wrote, "I felt a degree of relief scarcely ever equalled since." He added:

I was now in the enemy's country, with a vast river and the stronghold of Vicksburg between me and my base of supplies. But I was on dry ground on the same side of the river with the enemy. All the campaigns, labors, hardships and exposures from the month of December previous to this time that had been made and endured, were for the accomplishment of this one object.[4]

Tenaciousness, singlemindedness, and a willingness to take risks had gotten Grant across the river, and like all good fighting generals, he planned to exploit his advantage.

On the evening of April 30, 1863, Grant began moving toward Grand Gulf because he needed the town for a base for supplies that had to be either brought down the west bank of the river or run past the batteries at Vicksburg. The next day Grant's force, which now numbered about 23,000 soldiers, met about 5,200 Confederates six miles southeast of Grand Gulf near Port Gibson. After a sharp fight which cost each side about 800 casualties, the outnumbered Rebels began retreating to Grand Gulf. The commander of the Confederate forces at Grand Gulf, Brig. Gen. John S. Bowen, evacuated the town on May 2, 1863.

In Vicksburg the news that Grant had landed a substantial force south of Vicksburg and had driven Bowen from Grand Gulf touched off a flurry of activity. Pemberton now had some idea of both the size of the Federal force to the south and the threat that it posed to his theater of operations, and he began concentrating his forces.

Grant reached Grand Gulf on May 3, 1863. Having had neither a change of clothes nor a hot meal since April 27, he borrowed some underwear from a naval officer, took a bath, and ate dinner with Admiral Porter. Originally, Grant had planned to use Grand Gulf as a logistical base and then send troops to help Banks reduce Port Hudson. Once that garrison had been captured, Banks and Grant could then march against Vicksburg with an overwhelming force. However, early the next morning Grant was surprised to learn that Banks, rather than moving to invest Port Hudson, was on the Red River. Grant was too deep in enemy territory to wait for Banks: Such a delay might allow Pemberton to concentrate a superior force against the Federals in Grand Gulf. Rather than remain idle, the commanding general decided to "cut lose from my base, destroy the rebel force in rear of Vicksburg and invest or capture the city."[5]

By May 7, 1863, Pemberton had concentrated most of his forces ten miles south of Vicksburg in a shallow arc that ran eastward from the Mississippi River to Baldwin's Ferry on the Big Black River. Eight miles north of Baldwin's Ferry Confederate troops also guarded the Big Black River Bridge. Thirty miles east of Big Black River, at Jackson, additional Confederate forces were being scraped together to operate against Grant. Pemberton believed that Grant would avoid attacking the line between the Mississippi River and Baldwin's Ferry. Instead, he thought the Federals would attack Big Black River Bridge, while simultaneously conducting a major raid against Jackson.[6] Pemberton was only partially correct in his assessment, since Grant's first goal was to destroy the Southern Railroad of Mississippi, Pemberton's main supply line. Only then would he move against Vicksburg.

On May 7, 1862, two corps of Grant's army began moving in the direction of Jackson. He planned to sever the railroad somewhere west of the city. Pemberton had anticipated some move in that direction and ordered Brig. Gen. John Gregg to take his brigade to Raymond, Mississippi, to contest the Union advance. On May 12, 1863, two Union divisions, after a hard fight, drove Gregg's men back toward Jackson. Gregg's determined resistance convinced Grant that even larger forces must be gathering in Jackson. He therefore decided to attack the capital city before either cutting the railroad or turning to face Pemberton.

The next day Gen. Joseph E. Johnston, Pemberton's immediate superior, arrived in Jackson to assume direct command of operations. Johnston was faced with a mounting crisis, and he believed that it was more important to save Pemberton's army than to defend Vicksburg. He therefore immediately informed Pemberton that four Union divisions at Clinton, Mississippi, were now between Johnston's troops and the Vicksburg garrison. He urged Pemberton to march on the Union divisions and destroy them before all hope of uniting the Confederate forces was lost.[7] Pemberton, acting under explicit orders from Jefferson Davis to save both Vicksburg and Port Hudson, replied that he thought it would be better to take his forces southeastward to cut Grant's supply lines. The next day, two Federal corps advanced on Jackson so rapidly that Johnston was forced to hastily evacuate the city. Again Johnston urged Pemberton to move in the direction of Clinton to try to unite with Johnston's eleven thousand troops. Pemberton reluctantly agreed to the order but added "I do not think you fully comprehend the position that Vicksburg will be left in ..."[8]

On the evening of May 15, 1863, Pemberton had gotten no further than Champion's Hill, Mississippi, some twelve miles west of Clinton. By then two Federal corps stood in front of

Pemberton, and a third Union corps in Jackson was destroying anything of military value to the Confederacy. The last fleeting opportunity to unite the two Confederate forces was gone. Pemberton, realizing that he now could not obey Johnston's orders, planned to withdraw the next day, but he was attacked before the move got underway. By 4 P.M. on May 16, Pemberton had suffered over thirty-eight hundred casualties out of a total force of twenty-two thousand men who fought at Champions' Hill. The Federal forces, numbering about twenty-nine thousand soldiers, had suffered almost twenty-five hundred casualties.

By nightfall most of Pemberton's beaten army was across the Big Black River Bridge and headed toward Vicksburg, but he left five thousand men to guard the crossing. On May 17 Union forces smashed the five thousand troops defending the Big Black River Bridge and took several thousand prisoners. Many of the Southerners were captured because their comrades on the west bank burned the bridges before the defenders could retreat across them. Federal engineers quickly threw a pontoon bridge over the river, and the pursuit continued.

The first Union troops arrived before Vicksburg on May 18, 1863, and Grant swiftly established a supply line north of the city on the Yazoo River. Since landing near Bruinsburg eighteen days before, Grant's men had been living and fighting with little more than the material brought down

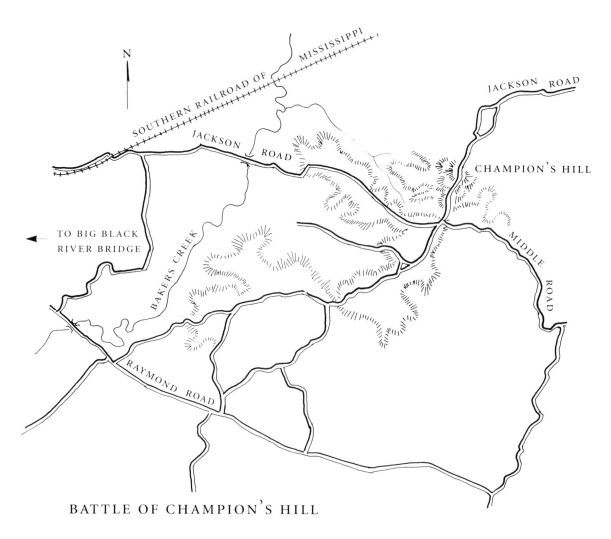

BATTLE OF CHAMPION'S HILL

earlier by Porter's boats, the few supplies that trickled in from Grand Gulf, and what sustenance they could scrounge from the countryside. During that time they had won four engagements and marched over two hundred miles. It was, perhaps, the most spectacular eighteen days of the Civil War, and now Pemberton's army was trapped in Vicksburg.

Even though Pemberton's troops had been outmaneuvered and defeated, they were far from impotent, as Grant was to learn on May 19, 1863. In front of the Federal army were more than eight miles of trenches which had been strengthened at strategic points with an assortment of batteries, lunettes, redoubts, and redans. The major roads that led to the city were protected by powerful bastions, and in many places the trees in front of the positions had been cut to create a clean field of fire for the defenders.[9] Inside the entrenchments were twenty thousand troops with adequate supporting artillery. Despite these formidable obstacles, Grant believed that Pemberton's forces were so demoralized that they could be overrun by a determined attack. At 2 P.M. on May 19, 1863, Samuel Swan, a Tennessean in Brig. Gen. Stephen D. Lee's brigade, heard the "continuous roar of heavy guns and small arms." He knew that a general assault was now underway, but in less than an hour the fire slackened, and he heard "a hearty cheer" from the defenders.[10] Grant's first assault had been stopped cold with a loss of almost one thousand men. "This is hard work to take this position by storm," wrote Lt. Col. Henry C. Warmoth of the 32nd Missouri (U.S.), "I don't think it can be done by such weak lines." But he added, "By a more concentrated movement and with great loss of life we may be able to take them by charge. . . ."[11] His commanding general believed the same thing.

On May 22, 1863, Grant ordered a second attack, which was better organized and larger than his earlier effort. His men met the same fate

as before. "No troops in the world," wrote the Rebel general, Stephen D. Lee, "could stand such a fire, and it took but a little time to see, that the general assault was repulsed."[12] Even in defeat, isolated Federal regiments continued the attack until dark when they finally pulled back after suffering thirty-two hundred casualties. Confederate losses in the two assaults totaled about six hundred men.

The two failed attacks finally convinced the stubborn Grant that Vicksburg could only be taken by a protracted siege. For the next six weeks hundreds of artillery pieces joined the gunboats in shelling the city. Meanwhile, Union infantry pushed their saps as close to the Confederate entrenchments as they dared. Inside Vicksburg the defenders countered these tactics by digging secondary lines of entrenchments and keeping up a continuous fire against the sappers and miners on their front.

Within a few weeks most of the encircled Confederates were living off an unappetizing mush of corn meal, peas, and rice. During the day, many suffered in hot trenches that were being peppered with Minié balls and artillery shells. Troops in the rear areas were generally safe from the sharpshooters, but mortar and artillery rounds often fell among them. Night brought some relief from the intense heat and rifle fire, but the desultory fire from the big guns continued. Casualties mounted daily, and diseases began to spread through the undernourished regiments. "It may sound very romantic to read in history of the hardships of a siege," Swan wrote in his diary, "but there is no romance for the actors."[13]

Conditions were not much better among the thousands of civilians who were trapped in Vicksburg with Pemberton's troops. Lida Lord Reed, like hundreds of other citizens, tried to escape from the constant shelling by burrowing into the ground. "Our refuge," she remembered, "consisted of five short passages running parallel into the hill, connected by another crossing them at right angles, all about five feet wide, and high enough for a man to stand upright. Inside she was "almost eaten up by misquitos [sic]" and remained in constant fear of snakes. Eleven people lived with Lida, and eight other families were in nearby caves.[14]

Outside Vicksburg, the besiegers also suffered from the heat and mosquitos. Those near the front were plagued by sharpshooters and sporadic artillery fire. Casualties occurred daily, and even though the Union soldiers were better fed, many became ill from dysentery, malaria, and other diseases. Drinking water often was in short

supply. During the day, a Union sharpshooter might fire as many as 150 rounds at the Rebel entrenchments. "We spent most of our time firing across the valley," wrote a soldier in the 12th Wisconsin Infantry, "and they over yonder busied themselves in the same way."[15]

By the middle of June, Grant had seventy-one thousand men before Vicksburg, and Pemberton's dwindling force had no hope of breaking out of the city. Meanwhile, Johnston was trying to assemble a relief force, and near the end of June he had thirty-one thousand troops under his command. Grant could not ignore Johnston, and throughout the siege he had to detach thousands

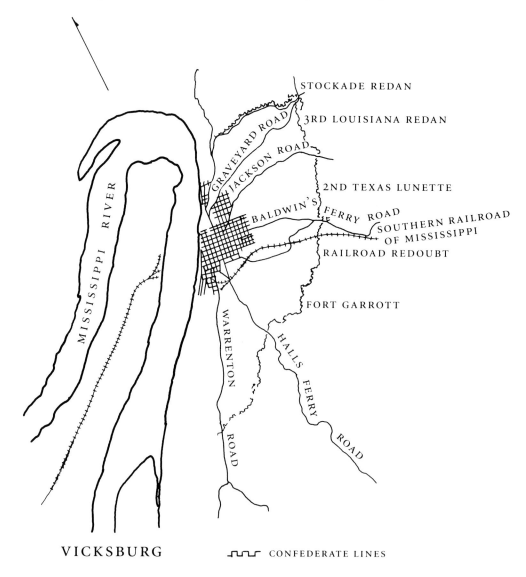

VICKSBURG   ⊓⊔⊓ CONFEDERATE LINES

of troops to protect his rear. On June 29, 1863, Johnston finally began moving slowly toward Vicksburg, but Pemberton's force was now too weak to participate in any foray against Grant.

On July 4, 1863, Pemberton, recognizing the futility of further resistance, surrendered the garrison, which had been reduced to ten thousand effectives. Fraternization began almost immediately among the soldiers. On July 5, 1863, Pvt. Richard Lewis of the 19th Iowa Infantry wrote his cousin that the Rebels "seemed as glad to see us as if we was their brothers." Lewis added that the surrendered men said that the Union had two good generals, "General Grant and General Starvation."[16] Until the conditions of parole could be arranged, Grant allowed the Confederates to stay in their old camps and to draw rations from the Federals.

On July 8, 1863, the Confederate garrison at Port Hudson surrendered and the Mississippi River was now firmly under Federal control. Many of the defenders of Vicksburg and Port Hudson were soon exchanged and returned to the Southern armies. However, thousands of other Rebels had seen enough of war and never rejoined their regiments.

The capture of Vicksburg freed thousands of troops that could now be used to deal with Johnston, who soon fell back on Jackson. By July 10, 1863, elements of Grant's army were in front of the capital city. Johnston, who had no plans to be trapped like Pemberton, withdrew from Jackson six days later.

The campaign for Vicksburg was over, and the Confederacy was split in two. Grant, who was now the hero of the Union, would go on to win more victories in Tennessee and Virginia, but none would be as skillfully conducted as his ultimate triumph at Vicksburg. Pemberton quickly became the scapegoat for the loss of the city, and he never again held a major command in any Confederate army. On May 18, 1864, Pemberton resigned as lieutenant general and offered his services as a private. Instead, Davis commissioned him as a lieutenant colonel of artillery, and the defender of Vicksburg served out the remainder of the war in obscurity.

WILLIAM H. CHANDLER
copy print

On August 5, 1862, William Chandler, a twenty-six-year-old carriagemaker from Huntsville, Ohio, joined the 96th Ohio as a lieutenant in Co. I. Chandler's regiment was assigned to Maj. Gen. John McClernand's Corps, and it helped capture Arkansas Post on January 11, 1863. During the engagement, the regiment had ten men killed and another twenty-five wounded. After the campaign, the 96th Ohio moved to Young's Point, Louisiana. Conditions in the camp were deplorable, and when the regiment left for Milliken's Bend on March 12, 1863, 196 men remained behind in graves on the levee.

On March 29, 1863, McClernand began moving his corps southward from Milliken's Bend in the first step of Grant's plan to get his army below Vicksburg. Chandler's regiment began marching southward through the cypress swamps on April 12, 1863. After the men had traveled about forty miles, they reached a swift bayou. There they boarded the *Empire City,* which had recently run past the Vicksburg batteries. The boat carried the men to their rendezvous with the rest of McClernand's troops. By late April, Grant had almost thirty thousand soldiers concentrated in the vicinity of Hard Times.

When Grant's forces finally crossed the river, the 96th Ohio remained behind to guard his supply depots. It was picked for this duty because McClernand's ordnance officer had neglected to procure any ammunition for the regiment's Belgian rifles.[17]
Photo courtesy of Don W. Scoggins

On the morning of April 17, 1863, Col. Benjamin Grierson and seventeen hundred cavalrymen left La Grange, Tennessee. He had orders to distract Pemberton by raiding the Southern Railroad of Mississippi, which ran from Vicksburg to Meridian. Among his troopers was Pvt. Clarkson C. Eves of Co. G, 2nd Iowa Cavalry. Eves was from Attalissa, Iowa, and had enlisted on September 21, 1861, at the age of twenty-two.

By the evening of April 20, 1863, Grierson was near Houston, Mississippi, but he was being closely followed by Confederate cavalry. The next morning Grierson ordered Col. Edward Hatch to take the 2nd Iowa and turn southeast to destroy a railroad bridge near West Point, Mississippi. He was then to follow a circuitous route that would eventually bring him back to La Grange. Grierson hoped that the detached column would distract the pursuing Confederate cavalry, so that the main raid could continue. Around noon on April 21, 1863, Hatch's column was several miles northwest of West Point at Palo Alto, Mississippi, when it was attacked by Rebel cavalry. Eves and most of his fellow troopers in Co. G were captured in the brief fight.

After the attack Hatch abandoned the plans to take West Point and turned northward. The Confederate cavalry mistakenly followed the 2nd Iowa, and Grierson was free to continue his raid. Eves and the troopers captured near Palo Alto were paroled on the same day of their surrender. *Photo courtesy of Dale Snair*

CLARKSON C. EVES
gem tintype

B. B. STARNS
carte de visite
S. Anderson's Gallery, New Orleans

Grierson now had only 950 troopers under his command, but he had eluded the main column of Confederate cavalry that was searching for him. On April 24, 1863, Grierson reached Newton Station on the Southern Railroad of Mississippi. There he destroyed all the railroad equipment, bridges, and military supplies in and around the town. Grierson knew that large Rebel cavalry forces were gathering to his rear, and he therefore decided to continue southward to Baton Rouge, Louisiana, a distance of approximately 180 miles.

By May 1, 1863, Grierson's weary column was approaching a bridge over the Tickfaw River in Louisiana. Baton Rouge was fifty miles away. Lt. B. B. Starns of the 9th Louisiana Partisan Rangers was part of a hastily assembled Rebel force of 115 men who were searching for Grierson. The men were resting near the bridge when Grierson's scouts came in sight. Starns' men fired two volleys into the surprised cavalrymen, but Grierson's main column quickly moved forward and charged across the bridge. Starns and most of the defenders escaped capture. The next day Grierson's troopers entered the Union lines at Baton Rouge. In sixteen days his men had ridden over six hundred miles and destroyed at least fifty miles of railroad track. More important, they had tied down Pemberton's cavalry, which should have been searching for Grant's main force.[18]
Photo courtesy of L.L.M.V.C., L.S.U., Civil War Album

On April 29, 1863, Grant made his first attempt to cross to the Mississippi side of the river. At 8 A.M. seven gunboats that had recently run past the Vicksburg batteries opened fire on the Confederate forces defending Grand Gulf. In the channel of the Mississippi River, ten thousand troops huddled aboard transports waiting for the signal to land.

Col. William Wade, a Missourian, who had earlier commanded a battery at the Battle of Pea Ridge, was Brig. Gen. Bowen's chief of artillery. On the bluffs at Grand Gulf, Wade had constructed four batteries with a total of thirteen guns, and for more than five hours his men dueled with the Federal gunboats. During the attack the Union flotilla fired at least three thousand shells without doing any serious damage to Wade's batteries. Late that afternoon the gunboats broke off contact and steamed away. Seven Federals had been killed and another nineteen wounded. Three Confederates died in the unsuccessful attack on Grand Gulf, and at least twelve more were injured. Colonel Wade was one of the dead. He had been struck and killed by a fragment from a Union shell.

That evening the gunboats and transports ran past the Grand Gulf batteries. The next morning the transports began landing Grant's troops on an unoccupied section of the riverbank near Bruinsburg. *Photo courtesy of the Grand Gulf Military Monument Park*

WILLIAM WADE
copy print

LYMAN MARTIN
copy print

Lyman Martin was a twenty-one-year-old farmer from Indiana when he volunteered for military service. On August 16, 1861, he mustered into the army as a private in Co. G, 18th Indiana Infantry.

On the morning of April 30, 1863, Martin's regiment was with one of the first brigades that crossed the river and landed near Bruinsburg. For the past two weeks he had been slogging through the mud in Louisiana. As soon as Martin's brigade landed on the Mississippi side of the river, they began moving toward Grant's first objective, Grand Gulf.[19] His regiment was part of McClernand's Corps, which was trying to reach the crossroads village of Port Gibson, six miles southeast of Grand Gulf. Martin's regiment made contact with Rebel skirmishers about five miles west of Port Gibson and was engaged in skirmishing until 3 A.M.

At daylight on May 1, 1863, the 18th Indiana moved forward and deployed with the right flank of the Federal infantry. Heavy fighting began about 10 A.M., and Martin's regiment helped drive the Confederates back. The bloodiest combat during the Battle of Port Gibson occurred on the Federal right, and Martin was wounded during the struggle. The 18th Indiana suffered eighty-three casualties—the highest number of losses of any Federal regiment which fought at Port Gibson. *Photo courtesy of U.S.A.M.H.I.; original* carte de visite *in the Grand Army of the Republic Memorial Museum, Springfield, Illinois*

At the time of the Union advance, only a thin line of one thousand men under Brig. Gen. Martin Edward Green was in front of the Federals. Green's men fought hard, but they could not hold against odds of at least five to one. His men had already fallen back almost a mile and a half when they met Brig. Gen. William Baldwin's brigade coming forward to reinforce them.

Baldwin, a native of South Carolina, had moved to Mississippi as a child. He eventually settled in Columbus, where he owned a book and stationary business. In 1861 Baldwin was elected colonel of the 14th Mississippi Infantry and commanded the regiment when it was captured at Fort Donelson. Baldwin was commissioned brigadier general while in Fort Warren Military Prison, and after his release he received command of a brigade.

Baldwin's men had heard the sound of fighting as they marched toward the Port Gibson battlefield, and for the last two miles the brigade had been marching at the double quick. When the exhausted soldiers arrived at the front, Green's men were "falling back from all points, pressed by greatly superior numbers." Baldwin quickly deployed his regiments, and the Confederate resistance began to stiffen. By the end of the fight Baldwin had lost eighty-seven men.[20] *Photo courtesy of U.S.A.M.H.I., MOLLUS, Mass., Collection*

WILLIAM EDWIN BALDWIN
albumen print

227

WILLIAM HAINES
copy print

Pvt. William Haines, a twenty-year-old farmer from Iowa City, enlisted in Co. I, 22nd Iowa Infantry on August 5, 1862. On April 30, 1863, his brigade was also among the first troops ferried across the river, and they too made contact with Rebel skirmishers that evening.

At sunrise on May 1, 1863, Haines' regiment went into the line of battle on the left flank of the Union line. Around 10 A.M. the regiment joined the general push that eventually drove the Rebels back almost three miles. About 4 P.M. the 22nd Iowa advanced into a "dense and impenetrable growth of cane" as the men tried to close with the enemy.[21] The Union infantry finally broke Baldwin's right flank, and the Rebels began withdrawing toward Grand Gulf.

Port Gibson was the 22nd Iowa's first fight, and Haines was unharmed. However, two of his comrades were dead and another twenty had been wounded. Union losses on McClernand's front totaled about six hundred men. *Photo courtesy of U.S.A.M.H.I., MOLLUS, Mass., Collection*

A few thousand yards north of McClernand's position, a second Union column was simultaneously pushing down the Bruinsburg Road, which also led to Port Gibson. The 20th Alabama Infantry, under the command of Col. Isham W. Garrott, and two other Alabama regiments stood in the way.

Before the war Garrott was a lawyer in Marion, Alabama, and as a past state legislator he had been a staunch supporter of states' rights. In 1861 Gov. Andrew Moore sent him to North Carolina to encourage that state to join the secession movement. When the Civil War began, Garrott raised the 20th Alabama Regiment and became its colonel, but neither he nor his regiment had seen much combat.

When Garrott's brigade commander was killed at Port Gibson, the Alabamian suddenly had to assume command of the three regiments. Throughout the morning of May 1, 1863, Garrott held his position, but by 11 A.M., he could see heavy columns moving toward him. Garrott slowly gave ground. By 3 P.M. he had been reinforced by only one regiment, and the Federal infantry was pressing hard. However, before Garrott's meager force was overwhelmed, Baldwin's position to the south collapsed. Garrott then received orders to withdraw toward Grand Gulf, which was evacuated the next day. For almost eleven hours the 1,400 soldiers under the inexperienced Garrott had held their ground against at least 5,000 Federals. He had suffered 272 casualties and inflicted an equal number of losses on the enemy.[22]

Photo courtesy of the Library of Congress, no. LC USZ62-83386

ISHAM GARROTT
albumen print

JOHN GREGG
albumen print

On May 7, 1863, Maj. Gen. James McPherson's Corps began advancing in the direction of Jackson with orders to cut the Southern Railroad of Mississippi. Pemberton had correctly deduced that Grant would next move toward Jackson, but he persisted in believing that such a maneuver was only a feint to draw the Confederates away from Vicksburg. At 3 A.M. on May 10, 1863, Pemberton ordered Brig. Gen. John Gregg to move promptly to Raymond and block any Union raid on Jackson. Meanwhile, Pemberton held his main forces along the Big Black River to protect Vicksburg.

Before the Civil War, Gregg had been a district judge in Texas. He later served in the Secession Convention and was a member of the Confederate Congress. Gregg resigned his seat after First Bull Run and was elected colonel of the 7th Texas Infantry. Gregg was later captured at Fort Donelson, and after his exchange he was promoted to brigadier general.

Gregg's twenty-five hundred men arrived near Raymond at 4 P.M. on May 11, 1863. Early the next morning he learned that the enemy was nearby, but he was unable to determine the size of the force because he had no cavalry. Gregg, acting on Pemberton's belief that the move toward Jackson was little more than a raid, assumed that all he faced was "a brigade on a marauding expedition."[23] He therefore immediately deployed his men for battle. *Photo courtesy of the Library of Congress, no. LC B812-2722*

The soldiers who fought at Raymond were surrounded by a dense undergrowth, which was permeated with the boiling dust generated by the movement of more than fourteen thousand soldiers and with the smoke from the discharge of thousands of weapons. Under these conditions it was impossible for commanders to maintain control or even to see what was going on around them. For men like Pvt. Allen Morgan Geer of Co. C, 20th Illinois Infantry, it came down to a struggle between soldiers who fought each other in isolated groups with little idea about what was going on elsewhere. Early in the battle, Geer's regiment was bushwhacked by a line of Rebel infantry and driven back in confusion. Geer and some of the frightened men rallied near a fence. Geer was busily firing his weapon when he suddenly noticed that he was one of the few men still left behind the fence. He moved back a few feet and continued firing. Suddenly a bullet hit Geer in the neck and spun him around. A few seconds later Geer felt the pain and found blood flowing down his neck; he then prayed for "mercy, life, & victory." Geer finally reached an aid station, even though "several cowardly dogs . . . passed me without notice saying that I was not worth getting off the field."[24]

Around 3:30 P.M. Gregg finally realized that he was facing overwhelming numbers and began retreating back to Jackson. The Battle of Raymond cost Gregg 514 casualties, while McPherson lost 442 men.

ALLEN MORGAN GEER
copy print from Mary Ann Andersen, ed.,
The Civil War Diary of Allen Morgan Geer

JAMES M. TUTTLE
albumen print

The news of the Union victory at Raymond reached Grant about sundown. He immediately decided to march on Jackson to "destroy or drive any force in that direction," before he turned on Pemberton.[25] On May 13, 1863, Grant left a force to block any move toward Jackson by Pemberton, and he sent two corps eastward in a converging advance on the capital city. Brig. Gen. James M. Tuttle led the 3rd Division of Maj. Gen. William T. Sherman's Corps as it rapidly marched toward Jackson from the southwest.

Tuttle, a farmer and local elected official from Van Buren County, Iowa, had entered the service on May 31, 1861, as lieutenant colonel of the 2nd Iowa Infantry. At the Battle of Shiloh, he temporarily commanded a division in the fighting around the Hornet's Nest. On June 9, 1862, Tuttle was promoted to brigadier general; he had commanded the 3rd Division since April 3, 1863.

During the evening of May 13, 1863, torrents of rain fell on the Mississippi countryside. The next day the Union columns marched over muddy roads that were sometimes covered with more than a foot of water. When Tuttle arrived in front of Jackson, Johnston was already withdrawing his forces, but the Union division charged forward. The retreating Confederates put up little resistance, and Tuttle's men easily overran the entrenchments, capturing ten field pieces. He had only four men killed and nine men wounded in the assault. *Photo courtesy of U.S.A.M.H.I., MOLLUS, Mass., Collection*

232

Lt. Col. Ellison Capers commanded the 24th South Carolina Infantry in Johnston's army. It was one of several regiments deployed three miles west of Jackson with orders to stop the second prong of the Federal advance.

Capers was a native of Charleston who graduated from the South Carolina Military Academy in 1857. In 1860 Capers, who was teaching at his alma mater, was elected major of the First Carolina Rifles, a state regiment that was later present at the bombardment of Fort Sumter. In early 1862, Capers helped raise the 24th South Carolina Infantry and was subsequently elected lieutenant colonel of the new regiment. The 24th South Carolina remained at home until it received orders to reinforce Johnston.

At the beginning of the attack on Jackson, Capers' troops were deployed as skirmishers, and his men stopped the first Federal patrols on their front. However, the Union infantry soon came up and drove the South Carolinians back. During the retreat Capers' horse was shot from under him, and the lieutenant colonel was wounded in the leg shortly afterward. Capers' aides carried him to the rear as the Federals continued their push. The Confederates received orders to withdraw around 2 P.M. In the engagement the 24th South Carolina lost 105 men, which was the highest number of casualties for any command in the Battle of Jackson. Still, Jackson had fallen after only a token defense, and Grant could now turn his full attention to Pemberton.[26] *Photo courtesy of the Library of Congress*

ELLISON CAPERS
albumen print

233

ALVIN PETERSON HOVEY
albumen print

Alvin Peterson Hovey, the youngest of eight children, was born near Mount Vernon, Indiana, on September 26, 1821. Hovey's parents died when he was fifteen, and the teenager was forced to earn a living as an apprentice bricklayer. He later taught school, read law, and was admitted to the Indiana Bar. In 1854 Hovey became the youngest Indianian to be appointed to the state supreme court. In 1861 Hovey, now a prominent political figure in his home state, was commissioned colonel of the 24th Indiana Infantry. His only prior military service had been as a volunteer officer in the Mexican War, but he had seen no action. Despite Hovey's lack of experience, he proved to be a good officer; after the Battle of Shiloh, he was promoted to brigadier general, and since February 26, 1863, Hovey had commanded the 12th Division of McClernand's Corps.

At 9:45 A.M. on May 16, 1863, Hovey's Division arrived in front of a seventy-foot slope known as Champion's Hill. His division contained 4,180 soldiers and was assigned to lead the attack against the position which dominated Pemberton's line. On Hovey's right, Maj. Gen. John Logan's Division was to advance alongside the 12th Division. A third division, under the command of Brig. Gen. Marcellus Crocker, was marching to support Logan's and Hovey's men. Hovey's soldiers began advancing about 10:30 A.M. During the next six hours, his command would lose 1,202 men, or 29 percent of all the Federal casualties, in the Battle of Champion's Hill.[27] *Photo courtesy of U.S.A.M.H.I., MOLLUS, Mass., Collection*

234

JOSEPH WILLIAM MATHEWS
salt print

Facing Hovey, Logan, and Crocker's troops was a lone division under the command of Maj. Gen. Carter L. Stevenson. Capt. Joseph W. Mathews had begun his military service as an assistant quartermaster for the 23rd Alabama Infantry, but since August 12, 1862, he had been acting assistant adjutant general on Stevenson's staff. The duties of the adjutant general and his staff were largely administrative except during battle, when they often communicated the orders of the divisional commander to his subordinates.

Stevenson's soldiers were posted in strong defensive positions on Champion's Hill and the ridge to its left, but he had only 6,500 men to cover a front of at least twenty-five hundred yards. Between 10:30 A.M. and 1:30 P.M. Stevenson's men singlehandedly fought against the better part of three Federal divisions. When reinforcements finally arrived, his command was already wrecked. By the end of the day, 332 men in Stevenson's Division were dead and another 525 had been wounded; at least 2,000 more soldiers were either missing or captured. Mathews retreated with the survivors of his division, and Stevenson later cited the captain for being "prompt, daring, and energetic in the discharge" of his duties.[28] *Photo courtesy of George Esker*

235

JOHN Q. WILDS
carte de visite

Pennsylvania-born John Q. Wilds originally joined the 13th Iowa Infantry when he was thirty-seven, but on April 19, 1862, he transferred to the 24th Iowa. Wilds was lieutenant colonel of his regiment during the Battle of Champion's Hill. The Iowans were part of Col. James R. Slack's brigade, 12th Division, which deployed on the left of Hovey's line. Slack's men met little opposition as they worked their way through the thick underbrush that choked the ravines on the slope of Champion's Hill. However, once Slack was on top of the ridge, he saw a Confederate battle line in the woods about two hundred yards away. An open field lay between him and the enemy. Wilds and the 24th Iowa charged across the field and captured a five-gun battery. During the brief engagement, the regiment's three field officers, including Wilds, were wounded, and the men were almost leaderless. Some of the Iowans continued pursuing the retreating Rebels, but others milled aimlessly around. About fifty yards beyond the captured battery, a reinforced Confederate line emerged and "opened a most murderous fire" on the Federals. The brunt of the attack fell on the disorganized 24th Iowa. After fifteen minutes of hard fighting, Slack withdrew his men to the crest of Champion's Hill, where they remained until the battle ended that afternoon. The 24th Iowa had taken 417 men into battle on May 16, 1863; 35 men died and another 120 soldiers were wounded at Champion's Hill.[29] *Photo courtesy of Roger Davis*

When the Civil War began, twenty-two-year-old Charles Brown, a native of Rutland, Vermont, was working as a carpenter in Indianapolis, Indiana. On August 3, 1861, he enlisted as a private in Co. K, 11th Indiana Infantry, and prior to the Battle of Champion's Hill he had been promoted to corporal.

On the morning of May 16, 1863, the 11th Indiana was part of Brig. Gen. George F. McGinnis's brigade of Hovey's Division as it fought its way up Champion's Hill. By 2:30 P.M. McGinnis was being pressed by superior numbers, and he began to urgently call for reinforcements. After almost four hours of fighting his men were exhausted, and they were running low on ammunition. McGinnis's brigade was slowly driven back, but just when it appeared that the brigade would be overwhelmed, reinforcements arrived. Still the Rebels continued to attack until they were finally stopped by Union artillery fire. By then Corporal Brown was dead. The fight for Champion's Hill had cost the 11th Indiana 167 men, or 36 percent of its total strength.[30] *Photo courtesy of the Indiana Historical Society Library*

Col. Thomas P. Dockery's regiment, the 19th Arkansas, was part of Green's brigade, which attacked alongside Cockrell's men. In 1861 the twenty-seven-year-old Dockery, who had no prior military experience, commanded the 5th Arkansas State Troops at Wilson's Creek, Missouri. After the battle, the state units disbanded, and Dockery returned home. On May 12, 1862, he rejoined the Confederate army as colonel of the 19th Arkansas Infantry and led his men with distinction at Corinth and Hatchie Bridge.

On the afternoon of May 16, 1863, Dockery waited with his regiment in the woods slightly to the left of Champion's Hill. He could hear the battle raging in the distance. Around 2 P.M. Dockery received orders to advance, and after he had gone about a mile he encountered Stevenson's retreating soldiers. Dockery pressed forward, drove back the enemy on his front, and recaptured several Rebel artillery pieces that had recently been overrun by the enemy. However, he was now low on ammunition and in danger of being outflanked. Around 4 P.M. Dockery began withdrawing to the rear, along with the rest of Green's brigade. *Photo courtesy of the U.A.L.R. Archives, J. N. Heiskell Collection*

Thomas Dockery
copy print

Henderson Duval
copy print

Pvt. Henderson Duval and his brother Thomas (see page 169) were among the fresh troops that helped drive Slack and McGinnis back. Both men were members of Co. C, 3rd Regiment, Missouri State Guard, which was part of Col. Francis M. Cockrell's brigade of Bowen's Division. Since early morning Bowen's men had been deployed southeast of Champion's Hill, but the enemy had not pressed hard. At 1 P.M. Cockrell received direct orders from Pemberton to move immediately to assist Stevenson's beleaguered division. Around 2:30 P.M. Cockrell's men, supported by Green's brigade of Bowen's Division, charged into Slack's men, pushed them back, and recaptured the artillery battery that had been taken by the 24th Iowa. The Rebel infantry turned next on McGinnis's brigade and drove them back also. In less than an hour, Bowen's two brigades had driven the Federals more than three quarters of a mile.[31] During the fighting Cockrell lost over 600 men, including both Duval brothers. *Photo courtesy of Tom Sweeney*

FINLEY SMACK
carte de visite

Pvt. Finley Smack of Co. F, 5th Iowa Infantry, was one of the men who helped stop the furious attacks by Green's and Cockrell's brigades. Smack had enlisted in the army on July 3, 1861, at the age of eighteen. On May 16, 1863, his regiment numbered only 350 men, and it was with Col. George B. Boomer's brigade as it rushed forward to support Hovey's mauled division. The men of the 5th Iowa came running onto the battlefield "shouting defiance to the enemy." They planted the regiment's colors on a small ridge and began firing on the advancing Confederates. Eventually, the 5th Iowa gave ground, but it still held the Rebels at bay. The Iowans continued to load and fire "while their comrades were continually falling around them." When their ammunition was exhausted the men obtained more from the "cartridge-boxes of the dead and wounded." At least 111 Federals died from Boomer's brigade, but their fierce defense gave Hovey time to re-form his division and return to the battle. By 4 P.M. the Confederate assault was spent, and the Federals were rapidly pushing Bowen's men off Champion's Hill. Smack had been seriously wounded in the thigh; ninety-three of his comrades were also casualties.[32] *Photo courtesy of Roger Davis*

SETH BARTON
copy print

Seth Barton, a native of Virginia, graduated from the United States Military Academy in 1849 and subsequently spent most of his career in the West. In June 1861, he was appointed colonel of the 3rd Arkansas Infantry and later served as Brig. Gen. Stonewall Jackson's engineering officer in the Shenandoah Valley. Barton was promoted to brigadier general on March 11, 1862, and at Champion's Hill he commanded a brigade in Stevenson's Division.

Most of Barton's Georgians remained in reserve until noon, when they received orders to support the left of Stevenson's line that was about to be outflanked. Barton's men covered a mile and a half at the double-quick and arrived just after the Federals turned the left flank of the Confederate line. Barton sent three regiments forward and stopped the advance. However, a reinforced Federal line drove into Barton's men, and he sent his last reserves to help stop the Union attack. Within a few minutes, both of Barton's flanks were turned, and his men fell back in confusion. By 4 P.M. Barton's beaten brigade was retreating to safety down the Jackson Road, the same route that Pemberton planned to use if he had to retreat. Barton lost 901 men, or 42 percent of the brigade's total strength, during the fight at Champion's Hill, and he failed to hold the vital road for Pemberton.[33] *Photo courtesy of the U.A.L.R. Archives, J. N. Heiskell Collection*

GEORGE A. SNOW
sixth-plate ambrotype

One of the regiments that helped defeat Barton's men was the 124th Illinois Infantry, which was part of Brig. Gen. John E. Smith's brigade of Logan's Division. Pvt. George A. Snow was with Co. H, 124th Illinois, when the fight began for control of the Jackson Road.

Eight days before the Battle of Champion's Hill Snow wrote his parents, telling them that he "was still further away from home which I love so dearly" and that he had recently "seen the elephant." The last phrase was often used by Civil War soldiers after they had first experienced combat; Snow was likely referring to his recent participation in the battles of Raymond and Jackson.

Snow was killed in the successful attack against Barton's brigade, but as late as two weeks after the battle his parents had not yet learned of his death. On May 30, 1863, his mother wrote the following to her son:

Although we have had no letter from you since the 8th and we know not where you are or what situation you are now in, still we always hope for the best and although we know that many of your brave army have lost their lives, yet we hope that these lines will find you still safe and well. We are very anxious about you my boy . . .[34]

Photo courtesy of the South Carolina Relic Room and Museum; original owned by Sarah Escott

LLOYD TILGHMAN
carte de visite
E. & H. T. Anthony, New York

Barton's men were safe, but the rest of Pemberton's army was cut off from the Jackson Road and could only escape if the Rebels continued to hold the Raymond Road. Brig. Gen. Lloyd Tilghman of Maj. Gen. William W. Loring's Division commanded a Mississippi brigade which protected that escape route.

Tilghman was born in Maryland and graduated from West Point in 1836. However, he almost immediately resigned his commission to pursue a career as a railroad construction engineer. On October 18, 1861, Tilghman was commissioned as a brigadier general in the Confederate army and sent to command Fort Henry. He was captured there on February 6, 1862, and later exchanged.

On May 16, 1863, Tilghman's brigade was on the extreme right of Pemberton's line. All day he had faced a powerful force of Federal infantry, but it had done little more than harass his men. When the retreat began, Tilghman received orders to hold his position until sundown. Throughout the waning hours of the day his batteries held back the timid probes of the Union forces. Behind Tilghman's thin screen, Pemberton's beaten army withdrew toward Vicksburg. At 5:20 P.M. Tilghman was directing a change in elevation on one of his guns when he was killed by a Federal shell. Loring's Division, which had been cut off from the rest of the retreating army, eventually escaped capture and joined Johnston's forces near Jackson.[35]
Photo courtesy of Daniel J. Stari

MEN OF CO. C, 34TH INDIANA
carte de visite

Almost eight hundred Americans died at Champion's Hill, and at least thirty-six hundred more men were wounded there. It was the bloodiest battle in the campaign that finally isolated Vicksburg.

Even veteran troops sometimes found it difficult to control their fear amidst the carnage that occurred on Civil War battlefields, and it was especially difficult for green troops to maintain their discipline. Sgt. John B. Harris (*kneeling on far left of the second row*) posed for this image with his fellow soldiers of Co. C, 34th Indiana Infantry. He was among the men of the 34th that fought at Champion's Hill; it was their first battle.

The regiment managed to reach the crest of Champion's Hill, but many of the men were badly frightened. Some of the Indianians had already started to run when Major General Logan rode up to the shaken regiment. Harris recalled that Logan shouted that he "had been wounded five times and never turned his back to the foe yet." Sergeant Harris thought that the general's "voice was forcible, inspiring, and savored with a little brimstone." An officer of the regiment, who was as shaken as his men, replied that "the Rebels are awful thick up there." Logan curtly informed him, "Damn it, that's the place to kill them—where they are thick."[36] The regiment, cowed by Logan's intimidating presence, calmed down. At the end of the day they had lost sixty-nine men. *Photo courtesy of Mark A. Warren*

On the night of May 16, 1863, the majority of Pemberton's beaten troops passed by the Big Black River Station as they withdrew toward Vicksburg. The station, which was located near a meandering turn in the Big Black River, consisted of little more than a few rough wooden buildings, but it sat on the main land route to Vicksburg. Here both the tracks of the Southern Railroad of Mississippi (*on the right of this image*) and a bridge crossed the Big Black River.

Before the Battle of Champion's Hill the Confederates had constructed a series of rifle pits and cotton-bale breastworks across the neck of land in the bend on the east bank of the Big Black River. Immediately in front of most of the fortifications was a long bayou which had been obstructed with brush and felled trees. In front of the bayou, cleared fields ran for a distance of four hundred to six hundred yards. The line, with its left flank resting on the Big Black River and its right on Gin Lake, was a strong position. Pemberton, still thinking that he would be joined by Loring, left behind three brigades and eighteen guns to protect the crossing until the wayward division arrived. *Photo courtesy of the Library of Congress, no. B 8171-392*

Big Black River Station
albumen print

WILLIAM KINSMAN
carte de visite

On the morning of May 17, 1863, Col. William Kinsman of the 23rd Iowa arrived in front of the Confederate entrenchments at Big Black River Bridge. Kinsman, a native of Nova Scotia, was twenty-nine years old when he joined the Union army in 1861. Prior to that time he was a restless soul, having already been a sailor, a student, a lawyer, a schoolteacher, a newspaper man, and a member of the 1858–59 rush to the Pike's Peak gold fields. When Kinsman got over the gold fever, he returned to his home in Council Bluffs, Iowa. In 1861 he joined the army as a lieutenant in the 4th Iowa and fought at Pea Ridge. In August 1862, Kinsman accepted a lieutenant colonel's commission in the 23rd Iowa, and the next month he became colonel of the regiment.

Throughout the morning of May 17, 1863, the two Union brigades facing the left of the Confederate lines worked their way as close to the Rebel entrenchments as they dared. Around noon, the Federals, who were about five hundred yards from the Confederate entrenchments, advanced at the run. The men were under orders not to fire until they reached the Rebel works. Before Kinsman had covered half the distance he was hit in the abdomen by a Minié ball and knocked down. Kinsman got up unsteadily and advanced a few yards before he was killed by a shot through the lung.[37] Within minutes the 23rd Iowa had suffered 101 casualties. *Photo courtesy of Roger Davis*

Twenty-six-year-old Pvt. Jacob Miller was also with the men that charged the left wing of the Confederate line. Miller, a native of Switzerland, was a blacksmith in Abingdon, Illinois, before the war. On October 10, 1861, he joined Co. H of the 33rd Illinois Infantry. His regiment had been on the battlefield at Champion's Hill, but it had remained in reserve until near the end of the fight.

Throughout the morning of May 17, 1863, four companies of the 33rd Infantry acted as skirmishers and sharpshooters. Some of the men "devoted themselves to the rebel artillery horses, getting under cover in some ditch or tree top, and firing at nothing else." Other soldiers "crept up almost to the embrasures and shot down the cannoniers [sic] as fast as they attempted to load." In a short while the regiment, "with a loud shout," headed toward the Confederate entrenchments. The 33rd Illinois quickly crossed the open fields, and within a few minutes the men, along with the other advancing regiments, had fought their way into the Rebel lines and shattered the entire left wing of the brigades defending Black River Bridge.[38] Miller was unharmed, and his regiment lost only 13 men in the quick assault. Total Union losses at the Big Black River Bridge were 279 men. *Photo courtesy of U.S.A.M.H.I., Randy Beck Collection*

JACOB MILLER
copy print

JAMES J. MARTIN
copy print from *Confederate Veteran*,
Vol. XVIII (July 1910)

Shortly before midnight on May 16, 1863, Lt. James J. Martin, of Co. K, 21st Arkansas Regiment, Green's brigade, arrived at Big Black River. At Champion's Hill the regiment had suffered heavy casualties when it reinforced Stevenson's broken lines, and the men were exhausted as they filed into the trenches along the river.

Martin was farming near Batesville, Arkansas, when the Civil War began. On October 7, 1861, he enlisted in the Confederate army as a private in Co. D, 14th (McCarver's) Arkansas Infantry. On June 15, 1862, McCarver's command was consolidated with another unit and redesignated the 21st Arkansas Infantry. Martin's company became Co. K in the new command, and he was assigned to duty as a second lieutenant. Martin later fought at the battles of Iuka and Corinth; he was captured and paroled in both engagements.

On May 17, 1863, Martin was on the right wing of the Confederate line when the Federals broke into the Big Black River Bridge defenses and immediately moved to cut off the Rebels' line of retreat. Before all the Confederate troops could be extracted, panicky soldiers on the west bank of the river began burning the bridge. At least 250 Rebels were wounded or killed at the Big Black River Bridge. Martin and perhaps 2,000 other soldiers were trapped on the east bank of the river and captured. Within hours Union engineers had thrown pontoon bridges across the river, and the pursuit continued.

METELLUS CALVERT
carte de visite

By the morning of May 19, 1863, Grant had most of his troops in front of Vicksburg. The general believed that Pemberton's soldiers were demoralized by their recent defeats and "would not make much effort to hold Vicksburg." Therefore, he decided to attack the Confederates in their fortified positions. Grant planned to make his major effort where the upper line of entrenchments began turning westward toward the Mississippi River. There the Confederates had constructed the bulging Stockade Redan to strengthen the line.[39] Much of the ground in front of the dirt-and-timber strongpoint was littered with trees that the Rebels had cut to impede the progress of any advancing troops. Thirteen Federal regiments were assigned to take the redan. Thirty-five-year-old Capt. Metellus Calvert of Co. C, 83rd Indiana Infantry, was one of the soldiers who assaulted the Stockade Redan.

About 2 P.M. on May 19, 1863, Calvert began moving through the tangled brush on his front. The 83rd Indiana was soon pinned down near the base of the redan, where Rebel sharpshooters "were picking off our officers with devilish skill." There, Calvert and one other officer of the 83rd Indiana were shot and killed. Eight other men from his regiment died in the futile attack, and forty-six more were wounded.[40] *Photo courtesy of the Indiana State Library*

249

A. W. HENLEY
copy print

First Lt. A. W. Henley of Co. E, 36th Mississippi Infantry, was posted in a salient near the southern edge of the Stockade Redan. The position was designed to allow troops to deliver a flanking fire against any force that tried to advance against the main section of the redan.

In March 1862, the twenty-seven-year-old Henley joined the Hazelhurst Fencibles and then marched 143 miles with his company to muster into the service at Meridian, Mississippi. Henley was elected first lieutenant of his company on May 11, 1862, but seven days later he was back in Hazelhurst in a military hospital. Henley remained sick and absent from the regiment until at least February 1863, when he apparently rejoined his unit.

During the Federal assault against the Stockade Redan, the flanking fire of the 36th Mississippi helped pin down the 83rd Indiana; it is likely that one of the soldiers from Henley's regiment killed Metellus Calvert. The 36th Mississippi suffered light casualties, and Henley was not harmed. However, when the siege ended, twenty-eight men from the 36th Mississippi had died and another seventy-two were listed as wounded.[41] *Photo courtesy of Gary Hendershott*

Capt. John J. Shaffer of Lafourche Parish, Louisiana, had joined the Confederate service on March 27, 1862. His unit, the Grivot Guards, became Co. F of the 26th Louisiana Infantry. Shaffer's regiment arrived in Vicksburg on May 19, 1862, and was one of the first commands assigned to the garrison. Since then it had not ventured very far from the city. When Grant's army began closing on Vicksburg, Shaffer's regiment was only a few miles north of town.

At 3 A.M. on May 19, 1863, the 26th Louisiana moved back into the Vicksburg fortifications and occupied a position about eight hundred yards west of the Stockade Redan. The men found that the rifle pits that had been previously dug for the regiment would only accommodate two companies; they set to work with spades and picks to strengthen the position. By morning the entire regiment was entrenched, and the 26th Louisiana's colonel, Winchester Hall, could see several Union officers on a distant hill "taking observations with their field glasses." Shortly after 2 P.M. a brigade emerged from the woods, but it was soon "driven to cover by the fire" of the 26th and 27th Louisiana.[42] All along the line, Grant's hasty attack had been a costly failure. In less than three hours of fighting 157 Union soldiers had died and another 777 were wounded. Confederate casualties numbered about 250 men. The 26th suffered light casualties, and Shaffer was not injured.

JOHN J. SHAFFER
copy print from *Confederate Veteran*,
Vol. XXVII (April 1919)

THOMAS KILBY SMITH
albumen print

The attack on May 19, 1863, should have proven that the Confederate garrison still had plenty of fight left in it, but Grant remained unconvinced, and three days later he ordered a larger attack against the defenders. Col. T. Kilby Smith of the 54th Ohio Infantry commanded one of the brigades that participated in both assaults at Vicksburg.

In 1837 Smith graduated from Cincinnati College and then clerked for Salmon P. Chase, a rabid abolitionist who was now Lincoln's secretary of the treasury. After leaving Chase's employment, Smith held several patronage jobs, including that of U.S. Marshall for the Southern District of Ohio. Since the beginning of the war, Smith had led troops at Shiloh, Chickasaw Bluffs, Arkansas Post, and Steele's Bayou Expedition. On May 19, 1863, his brigade lost 155 men in front of the Stockade Redan, and he now had orders to attack the position again.

On May 22, 1863, Smith deployed his regiments in a protected spot behind the brow of a small hill slightly to the right of the redan. His men went over the top of the hill under heavy fire and then entered a ravine in front of the Confederate entrenchments. By noon the brigade was pinned down. That evening Smith withdrew, after losing fifty-six men in his second unsuccessful assault against the Stockade Redan. Shortly after the failed attack, Smith was appointed to Grant's staff. *Photo courtesy of U.S.A.M.H.I., MOLLUS, Mass., Collection*

252

CHARLES THOMAS INGRAM
ninth-plate ruby ambrotype

About 3 P.M. on May 22, 1863, the 11th Missouri Infantry (U.S.) spearheaded a second attack against the Stockade Redan. Pvt. Charles Ingram of Co. F, 3rd Missouri Infantry (C.S.), waited inside the redan as his fellow Missourians advanced toward him.

Ingram was twenty-four years old when he enrolled in the Confederate service on December 31, 1861, at Green County, Missouri. Since then he had been through some hard campaigns, having served at Pea Ridge, Iuka, Corinth, Hatchie Bridge, Grand Gulf, Champion's Hill, and Big Black River Bridge. At Champion's Hill his regiment lost 120 men in Cockrell's aggressive attacks, and the next day several hundred more soldiers were captured at Big Black River Bridge.

During the assault on May 22, 1863, the 11th Missouri fought its way into the ditch in front of the redan. Soldiers of the 3rd Missouri, using fuse-shells as hand grenades, tossed the projectiles into the ditch, killing and wounding twenty-two of the enemy. Ingram helped stop the final assault against the Stockade Redan, but the losses in his regiment were heavy; twelve men died in the fighting and another fifty-two were wounded.[43] *Photo courtesy of George Esker*

253

LEWIS OBERT
carte de visite

Four hundred yards west of the Stockade Redan, Brig. Gen. John Thayer's three Iowa regiments were assigned to assault a section of the line held by an equal number of Louisiana units. Third Corp. Lewis Obert of Co. H, 9th Iowa, had joined the army at Waterloo, Iowa, on September 10, 1861. Obert's regiment had been part of Grant's army since December 1862, and it had fought at Chickasaw Bluffs, Arkansas Post, and the May 19, 1863, assault at Vicksburg. The 9th Iowa had sustained just twenty-one casualties in more than five months of campaigning.

On May 22, 1863, Obert's regiment, which had less than three hundred men in its ranks, began advancing about 2 P.M. Inside the Confederate entrenchments, the Louisianans watched as two columns of Union infantry came out of a deep gorge, dressed their ranks, and began moving forward. The 9th Iowa, intent on planting its flag on the Rebel parapet, lost four color bearers during the advance. When the assault ended, the regiment's dead and wounded totaled seventy-eight. Obert was slightly wounded in the leg but managed to retreat with his beaten regiment. The attack, wrote the commander of the Confederate troops, had been "promptly repulsed with heavy loss."[44] *Photo courtesy of Roger Davis*

Sgt. James Brownlee was with the 35th Mississippi Infantry, which was posted about sixteen hundred yards south of the Stockade Redan. Brownlee had mustered into the service on March 1, 1862, as a private in Co. K. He saw his first action at the Battle of Corinth, where he was wounded and subsequently captured. Brownlee rejoined his regiment after being exchanged.

For the men of the 35th Mississippi, the early daylight hours of May 22, 1863, began with the usual "popping of small arms & the booming of cannon," but by mid-morning the volume of Federal firing had dramatically increased. During the bombardment, the Mississippians lay in the hot dust as the breastworks above them were "torn down over their heads" by the Federal barrage. Around 10 A.M. the shelling slackened, only to be replaced by the crackling rifle fire of advancing skirmishers. Behind them columns of assault troops made their way through the winding ravines until they were within several hundred yards of the 35th Mississippi's entrenchments. The assault troops then moved out of their cover and began rapidly advancing. The Mississippi soldiers raised their heads above the parapet and unleashed "a withering, consuming fire" against the crowded ranks. Before the day ended Brownlee and the other riflemen of his regiment had stopped three attacks on their front.[45] *Photo courtesy of Gary Hendershott*

JAMES M. BROWNLEE
copy print

Corp. Charles Brown of Co. E, 33rd Illinois Infantry, was several hundred yards south of the 35th Mississippi's position. The 33rd Illinois was one of five regiments that had been assigned to attack the 2nd Texas Lunette. Brown, a twenty-three-year-old farmer from Princeton, Illinois, had enlisted on September 2, 1861. On the morning of May 22, 1863, his regiment followed the 99th Illinois out of a ravine and began deploying for battle. "Bullets were falling like hail" as the two regiments moved forward, but some of the men managed to reach the ditch in front of the position occupied by the 2nd Texas Infantry. For the next few hours the 33rd Illinois fought vainly to penetrate the lunette.[46] Brown was among seventy-two men in his regiment who were wounded in the assault; another thirteen of his fellow soldiers died in the fighting. *Photo courtesy of U.S.A.M.H.I., Richard Tibbals Collection*

Inside the lunette, Col. Ashbel Smith commanded the 2nd Texas Infantry. The 500 men in the regiment were protected by a four-foot-high parapet which, in places, was fourteen feet thick. Behind the parapet, Smith's soldiers had dug a two-foot-deep ditch which allowed the riflemen to "stand erect without being exposed to the enemy's fire." Smith had ordered embrasures cut in the parapet for two artillery pieces, and these holes were strengthened by dirt-covered cotton-bag revetments. The entire front of the parapet was surrounded by a six-foot-deep ditch, which meant that an attacking force would have to scale a ten-foot dirt slope to enter the lunette. The 2nd Texas was ready when the Union regiments began advancing, but they could not prevent several hundred Federals from reaching the ditch in front of the parapet. Inside the lunette, Smith's men were pinned down by Federal sharpshooters and consequently could not maintain a steady fire into the ditch. Early in the assault, Federal shells blew the cotton-bag embrasures to pieces and scattered burning lint everywhere. For a few moments the smoldering material threatened Smith's ammunition dump, but his men managed to brush the burning lint away with their hands. By 4 P.M. Smith's men were exhausted and in desperate need of support.[47]

GEORGE H. CHILDS, JR.
carte de visite

The only real Federal success of the day occurred five hundred yards south of the 2nd Texas Lunette where the tracks of the Southern Railroad of Mississippi passed through the Confederate lines. About one hundred yards in advance of the main Rebel entrenchments, there was a small redoubt that guarded the point where the railroad track entered the Confederate lines.

Second Lt. George H. Childs, Jr., of Epworth, Iowa, was with Co. F, 21st Iowa, one of four regiments assigned to attack the Railroad Redoubt. The Federal columns began their movement from a protective ravine which was only one hundred yards from their objective. The advancing regiments were met by "a terrible fire from the enemy," which checked the advance of the 21st and 22nd Iowa. However, a few daring soldiers from the two regiments rushed into the ditch, climbed the steep sides of the parapet, and seized a portion of the redoubt. All afternoon, Confederate and Union forces struggled for control of the vital position. During the initial charge, Lieutenant Childs was badly wounded in the chest. Total losses for the 21st Iowa were twelve killed, eighty wounded, and thirteen missing.[48] *Photo courtesy of Roger Davis*

On August 3, 1861, John C. Rye, of Marion County, Arkansas, joined Co. A of the 1st Battalion of Arkansas Cavalry. Rye's unit actually saw little cavalry service, and by the time of the Vicksburg Campaign the men were fighting as dismounted sharpshooters.

At daybreak on May 22, 1863, Green's brigade, which included Rye's unit, was in reserve. Late that morning the men were ordered to support the 2nd Texas Infantry. Before Green reached the Texans, he received new instructions to reinforce the Confederates who were counterattacking at the Railroad Redoubt. When Green arrived at his new position, the redoubt had already been recaptured by the Rebels. Nevertheless, Green sent the 1st Arkansas Battalion forward to clear out the few Federals who were still huddled in front of the redoubt. Rye's battalion drove the remaining soldiers out of the ditch. The brigade then retraced its steps to the 2nd Texas Lunette, which was still under heavy attack. Two of Green's regiments joined the 2nd Texas, while the 1st Arkansas Battalion, along with the 1st and 3rd Missouri Cavalry, filed into the entrenchments that flanked the lunette. Shortly after 4:30 P.M. the three dismounted cavalry units advanced into the ditch in front of the 2nd Texas Lunette. After a short but hard fight, they drove the Federals back.[49] By sunset Grant had suffered thirty-two hundred casualties, and all his attacking columns had been defeated.

JOHN C. RYE
copy print from *Confederate Veteran*, Vol. XVIII (August 1910)

The failure of the attack on May 22, 1863, finally convinced Grant he would have to reduce Vicksburg by siege. Facing the Union army was a series of rifle pits and dirt parapets that snaked across more than eight miles of rugged terrain. At strategic points the Rebels had constructed powerful redoubts and protected artillery batteries that could deliver enfilading fire against any column that dared to approach the main line of entrenchments. During the siege the defenders constantly worked to improve their homes in the dirt. "Everywhere," wrote Brig. Gen. Stephen D. Lee, "the trenches were made more comfortable. . . . Head logs and sand bags were used along the rifle pits to protect the heads of men in the trenches, and arrangements made to shade the men with their blankets overhead, from the sun. Openings were made to the rear for convenience in getting back to the trenches, and to let water run off in case of rain."[50]

This image, taken after the fall of Vicksburg, shows a typical section of the Confederate trenches. The old Rebel gun emplacement on the hill to the left contains two artillery pieces that were probably placed there by the Federals after the siege. It is surrounded by a network of protective ditches. Below and to the right of the position is a parapet that has been strengthened by a wooden revetment. Additional fortifications zigzag through the gorge below the fort and continue along the hill in the background. *Photo courtesy of U.S.A.M.H.I., MOLLUS, Mass., Collection*

CONFEDERATE ENTRENCHMENTS
EAST OF VICKSBURG
albumen print

During the siege, thousands of Union soldiers slowly pushed their entrenchments closer to the Rebel positions by digging zigzag trenches called saps. Most of the work was done at night.

This 1863 image shows a sap running toward the 3rd Louisiana Redan. The parapet on the left of the sap provided additional protection for the Federal soldiers in the trench. Along the right of the photograph is a series of gabions, which were cylindrical baskets made of woven twigs and filled with dirt. The devices helped protect the men working on the sap. The first gabion was usually placed out of range of the enemy's fire. Then soldiers rolled a second twig basket alongside its neighbor and filled it with dirt. The process was repeated again and

again until a wall like the one shown had been constructed. After a sap had been pushed as far forward as possible, the soldiers then constructed a redoubt and man-handled several artillery pieces into the new fortification. The redoubt and battery in the background of this image provided covering fire as the soldiers dug a new sap that was even closer to the besieged soldiers. Sometimes the men would construct an observation tower like the one in the upper left of this image. This particular structure was built with railroad iron and crossties. Its designer, Lt. Henry C. Foster of the 23rd Indiana, was fond of wearing a raccoon cap, and his work was popularly known as "coonskin's tower."[51] *Photo courtesy of the Library of Congress, no. B 8184-8522*

Union sap near the 3rd Louisiana Redan
copy print

261

Many of the soldiers who worked on the sap in front of the 3rd Louisiana Redan were with the 45th Illinois Infantry. One of their camps was near the Shirley House. Wilbur F. Crummer, an officer in the regiment, lived behind the house during the siege. Years later he wrote the following description of the men's accommodations:

They were encamped along the steep hillside, mostly sheltered from the enemy's shot. A place was dug against the hill, and in many cases, into it, forming a sort of cave. Poles were put up and covered with oil cloths, blankets or cane rods . . .

On the ridge in this image is a parapet that could be manned in the unlikely event of a Confederate sortie against the 45th Illinois. Generally, the camps were safe from artillery fire, but a stray round sometimes reached the rear areas. One day the men of Crummer's mess had just finished cooking a pot of beans when they heard the "sharp whirr of a piece of shell from overhead." The fragment "went crashing through the bottom of the kettle, carrying beans and all with it, burying it in the earth." "Boys," exclaimed one of the cooks, "your beans have gone to h——l."[52]

Federal soldiers had plenty of hardtack, beans, and bacon to eat, but good water and tobacco were in short supply. "The narcotic properties of tobacco," wrote a soldier in the 12th Wisconsin Infantry, "seemed to have so soothing an effect upon the nervous system that the weed was in general demand."[53]
Photo courtesy of the Old Court House Museum, Vicksburg

Shirley House and camp
of the 45th Illinois
copy print

Pvt. Samuel H. Wells of Co. H, 31st Tennessee, was eighteen years old when he joined the Confederate army at Midway, Tennessee, on March 19, 1862. The regiment had been with the Army of Mississippi since January 1863, and Wells was now trapped in Vicksburg. Adequate rations and clothing had always been in short supply in the Confederacy. In February 1863, for example, Wells' company clerk noted that the men were "in great need of clothes and shoes. Miserably fed on very poor and unhealthy beef." He added that "The beef is so bad that the men refuse to eat or draw it and is generally thrown away." When the garrison was thrown back on its own resources, edible food quickly became a scarce commodity. In June 1863, Wells' company clerk recorded that "our issue is 1/4 lb. bacon & flour, 6 oz sugar, 5 oz peas, 1 1/2 oz lard, rice, salt, tobacco, etc."[54] In the trenches, soldiers had to endure stifling heat, dust, and the unremitting shelling from Federal guns. "The firing is kept up with but little intermission day and night," wrote a fellow Tennessean. "When we lie down at night the chances are that a ball or fragment of shell may strike us at any moment."[55] Inadequate food, constant exposure to the elements, and the Union shells took their toll on the defenders. Within weeks thousands of Confederate soldiers were in hospitals, and those who remained on duty were in scarcely better condition. *Photo courtesy of Lawrence Jones, Confederate Calendar Works; original owned by Mildred S. Archer*

SAMUEL H. WELLS
copy print

LEVI W. HALL
copy print

The majority of Federal casualties at Vicksburg occurred during the assaults of May 19 and 22, but hundreds of other soldiers died or were wounded during the siege. On some days the opposing artillerymen and sharpshooters blazed away at each other as if they were fighting their own private war. At other times, as Pvt. James K. Newton of the 14th Wisconsin Infantry noted, "neither side will fire more than two or three cannon shots all day," but, he added, "like as not the next day there will be a continual roar for hours together. . . ." One of the casualties of such indiscriminate fighting was Pvt. Levi W. Hall of Co. G, 33rd Illinois Infantry.

Hall was a twenty-year-old farmer from McLean County, Illinois, when he joined the army on August 5, 1861. Hall later fought at Big Black River Bridge and in the assault on May 22, 1863. The two engagements cost the regiment eighty-five men, but Hall had not been hurt.

At Vicksburg the 33rd Illinois was entrenched in front of two Union siege guns that constantly fired over the men's heads. Occasionally, the shells burst prematurely and injured soldiers in the regiment. During the daylight hours the 33rd Illinois's sharpshooters fired at the enemy, and at night the men stood picket duty. On June 13, 1863, Hall was in the trenches when he was wounded by a Rebel sharpshooter. He was eventually transferred to the General Hospital in Memphis and was there when the siege ended.[56] *Photo courtesy of U.S.A.M.H.I., Richard Tibbals Collection*

While Grant's army kept the pressure on Vicksburg's landward approaches, the Union navy harassed the garrison from the Mississippi River. At night soldiers in the trenches could see the red trail of the blazing fuses of mortar shells and hear the two-hundred-pound projectiles crash into the houses in the besieged city. During daylight hours the big ironclads such as the USS *Cincinnati* sometimes dueled with the heavy river batteries that protected Vicksburg. She and the other Eads boats were powerful vessels, but they were not invulnerable.

On May 10, 1862, at the Battle of Plum Bayou, the *Cincinnati* had been so badly damaged by Rebel rams that her crew had had to run the ironclad aground to keep the vessel from sinking. The *Cincinnati* was subsequently refloated and joined the fleet in front of Vicksburg. On the morning of May 27, 1863, the *Cincinnati* was under a full head of steam as she engaged the Vicksburg batteries. During the duel she was riddled by eight- and ten-inch shells, and sank in eighteen feet of water. Twenty-five men were either killed or wounded aboard the stricken vessel, and another fifteen sailors drowned while trying to swim to shore. After Vicksburg fell, the *Cincinnati* was raised for a second time and returned to duty.
Photo courtesy of the Old Court House Museum, Vicksburg

USS *Cincinnati*
cabinet card

LEMUEL PRIOR COSBY
copy print

For almost a month Union soldiers had been pushing a sap toward the 3rd Louisiana Redan. By June 25, 1863, a tunnel from the sap had been dug under the redan and packed with explosives. That afternoon, Corp. Lemuel Prior Cosby's regiment had a detail working in a shaft which the Confederates were digging in an attempt to locate the Union tunnel. Since the Rebels had been unable to find the tunnel, they had taken the added precaution of constructing a second line across the base of the 3rd Louisiana Redan. It is likely that Cosby was stationed behind that parapet.

Cosby had originally been a member of the Lowndes Southrons, which became Co. D of the 10th Mississippi Infantry. When that regiment was reorganized after its required year of service, Cosby reenlisted on April 29, 1862, in Co. F, 43rd Mississippi. Cosby's regiment had fought at Iuka and Corinth, but he was sick in the hospital during both battles.

Around 3 P.M. on June 25, 1863, the ground under the men in the 3rd Louisiana Redan ruptured from the force of an explosion beneath them. Six men from the 43rd Mississippi who were working in the shaft died immediately, and five others were buried in the debris. The explosion blew out a section of the redan, leaving in its place a rubble strewn crater.[57] A Federal column immediately rushed into the breach to attack the secondary line behind which Cosby stood. *Photo courtesy of U.S.A.M.H.I., C. N. Cosby Collection*

266

On the afternoon of June 25, 1863, 1st Sgt. James Code of Co. I, 17th Iowa, waited in the sap with orders to reinforce the assault troops as soon as possible. However, the crater was too small to accommodate any more men, and the advancing column was pinned down. Despite the failure of the attack, the Union high command refused to give up even such a small gain. At 10:30 P.M. the 17th Iowa received orders to begin relieving part of the troops in the crater. The commander of the Iowans could see the position he was to take "by the glare of the bursting shells which were constantly thrown over the broken parapet by the enemy." The 17th Iowa remained in the crater until it was relieved around 2 A.M. the next day. The regiment suffered thirty-seven casualties, including Code, who was badly wounded. The next day Grant withdrew his men. On July 1, 1863, miners exploded an even larger charge under the redan, but Union commanders made no attempt to rush the breach.

In September 1893, Code walked into the Wales Studio in Keokuk, Iowa, with a small tintype of himself that had been made thirty years earlier in Memphis, Tennessee. He had this print made for his grandchild. On the back of the print, Code wrote: "I carried said picture . . . to May 1865 when I was discharged. It is badly broken and scratched as you may see. I carried it through Battle(s) of Raymond, Jackson, Championsville [sic], Vicksburg, Miss., and Atlanta, Ga. and to Andersonville prison."[58] *Photo courtesy of Richard Holloway*

JAMES CODE
cabinet card

267

JOHN C. BOWEN
carte de visite

On July 3, 1863, white flags appeared along a section of the Rebel trenches, and hostilities temporarily ceased. Shortly afterward, Maj. Gen. John C. Bowen and another officer began walking toward the Union lines. Few Confederate officers had seen more action in Mississippi than Bowen: He had led troops in nine major battles in the state and had lost at least four thousand men to the enemy. Bowen also symbolized the deep division that the war caused in border states such as Missouri. At Vicksburg, for example, twenty-seven Union and fifteen Confederate commands from Missouri served in the siege; on several occasions they fought each other. Bowen was a dedicated soldier, but he was realistic enough to know that continued resistance was useless. He wanted Pemberton to surrender.

Bowen, a graduate of West Point, had been an architect in St. Louis before the war. There, Grant had once been his neighbor. On July 3, 1863, Grant declined to meet with his old friend, but he did agree to see Pemberton. The meeting did not go well, because Grant demanded unconditional surrender. Bowen tried to mediate between them, but his effort failed. That evening Grant relented and agreed to parole the entire army.[59] Pemberton accepted. The next day more than twenty thousand Rebels laid down their arms. Nine days after the surrender, Bowen, who had been physically worn down by the long siege, died near Raymond as a paroled prisoner of war. *Photo courtesy of the Library of Congress, no. B 813-6577*

268

Reinforcements joined Grant throughout the siege and by July 4, 1863, he had at least seventy-one thousand men in east-central Mississippi. However, many of these new units had to be detached to watch the relief force that Johnston was assembling in Jackson. By late June, Johnston had thirty-one thousand men under his command, and he felt compelled to try to relieve Pemberton. On July 1, 1863, the leading elements of Johnston's troops reached the Big Black River.

Lt. Col. Albert Heath commanded the 100th Indiana, which had reinforced Grant on June 11, 1863. Two weeks later Heath's men began scouting to ascertain Johnston's location, and they reported that he was still east of the Big Black River. After Johnston learned of Vicksburg's fall, he began withdrawing to the entrenched lines at Jackson. A few hours after the surrender of Vicksburg, Heath received orders to move on Jackson. Each of Heath's Indianians carried 150 rounds of ammunition and five days' rations. As the men marched eastward they "could trace the route of the retreating Rebel cavalry by the columns of dust seen in the distance." The 100th Indiana arrived in front of Jackson on July 9, 1863, and by the next day almost fifty thousand more Union troops were converging on the city. During the Siege of Jackson, Heath's regiment came under sporadic artillery fire, but the shells usually did little more than spray his men with dirt.[60] *Photo courtesy of the Indiana State Library*

ALBERT HEATH
carte de visite

ABNER H. MCMURTRIE
carte de visite

The biggest fight at Jackson occurred on July 12, 1863. That morning, Brig. Gen. Jacob Lauman was realigning his division to conform to confusing orders, which, among other instructions, directed him to carry out a reconnaissance in force. However, he had no orders to attack. During the movement, one of his brigades mistakenly advanced against the Rebel lines. Among the assaulting troops was 1st Lt. Abner McMurtie of Co. D, 3rd Iowa Infantry.

McMurtrie, a twenty-year-old native of Decorah, Iowa, enlisted as a second sergeant on May 20, 1861. On May 21, 1862, he was commissioned second lieutenant of his company.

The 3rd Iowa advanced on July 12, 1863, with 241 soldiers. When the Iowans emerged into a cleared field in front of the enemy's entrenchments, they were pounded by Rebel artillery fire. McMurtrie's regiment got within seventy-five yards of the Rebels, but the 3rd Iowa's line "rapidly melted away under this terrible fire." They fell back in disorder.[61] Seventeen Iowans died in the deadly assault and another fifty-seven were wounded. The attacking Federal brigade lost a total of 519 men in the forty-minute battle. That afternoon Lauman was removed from command and ordered to Vicksburg. He never again led troops in the Civil War.

McMurtie's legs had been broken by a shell fragment. Surgeons amputated his right leg below the knee and transferred him to the hospital ship *Nashville,* where he died on July 25, 1863. *Photo courtesy of Mark Warren*

270

Lauman's attack had been made against Brig. Gen. Daniel Adams' brigade. Supporting the brigade was the six-gun battery of the 5th Co., Washington Artillery, one of the best batteries in Johnston's army. One of the gunners was Pvt. Andy Swain. Swain liked music, and he had managed to find a piano, which now sat near the company's artillery. Just before the Union advance began, Swain was entertaining some of his fellow soldiers, who were grouped around him singing "You shan't have any of my Peanuts." Swain's performance was interrupted by the advancing Federals. The men rushed to their guns and opened fire on the columns. The Union infantry continued to advance until the men were "no longer able to endure the withering fire, principally from the artillery . . ."[62] Swain then returned to his piano playing.

Johnston knew that he could not survive a protracted siege, and on July 16, 1863, he decided to evacuate the city. By 1 A.M. the next day Johnston's troops were across the Pearl River. With Vicksburg and Jackson captured, it made little sense to maintain Johnston's force in Mississippi. Most of the men, including the Washington Artillery, eventually reinforced the Army of Tennessee. *Photo courtesy of Manuscripts Section, Howard-Tilton Memorial Library, Tulane University, Louisiana Historical Association Collection*

ANDY SWAIN
carte de visite

Chapter 8

Behind the Lines
in Mississippi

The Civil War years brought armed conflict to many parts of Mississippi. The war within the state was not limited to the battle front, however. From the beginning of the fighting those who remained at home were involved in another type of war. Civilians had to fight simply to survive as economic and human resources were drained away to support the war effort. Government and other social institutions collapsed, and the very fabric of life in some communities disintegrated. Federal armies forced some to flee their homes as refugees. Others faced the difficult problem of living behind Yankee lines in areas occupied by the Union troops. For all of these civilians, the Civil War ultimately threatened to destroy the Mississippi that had existed prior to secession.

Gov. John J. Pettus headed a state government in 1861 that faced immense problems on the home front as well as on the battlefield. Civilian authorities had approached the conflict with little regard for the potential social and economic problems that the war would create. When the war did not come to a quick conclusion, these difficulties mounted. Among the earliest problems encountered were economic ones. The absence of large numbers of citizen-soldiers left the state's farms short of labor and left families without food and necessary supplies. A major crop failure in the first year of the the war compounded the problem. Governor Pettus tried to solve the problem by encouraging farmers and planters to plant at least one acre of corn for every laborer. While the production of food grains increased, the farms never produced enough during the war to prevent suffering among the civilian population.

Other goods were also in short supply, and the state government and civilians were forced to use ingenious methods to meet their needs. Salt, essential to the preservation of meats, was one such item, and the state government tried various ways of securing it. Ultimately, the state established a salt works of its own in Alabama. Homespun cloth and handmade clothing replaced imported manufactured goods. Home-produced substitutes replaced scarce items such as coffee, tea, soda, candles, dyes, and some medicines. The sole source of supply for many medicines often was through Federal lines.

Those hardest hit by the problems that developed within the state usually were the poorest members of society, particularly the wives and children of the men who had joined the army. The plight of these individuals caused local and state governments to try to provide some relief. The burden of relief finally fell upon the state government alone because local governments tended to fall apart as the war progressed. The efforts of both were never adequate because of the enormousness of the problem, however, and suffering continued among these civilians throughout the war.

The governor's task of providing relief was compounded by the shortage of revenues during the war, as well as by the actual lack of goods to distribute. In 1861, in order to provide relief and meet other demands, the Secession Convention raised the state tax by 50 percent, then an additional 3 percent tax was imposed on money lent or used to buy securities. When these tax increases did not raise enough money, the legislature provided for the issue of $5,000,000 in currency in return for cotton at the exchange rate of five cents per pound. Three other efforts to finance state governmental operations amounted simply to printing money. Between 1861 and 1863 the amount of such paper authorized by the legislature totaled $5,500,000.

The state's monetary policy not only failed to provide the state with the necessary funds to deal with its many problems, it actually worsened the problems of civilians by driving up prices and ultimately producing a runaway inflation rate. Prices went upward rapidly. For example, a barrel of flour sold from $50 to $75 in northern Mississippi in December 1862, was $60 to $65 per barrel in October 1863, and then ranged from $90 to $100 by November 1863.

The ultimate failure of the state and Confederate governments was their inability to prevent the Union army from staging destructive raids into the interior of the state and from finally bringing much of the area along the Mississippi River under its control. After 1862 Federal gunboats operated freely along the river as far north as Vicksburg and supported army forays against targets in the interior. Areas in northern Mississippi came under long-term Federal control. In 1863 the occupation of Vicksburg and Natchez provided bases from which even more extensive operations could be carried out. Confederate officials could not stop the Federal advance and eventually abandoned large parts of the state to the Union or to anarchy. In 1863 the state government abandoned Jackson to begin an odyssey that lasted until the end of the war, as the executive officers and legislators moved to Meridian, Enterprise, Columbus, and then to Macon.

Federal armies brought widespread suffering to civilians as they moved into the state. James Lusk Alcorn recorded the impact of one raid into Coahoma County in the autumn of 1862 when the Federals drove east to Oakland on the Central Mississippi Railroad. Alcorn wrote to his wife:

The Yankees . . . made sad havoc on their march; burnt old man Shelby's gin house also Hulls—and Hatchez— burnt all Hull's fence, killed most of his stock, took all that they had left, clothes, bedding, burnt all his doors, broke out his window sash, and burnt two of his cabins; at Hills they broke all that fine furniture and threw it into the yard, searched the House and robbed it of ten thousand dollars in money. . . . They took off about twenty of Hill's negroes, and killed a great amount of the stock.[1]

Alcorn grimly predicted that the state could not

stand up against the onslaught for more than a year.

The state's towns and villages suffered particular destruction. Friars Point, Grand Gulf, and Prentiss were burned to the ground. Large portions of Holly Springs, Jackson, and Oxford were destroyed. Prentiss met its fate after two transports carrying members of the 33rd Illinois Infantry on the Mississippi River were fired upon. The soldiers were put ashore, and Capt. Charles E. Wilcox recorded the subsequent destruction. He wrote in his diary on September 14, 1862, that "We burnt every thing, a single thing not being allowed to be pillaged. . . . [A] store full of goods, the court house with all tavern, and about thirty dwellings . . . , all, all committed to the flames. . . . They have met a just retribution."[2] Writing of Jackson in February 1864, another Illinois soldier wrote, "[I]t is a heap of ruins. Some of the citizens call it 'Chimneyville,' from the great number of standing chimneys from which the buildings had been burned."[3]

Many residents simply abandoned parts of the state and headed for the eastern counties or Alabama. The inability of Confederate authorities to protect citizens led to a collapse of civilian morale. Writing from his unit's camp on the rail line north of Jackson, William L. Nugent informed his wife in March 1864 that the surrounding country was "a dreary spectacle indeed. The largest plantations are thinning out, grown up in woods & pastured upon by a few scattering cattle; fences are pulled down & destroyed; houses burned; negroes run off. A general gloom pervades everything and the people appear to be in a listless spirit, perfectly impassable, subjugated, in some instances by prospective want and suffering, and utterly devoid of any disposition to continue longer the struggle for Independence."[4]

In the autumn of 1863, John Pettus turned over the governorship to Charles Clark. With support of the Confederate government, the state militia was strengthened, and units were raised for regular service in the state alone. Many of the volunteers were old men and children. Such measures did not prevent the steady deterioration of conditions. Clark's administration was no more able than Pettus's in solving the problems of supply and morale.

Governor Clark also faced a new problem: the spread of disaffection with the Confederate cause. The roots of this discontent were broad and deep. Poorer citizens of counties such as Tishomingo, Pontotoc, and Itawamba had opposed the war from the beginning. The ranks of dissent within these counties were swelled by deserters, whose numbers increased after Confederate defeats in Tennessee and northern Mississippi in 1862 and who now sought refuge in this area. Following the imposition of conscription by the Confederacy in the autumn of 1862, the deserters were also joined by those seeking to resist service in the army.

After 1863 armed bands acted freely in many parts of the state. Some local officials supported such activities to resist the enforcement of Confederate conscription laws. The result was practically a civil war within the state itself. Military commanders were forced to send in Confederate troops to enforce conscription laws and to bring deserters back to their commands, and by the end of the war some Confederate cavalry units did little more than scour the countryside searching for deserters and resisters to conscription.

While civilians behind Confederate lines lived lives of desperation, other Mississippians faced different conditions in those areas occupied by the invading Federals. In northern Mississippi and along the Mississippi River, the Federals settled down for long periods of occupation, establishing permanent posts. Corinth in the northern part of the state was occupied from 1862 until the Federals finally abandoned it in 1864. Both

Vicksburg and Natchez fell into Federal hands in 1863 and remained under the National flag until the end of the war.

The river towns prospered under occupation. Merchants reopened stores, selling goods to the thousands of troops garrisoned along the Mississippi. In addition, a lively trade also existed at times between the town stores and the residents of the surrounding countryside. One resident recalled that "accommodating clerk[s]" sold brass buttons, cavalry boots, flannel shirts, and even pistols to whoever would buy them. Even the women of the communities participated in the bonanza. One wrote: "Every kitchen was converted into a confectioners shop and the avalanche of cakes and pies & pickles & molasses candy which poured into the Yankee camps for sale, must have been as astonishing as pleasing to hungry eyes."[5]

Federal occupation also saw a resurgence of the agrarian economy when the Yankees began a program of leasing plantation lands along the Mississippi River to loyal leasees. This was one way of handling the thousands of black refugees who fled to Union lines during the war years. Every raiding party and major operation brought more blacks out of Confederate Mississippi. One official estimated that at one point twenty thousand refugee blacks were in the Vicksburg area. Support of this population presented a major difficulty. To solve the army's problem and to help blacks make the transition from slavery to freedom, Gen. Ulysses S. Grant appointed John Eaton, Jr., educator and chaplain of the 27th Ohio Infantry, to direct work among the refugees. Among other projects, Eaton initiated the lease program that put many of the escaped slaves to work as wage laborers in Mississippi's cotton fields.

In the spring of 1863 the Federal government also began to recruit blacks for the army. Gen. Lorenzo Thomas worked along the Mississippi River Valley, where he encouraged whites to volunteer as officers for such regiments and worked to integrate black forces into the Union army. Ultimately, thousands of blacks served in regiments recruited from within Mississippi, Arkansas, and Louisiana. Designated as Mississippi units were one regiment of cavalry, two regiments of heavy artillery, and five regiments of infantry. All of these troops remained in Mississippi during the war, primarily serving as garrison troops at Vicksburg and Natchez.

In the Federal enclaves, renewed loyalty actually brought some white Southerners to join the Union army. In March 1864, the 1st Mississippi Mounted Rifles, the only white Union regiment from Mississippi, was organized at Memphis. Its officers were Northerners, just as with the black regiments, but for the most part the men were from Mississippi. The unit had a good record of service, including raids along the Mississippi River in the Grand Gulf and Port Gibson vicinity in July 1864; A. J. Smith's expedition to Oxford in August; and Benjamin Grierson's raid on the Mobile & Ohio Railroad that December.

Permanent Federal occupation encouraged some Mississippians to seek the return of their state to the old Union and to peace. After the fall of Vicksburg, prominent antebellum Whigs in that vicinity, such as William L. Sharkey, requested protection by Federal troops from Confederate soldiers. Gen. William T. Sherman reported that he found many men in Jackson and the area between the capital and the river ready for peace and asking him for a restoration of state government under the Union. In April 1864 the Federal commander at Vicksburg officially encouraged such individuals to hold a convention as a prelude to the reestablishment of a loyal civilian government. Nothing was done, but the peace movement amply demonstrated that many people of the state had tired of the war.

Permanent Federal posts in Mississippi proved

a major problem for the Confederates. Morale suffered, particularly as trade extended across military lines, thousands of slaves slipped out of Confederate control, plantation operations began again, and Mississippians began to speak out for the Union. Some efforts were made by Confederate authorities to stiffen the line between Unionists and secessionist Mississippians, but ultimately this division remained a nuisance to the Confederacy until the war's end.

While battles raged within the state and out, Mississippi's civilian population faced a war of their own. They fought for survival in the midst of trying circumstances. Their battle left its own mark on them, just as the armed conflict left its mark on the soldiers who fought.

Charles Clark, an attorney and planter from Bolivar County, was a war hero when he ran successfully for governor of the state in the 1863 general election. Clark had been a radical secessionist in 1861 and remained in 1863 a strong advocate of his earlier position. When he took office he promised a vigorous support of the war effort. Rather than submit ever to reconstruction of the nation, he admonished citizens in his inaugural address that they "like the remnant of the heroic Pascagoulas, when their braves were slain, join hands together, march into the sea, and perish beneath its waters."[6] Rather than achieving success, however, Clark fought simply to keep the state from devolving into chaos. The problem was immense. Judge Robert S. Hudson of Leake County expressed the near hopelessness of the situation in the spring of 1864 when he informed Governor Clark that, "the state is now under the tacit rule of deserters, thieves, and disloyal men and women."[7] *Photo courtesy of the Library of Congress, no. LC B8184-5835*

ARTHUR E. REYNOLDS
carte de visite

The development of widespread opposition to the Confederate conscription laws after the autumn of 1862 was a source of major trouble for civil and military authorities. Col. Arthur E. Reynolds, commander of the 16th Mississippi Infantry, was one of the many men who temporarily tried to enforce conscription when placed in charge of the Conscript Bureau in August 1863. This attorney from Jacinto had taken leave from his regiment following the capture of Vicksburg because of an illness and had been assigned temporarily to help round up conscripts. The task proved formidable, with draft dodgers securing help both from neighbors and local civilian authorities. Reynolds would return to his regiment and fight with it in northern Virginia, but his successors continued to encounter strong opposition to their efforts. Lt. Gen. Leonidas Polk complained in the spring of 1864 that the conscript laws had been inefficiently administered and the Bureau of Conscription had failed to perform its functions with "the necessary vigor and energy."[8] As a result, Polk appointed a provost-marshal general for his entire department, divided the department into sub-districts, and appointed wounded or sick officers to police their districts and require the men liable for military service to report. Regular cavalry was put to work supporting these officers in what would prove a never-ending task. *Photo courtesy of the Museum of the Confederacy*

The fate of Stephen Davenport of the 26th Mississippi Infantry, a merchant and farmer in Tishomingo County before the war, reflected the widespread breakdown of law and order. In August 1863, Davenport left his unit after being promoted to major and assigned to head a cavalry battalion that was being formed. He went on furlough prior to assuming that command and returned home. On the way he had to pass through Itawamba County, an area reported by Gen. Stephen D. Lee to be infected with political dissent and filled with independent companies authorized by Richmond, the governor, and even different generals and responsible to no one. He called these units "harbors for deserters and persons trying to avoid the military service."[10] Davenport ran into one such group of bushwhackers and was assassinated on November 8, 1863. *Photo courtesy of Margaret G. Rogers*

STEPHEN DAVENPORT
quarter-plate ambrotype

In June 1864, Brig. Gen. William L. Brandon was transferred from the Army of Northern Virginia and assigned to head the Conscript Bureau and the Reserve Corps of the state. The formation of the Reserve Corps indicated the extent of Confederate personnel problems by that time. The Corps consisted of all men able for duty under the age of eighteen and over forty-five. In his first order, Brandon pointed to the success of reserve forces in Virginia at Petersburg and Staunton and called upon Mississippians to follow their example. He wrote: "I appeal to you as fellow Mississippians to come forward and prove that you can also buckle on your armor to resist the encroachments of a foe who is now seeking to devastate our beloved country."[9] The Reserve Corps had difficulty recruiting enough men and never proved effective in preventing the easy movement of Yankees through the state. *Photo courtesy of the Library of Congress, no. LC 5880*

JOHN FRANK POU
sixth-plate ambrotype

Pvt. Johnson Harris enlisted in Co. A, 3rd Battalion Mississippi State Cavalry, in April 1864 at Simpson. Raised by Maj. D. G. Cooper, the company consisted totally of men between the ages of ten to eighteen and forty-five to fifty. As part of Brandon's Reserve, these troops were raised for short-term service authorized by the legislature. These units saw only limited service and were used primarily to aid the work of the provost marshal within the state and to keep order at home. *Photo courtesy of Kevin Hooper*

JOHNSON HARRIS
ninth-plate ambrotype

Pvt. John Frank Pou of Wayne County enlisted in Co. A, Moorman's Cavalry Battalion, later the 24th Mississippi Battalion, in July 1864, having just turned eighteen. Like many other units that formed late in the war, the 24th Battalion attempted to resist Federal raids, but spent much of its time trying to police the areas that remained under Confederate control. In July 1864, the 24th was assigned to the command of Major Denis, provost marshal general for the state. These units chased bushwhackers, hunted down deserters, and enforced conscription. Co. A was part of Denis's command used to suppress disturbances in Jones County. An expedition in March 1864 broke up bands operating there. The bands were back by the end of summer, and Co. A was sent back in again after the Conscript Bureau reported "serious disaffection and the apprehension of disturbances" from large numbers of deserters in that county."[11] *Photo courtesy of George Esker*

282

Pvt. Elliott W. Mudge enrolled in the "Ed Moore Rangers" at Iberville Parish, Louisiana, in the summer of 1861. The Rangers were known by the rattlesnake rattles that the troopers wore on their hats. The unit became Co. A of Col. John S. Scott's 1st Louisiana Cavalry. After extensive service in Mississippi and Tennessee, in 1864 Mudge and his unit were in Wilkinson County in southern Mississippi, where they would spend much of the rest of the war as raiders. They also tried to restore order in that section of the state. The 1st Louisiana's specific instructions at the time included "interrupting travel on the Mississippi River, and preventing the planting of cotton crops on the river lands and suppressing the trade with the enemy."[12] When they arrived, the Louisianans found a civilian population practically in arms against the Confederate government. Moreover, the Rangers' own sympathies were with the civilians. Such demoralization practically doomed the Confederate cause. *Photo courtesy of Manuscripts Section, Howard-Tilton Memorial Library, Tulane University, Louisiana Historical Association Collection*

ELLIOTT W. MUDGE
carte de visite

After the autumn of 1862 Mississippi civilians came into increasing contact with Federal forces. The town of Oxford was one of those that periodically saw Federal troops. This picture was made in the winter of 1862–63, when it was occupied by the army of Gen. Ulysses S. Grant. Grant was then trying to move against Vicksburg through the interior of the state, but he was thwarted by Gen. Earl Van Dorn's attack upon his supply lines at Holly Springs. Grant's response was to send out foraging parties into the surrounding countryside, leaving the people around Oxford with little to eat. Grant informed local citizens, "it could not be expected that men, with arms in their hands, would starve in the midst of plenty. I advised them to emigrate east, or west, fifteen miles and assist in eating up what we left."[13] *Photo courtesy of the Chicago Historical Society, no. ICHi-07966*

OXFORD COURT HOUSE
albumen print

RUINS OF OXFORD
albumen print

Oxford was visited again on August 22, 1864, faring worse than in its initial occupation. A Federal army under Gen. Andrew J. Smith marched in, searching for Nathan Bedford Forrest. Forrest was elsewhere, but before leaving, Smith's men devastated the town. The commander of the Confederate post at Oxford reported that General Smith's troops had been "made mad with whisky for the occasion," and their conduct to the civilians had been "brutal in the extreme." Before retiring, the Federals had burned "34 stores and business houses, court-house, Masonic hall, 2 fine large hotels, besides carpenter, blacksmith, and other shops; also 5 fine dwelling-houses among the latter that of Hon. Jacob Thompson."[14] *Photo courtesy of M.D.A.H.*

Following its central role in the battles of the spring and autumn of 1862, the town of Corinth continued to be an important staging area for occupying Federal troops until they abandoned it in January 1864. As with other Mississippi towns, it became a staging area for expeditions into the interior of the state—those searching for cotton as well as those with more purely military goals. The town square and the railroad platforms were often filled with cotton seized on Mississippi plantations to be shipped to the North.
Photo courtesy of the Chicago Historical Society, no ICHi-07848

CORINTH TOWN SQUARE
albumen print

286

As a result of the raids from the town, Corinth would be one of the first places where Federal armies encountered large numbers of runaway slaves. Situated in the rich black lands of northeastern Mississippi, the area was home to thousands of slaves. With the movement of the Union armies into the area, many slaves simply walked away from their owners, posing a major logistical problem for the military.

FREEDMEN AT PROVOST GUARDS
HEADQUARTERS, CORINTH
copy print from Francis T. Miller,
The Photographic History of the Civil War

CORINTH
albumen print

As with other Mississippi towns, Federal occupation brought renewed business activity to Corinth. In the wake of the occupying armies came an army of businessmen ready to sell provisions to the army and also cotton speculators anxious to acquire the cotton seized by the military. This photograph of Corinth's streets shows businessmen, possibly cotton speculators, posing for the photographer. *Photo courtesy of the Chicago Historical Society, no. ICHi-08016*

Natchez surrendered to the Union navy as ships steamed toward Vicksburg in May 1862. The city was occupied thereafter until the end of the war. The Federal soldiers who were stationed there liked the city and the surrounding countryside. The large houses within it particularly distinguished this Southern city. They included the "Parsonage," a house constructed across from "Rosalie" by Peter Little to house the large numbers of Methodist ministers who frequently visited his wife. By wartime, it was a private residence. Such houses allowed one Wisconsin soldier to describe Natchez as a "beautiful city,—one of the pleasantest we ever visited in the South. Its streets were clean and shady, its dwellings tasty, and some of them elegant."[15] *Photo courtesy of Natchez Trace Collection, Center for American History, University of Texas at Austin*

288

DWELLINGS ON MAIN STREET, NATCHEZ

THE PARSONAGE, NATCHEZ
carte de visite

In addition to the physical beauty of the city, many of the soldiers found other attractions. Kate D. Foster, a planter's daughter, wrote in her diary on September 10, 1863, that "some of the young ladies around Natchez are receiving attention from the Yankees. I think it shows *so* little character not to resist love of admiration more. I don't mean to say the Yankees are not gentleman enough to visit here, but we ought to remember that we all have relatives, friends or lovers in our army and if they heard of these things it might weaken a strong arm in time of battle and sicken a stout & loving heart."[16] Foster never fraternized, but many of the belles of Natchez apparently did. *Photo courtesy of Natchez Trace Collection, Center for American History, University of Texas at Austin*

A large force garrisoned Vicksburg from July 1863 until the end of the war. Unlike Natchez, Vicksburg was not a popular post for the occupying troops. One soldier wrote of the town: "Vicksburg is a miserable hole and was never anything better. A number of houses have been burned by our artillery firing, but altogether the town has suffered less than any secesh village I have seen at the hands of our forces. . . . no business whatever doing in the town, except issuing orders by generals, obeying them by soldiers and the chawing of commissary stores without price by the ragged citizen population."[17]
Photo courtesy of U.S.A.M.H.I., MOLLUS, Mass., Collection

VICKSBURG MARKETHOUSE
carte de visite

Many of Vicksburg's better houses were seized by Union forces and occupied by officers. The home of Dr. and Mrs. William T. Balfour had been built in 1835 and had survived the siege of the city. Mrs. Balfour was displaced following the fall of Vicksburg, and the home became the headquarters for Maj. Gen. James B. McPherson while he commanded the Federal forces there. *Photo courtesy of the Library of Congress, no. LC B816-8183*

Balfour House, Vicksburg
albumen print

As with other points occupied by the Federals, Vicksburg became a stepping-off point for many of the expeditions into the interior. Many of these were carried out by infantry who were carried to their point of attack by steamboats and supported by Federal gunboats. Boats such as these, seen at Vicksburg in February 1864, were typical of those used by the army in these raids. Steamboats like those pictured supplied Federal troops along the river. *Photo courtesy of U.S.A.M.H.I., MOLLUS, Mass., Collection*

Docked boats at Vicksburg
carte de visite

Many of the Federal troops were placed on the outskirts of Vicksburg, but a few were placed within the city itself. This photograph shows the barracks of the 124th Illinois. A soldier's life within the captured city took on the tone of a peacetime army. R. L. Howard, whose unit occupied these barracks, recalled: "The boys soon settled down into their routine of duty, which for the present was mostly picket, as the colored troops, of which there were several regiments in the city, had been hitherto called upon for fatigue, and the 72d Illinois were on provost duty. It was always deeply interesting to us to picket the line of our old approaches to the works, and guard our historic spots, and our picket line at this time was mainly the line of the old rebel breastworks."[18] *Photo courtesy of U.S.A.M.H.I., MOLLUS, Mass., Collection*

CAMP OF THE 124TH ILLINOIS, VICKSBURG
carte de visite

JOHN T. MURRAY
carte de visite
D. P. Barr, Vicksburg

Beginning in 1863 the Union army began efforts to organize regiments from among the freedmen moving into their lines. The officers of the new black units were all drawn from white regiments. Second Lt. John T. Murray was one of the many Yankee soldiers who signed up for these new units, joining Co. B of the 50th U.S.C.T. *Photo courtesy of John Wernick*

NAPOLEON SNYDER
carte de visite
A. Richmond, Memphis

One white regiment was raised in Mississippi, but like the black regiments all of its officers were Northerners who transferred from other units. Capt. N. Snyder was commander of Co. D, 1st Mississippi Regiment Mounted Rifles. Raised at Memphis, Tennessee, in March 1864, the unit was attached to the Cavalry Division, District of West Tennessee, throughout the war. The unit accompanied expeditions to Grand Gulf, Bolivar, Port Gibson, and Oxford. It was also on Grierson's raid against the Mobile & Ohio Railroad in December and January, 1864–1865. *Photo courtesy of Don W. Scoggins*

UNKNOWN UNIT OF BLACK TROOPS, VICKSBURG, 1864
copy print from Francis T. Miller, *The Photographic History of the Civil War*

While photographs of officers remain, few individual photographs of black soldiers exist. This photograph appeared in *The Photographic History of the Civil War*. Identified only as "colored troops at drill" at Vicksburg in 1864, it is probably a company of one of the four black infantry regiments both raised in Mississippi and garrisoned at Vicksburg—the 51st, 52nd, 58th, or 66th U.S. Colored Troops. A fifth black regiment, the 53rd, was raised in Mississippi but was assigned to the District of Northeast Louisiana and then Goodrich Landing.

Chapter 9

Meridian and the Campaigns in Northern Mississippi, 1864–1865

Following the fall of Vicksburg, Confederate forces in Mississippi established themselves in positions to respond to any further movements into the state by the strong Federal armies garrisoned at Vicksburg and at Memphis. Union strategy in 1864, however, no longer focused primarily on goals in Mississippi. In the Western Theaters of operation the major Federal effort was directed at protecting Chattanooga, then moving against Atlanta. Major Federal military operations in Mississippi were largely in support of these actions—attempting to disrupt Confederate logistics, preventing the release of Confederate forces to reinforce the beleaguered armies in Georgia, or keeping Confederate units, principally those of Maj. Gen. Nathan Bedford Forrest, from interfering with Yankee plans.

The Confederates, with limited resources, established a thin line arrayed against the Federal strong points and pursued a defensive strategy. In early 1864 the Confederates had only about six-teen thousand men along this line. Maj. Gen. William W. Loring's infantry division was at Canton; Maj. Gen. Samuel G. French's infantry division was at Jackson; Brig. Gen. William H. Jackson's cavalry division stretched from Yazoo City to Natchez; and Maj. Gen. Nathan Bedford Forrest's cavalry was in northern Mississippi along a line south of the Tallahatchie River. Even this limited force would be reduced further as the center of the war changed, but the fighting in Mississippi would continue, and men would die in combat until the very end of the war.

Although there were many expeditions, raids, and skirmishes from the summer of 1863 until the end of the war, during this period Confederate forces in Mississippi faced five major campaigns by the Federals into the state's interior. In October 1863, in the first such campaign, Gen. James B. McPherson advanced into central Mississippi with the intention of pinning down Confederate troops there in order to keep them from moving to support efforts at blocking Sherman's movement across the northern part of the state. In January 1864, Sherman initiated a second major invasion. This one was aimed at Meridian and was designed to destroy Confederate transportation facilities in eastern Mississippi. Three other major Federal operations in Mississippi also attempted to destroy Gen. Nathan Bedford Forrest's command in northern Mississippi. The first was led by Gen. Samuel D. Sturgis in May and ended with a Confederate victory at Brice's Crossroads on June 10. A second expedition commanded by Gen. Andrew J. Smith began in July and included the Confederate defeat at Tupelo on July 14. The third, also led by A. J. Smith, ended at Oxford when Forrest forced a Federal withdrawal by a bold raid into Memphis.

Confederate commanders faced the first major threat to the interior of the state when General McPherson marched a column consisting of sixty-five hundred infantry and fifteen hundred cavalry from Vicksburg toward Canton on October 14, 1863. McPherson's goal was to divert Gen. Joseph Johnston away from northern

Mississippi, where Sherman was moving troops to the relief of Chattanooga. Johnston's cavalry under Gen. Wirt Adams picked up the Federals as they moved to the northeast, and the Confederates rushed General Loring's infantry division to Canton to stop the Federal advance. McPherson accomplished his goal of occupying Johnston's army, but he did little else. This first movement into Mississippi (after Vicksburg) ended when McPherson decided that he would withdraw his force back to the Mississippi River rather than fight Loring at Canton.

A more serious threat developed in February 1864 when General Sherman sent another force into the state from Vicksburg. His goal was Meridian, where he intended to destroy what he could of the Mobile & Ohio and Southern railroads and the supporting facilities located there. On February 3, 1864, he set two corps, about twenty thousand men, from Vicksburg. This column was to unite at Meridian with a cavalry force of seven thousand men moving from Memphis under Gen. William Sooy Smith. Cavalry brigades under Gen. W. Wirt Adams and Col. Peter B. Starke met Sherman east of the Big Black River, while Gen. Leonidas Polk ordered his infantry to concentrate at Morton, east of Jackson. General Forrest's force remained in the northern part of the state.

In the Meridian Campaign Sherman's force was too large for his opponents to block his relatively easy advance. Gen. Stephen D. Lee's cavalry engaged the Yankees on February 4 at Baker's Creek, but the Federals pushed the three thousand men before them. On the evening of February 8, Sherman reached Jackson, and his force then pushed on to the east. General Polk decided that Sherman was too strong for the Confederate infantry available and ordered Morton abandoned, withdrawing his infantry to Demopolis, Alabama. Lee's cavalry harassed the Federals, but could do little but delay the march.

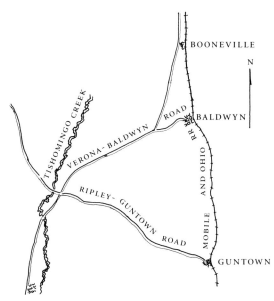

BATTLE OF BRICE'S CROSSROADS

On February 15, the Federal columns reached their objective at Meridian and immediately began to destroy the railroads and the facilities there. In his official report Sherman described his efforts, writing, "For five days 10,000 men worked hard and with a will in that work of destruction, with axes, crowbars, sledges, claw-bards, and with fire, and I have no hesitation in pronouncing the work as well done. Meridian, with its depots, store-houses, arsenal, hospitals, offices, hotels, and cantonments no longer exists."[1]

Sherman's campaign was not a complete success, however. Gen. Sooy Smith's cavalry was late getting out of Memphis, not leaving until February 11. By February 18 they had only reached Okolona on the Mobile & Ohio. On February 20 Smith's column ran into Forrest at West Point. While victorious on that day, Smith decided to retreat, and on the next day he began to move back to Okolona. On February 22, Forrest engaged Smith at Okolona and ensured that Smith would hasten back to his base at Memphis. At Meridian, Sherman's force waited for the cavalry, but hearing nothing from Smith, they completed the devastation of the rail facilities in the vicinity and began to withdraw to Vicksburg on the very day that Smith had first encountered Forrest. The Confederate forces could not prevent Sherman from achieving his principal goal, but General Forrest's forces proved particularly adept at dealing with a force such as Smith's in the northern part of the state.

Following the Meridian Campaign, Confederate forces in Mississippi were depleted further. Polk, two infantry divisions, and a major portion of the cavalry in the state were sent to Georgia to reinforce Gen. Joseph Johnston in his defense of Atlanta. The defense of Mississippi was left to Maj. Gen. Stephen D. Lee, named to command the Department of Alabama, Mississippi, East Louisiana, and West Tennessee; and Lee's princi-

pal force was that of Nathan Bedford Forrest. Lee faced Federal raids early in May, then a major expedition moved against his position on June 1, 1864. Gen. Samuel G. Sturgis advanced with a force of about 8,500 men from Memphis to engage General Forrest's men in northern Mississippi, and by June 7 the Federals were at Ripley. Lee ordered his cavalry to converge at Okolona to engage Sturgis. Forrest, however, decided that he had an opportunity to defeat Sturgis at Brice's Crossroads before Lee and reinforcements would arrive, and he went ahead wih his attack on the Federals on June 10. At mid-morning on that day, Forrest sent his own cavalry against the cavalry heading Sturgis's column at Brice's Crossroads. Forrest's attacks halted the cavalry and then sent Sturgis's cavalry and infantry running. At Tishomingo Creek the Federals began to abandon equipment as they dashed for safety. Sturgis's army reached Ripley before it could regroup. Brice's Crossroads brought an end to another Federal effort in Mississippi.

Federal officers remained concerned about Forrest's position in northern Mississippi and about his ability to strike at the supply lines of Sherman's army in northern Georgia. As a result, they ordered another expedition against the Confederate commander. Gen. A. J. Smith moved with fourteen thousand men from La Grange, Tennessee, on July 5, 1864, aiming for Forrest near Okolona. To keep Confederate forces occupied in central Mississippi, Gen. Henry Slocum led another Federal column eastward from Vicksburg, while another force landed at Rodney. Slocum's men moved to Jackson, then to Grand Gulf, to return by river to Vicksburg. By July 12 Smith's main force was outside of Pontotoc, on the move toward Tupelo. Forrest had waited for Smith at Okolona, but was now forced to pursue the Federals, attacking a Federal force that had dug in at Tupelo on July 14. In the Battle of Tupelo, fought on the fourteenth, Smith's force repulsed

Lee's and Forrest's attacks, but then began to withdraw because of short supplies. Forrest pursued Smith, but was unable to prevent his successful return to Memphis.

Smith returned to Mississippi again in late July upon Sherman's orders. This time Smith's force marched through Holly Springs toward Oxford to destroy the prairie farms of northern Mississippi and draw Forrest into a fight. Forrest, now in command of Confederate forces in Mississippi, hurried troops to Oxford. Forrest blocked Smith briefly at Hurricane Creek, but was unable to keep the Federal force from occupying Oxford on August 22. When Forrest realized that he could not stop Smith, he led two thousand of his cavalry on August 18 on a raid to Memphis, with the purpose of forcing Smith to pull back to protect this critical position. Forrest hit Memphis on August 21, and although unable to hold on to the city, he produced the desired result. Smith pulled back. Federal grand strategy had worked, however. Forrest was unable to operate in Sherman's rear flanks and was pinned down, responding to the repeated Federal expeditions.

In November Sherman abandoned his line of supply for his march to the sea, making Forrest's operations less important. There was little that remained within the state to attract large Federal forces, and Smith's August operation was the last major Federal incursion into the state. This is not to diminish the importance of the many smaller Federal expeditions, particularly by cavalry, that took place throughout this period in efforts to destroy the state's resources, including its farms, railroads, and industrial facilities, and at breaking up efforts to supply Confederate armies in Georgia and Alabama. These movements often involved large numbers of troops, but their goal was not to engage Confederate armies as much as it was to pillage. The raids increased in magnitude after the autumn of 1864. Among the more important were Col. Embury D. Osband's destruction of the Mississippi Central between Vaughan and Goodman that began on November 23, 1864. Gen. John W. Davidson led some four thousand cavalry from Baton Rouge, Louisiana, on November 27 in an attempt to break up the Mobile & Ohio. Davidson was stopped at Leakesville on December 20. On December 21, Gen. Benjamin H. Grierson commanded thirty-five hundred soldiers in a particularly devastating raid. Grierson's cavalry moved from Memphis to Ripley, tearing up the Mobile & Ohio Railroad south of Ripley, then headed toward Houston before crossing the Mississippi Central, which was destroyed between Grenada and Durant. Grierson's troops entered Vicksburg on January 4, 1865, completing a raid that had destroyed miles of railroad and also one of the state's largest textile mills at Bankston.

Federal raiders achieved success in part because Confederate Mississippi was left practically unprotected after 1864. The Confederacy continued to pull out troops to protect more critical positions such as the port of Mobile and the Confederate factories in Alabama. Others were moved to the east in an effort to block Sherman, who began what would be a decisive drive from Savannah northward into the Carolinas.

Sherman's advance, combined with Grant's

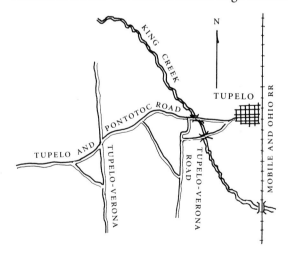

BATTLE OF TUPELO

fight in Virginia, brought the war to a close in battles fought far from Mississippi. The surrender of the armies of Robert E. Lee and Joseph Johnston meant that there was little that the Western armies could do to prevent the inevitable. On May 4, 1865, Gen. Richard Taylor officially ended the war in Mississippi when as commander of the Confederate forces in Alabama, Mississippi, and eastern Louisiana he surrendered to Gen. Edward R. S. Canby at Citronelle, Alabama. Soldiers of Mississippi had given their all, but there was nothing more to do. Nathan Bedford Forrest sounded the finality of the surrender in his farewell message to his troops. Forrest wrote:

I have never on the field of battle sent you where I was unwilling to go myself, nor would I now advise you to a course which I felt myself unwilling to pursue. You have been good soldiers, you can be good citizens. Obey the laws, preserve your honor, and the Government to which you have surrendered can afford to be and will be magnanimous.[2]

WILLIAM T. SHERMAN
paper print

Maj. Gen. William Tecumseh Sherman, promoted to that rank as a result of his role in the Vicksburg Campaign, succeeded Gen. Ulysses S. Grant to the command of the Army of the Tennessee in October 1863, as Grant was placed in command of the Army of the Mississippi. Sherman and the Army of the Tennessee would be the major factors determining military events in Mississippi after the surrender of Vicksburg. Beginning with Maj. Gen. James B. McPherson's expedition toward Canton in October 1863, the Federals acted aggressively in the local theater to ensure the success of their overall strategy. Confederate commanders were forced to respond or risk disaster. In the West the Confederates had lost the freedom to maneuver, except for the occasional bold raid at which Gen. Nathan Bedford Forrest excelled. Responding to moves by Sherman himself or by expeditions sent out in support of Sherman, Confederates met challenge after challenge from the invading Yankees. *Photo courtesy of U.S.A.M.H.I., MOLLUS, Mass., Collection*

JAMES B. McPHERSON
carte de visite

The commander of the first major expedition into the interior of Mississippi after the events of the summer of 1863 was Maj. Gen. James B. McPherson. With a force of eight thousand men, he advanced from Vicksburg on October 14. His column ran into the cavalry command of Brig. Gen. Wirt Adams at Brownsville on October 15, and pursued it to Bogue Chitto Creek several miles east of Brownsville. Adams withdrew to a strong position east of the creek. McPherson sent his cavalry under Col. Edward F. Winslow toward Canton to get behind Adams, but Winslow encountered another Confederate cavalry brigade where the Brownsville-Canton Road crossed Bogue Chitto. Confederate Brig. Gen. William H. Jackson described the two encounters as "a handsome fight."[3] As a result, McPherson proceeded with caution. On the afternoon of October 16, he sent two brigades of infantry to support Winslow in preparation for battle. That evening the Confederates concentrated their force on the brow of a hill overlooking the creek. *Photo courtesy of the Library of Congress, LC B8172-6415*

JOHN S. HADLEY
carte de visite

Pvt. John S. Hadley of Co. G, 45th Illinois Infantry, was part of the brigade of Brig. Gen. Manning F. Force that came up on the Confederates at Bogue Chitto Creek on October 16. Hadley and his unit arrived late in the day, but were thrown across the creek and deployed to advance. Sunset delayed the Federal advance. Early the next morning, the Yankee infantry on the eastern side of the creek was joined by another brigade, and McPherson's cavalry was sent to the left in an effort to flank the Confederate position. The Federal soldiers waited while Confederate artillery fired at them and their own men were placed in position. At 7 A.M. Hadley and a line of blue advanced against the Confederates. They faced no return fire, however, since the Confederates quickly withdrew to the north and northeast. McPherson sent his cavalry and one brigade of infantry in pursuit. *Photo courtesy of U.S.A.M.H.I., Randy Beck Collection*

WILLIAM H. JACKSON
carte de visite

The force McPherson had run into consisted of three brigades. The division commander was Brig. Gen. William H. Jackson. Jackson realized that he faced an overwhelming force and moved to delay McPherson's forward movement rather than engage the Yankees. At the same time, Jackson called for infantry support to be concentrated at Canton. Maj. Gen. William W. Loring rushed two brigades of his division, composed of troops from Alabama, Arkansas, Louisiana, Kentucky, and Mississippi to Canton. The brigade of Gen. John Adams arrived at Canton on October 17, just as Jackson's force fell back from his position along Bogue Chitto Creek. Jackson's delaying tactics worked for the Confederates. After destroying mills and a wagon repair shop along the Canton road, McPherson's troops began to pull back. Believing that he now faced a force larger than his own, McPherson ordered his men back to the Big Black River in order to protect Vicksburg from any possible Confederate attack. *Photo courtesy of U.S.A.M.H.I., MOLLUS, Mass., Collection*

PETER B. STARKE
carte de visite

On February 3, 1864, the Federals staged a larger expedition into Mississippi under the command of General Sherman himself. The force consisted of Stephen J. Hurlbut's XVI Corps and McPherson's XVII Corps. Some twenty thousand men marched out of Vicksburg toward the railroad junction of Meridian in eastern Mississippi, while from Memphis seven thousand cavalry moved out for the same goal under the command of Brig. Gen. William Sooy Smith. Confederate Gen. Leonidas Polk faced a force much larger than his own. While his infantry concentrated at Morton, Polk's cavalry attempted to slow down Sherman's advance. Directly in the path of the Federals were Brig. Gen. Wirt Adams' brigade at Raymond and Col. Peter B. Starke's brigade at Brownsville. Colonel Starke, a prominent antebellum politician from Bolivar County, faced the XVI Corps as it moved along the Queen's Hill Church road to Clinton road. On the morning of February 4 he deployed the 1st, 28th, and Ballantine's Mississippi cavalry regiments, along with supporting artillery to try to halt the Yankee tide. Fighting all day on the fourth and fifth, the cavalry was forced back. Jackson was abandoned, and, with the cavalry protecting their retreat, Confederate forces at the capital retreated toward Canton. East of Jackson, Starke found that "the roads and streets were much obstructed by large numbers of stragglers and hangers-on of the army in their flight."[4] The infantry gathering at Morton would attempt to halt the Federal raid. *Photo courtesy of the Library of Congress, LC US762-12085*

While the Confederate cavalry tried to delay the advance of Sherman's heavy columns, Polk's infantry began to arrive at Morton. Sylvester Fayard, a thirty-four-year-old private from Harrison County, was in Co. E of the 20th Mississippi Infantry as it dug in outside of Morton. Brig. Gen. William Loring was in command of the growing force there. His men established their defensive position along a line of hills two miles to the west of town. Rifle pits were dug, and infantry was moved into a defensive line about a mile long to await the Yankees. *Photo courtesy of Thomas Wixon*

JOHN B. LOVE
copy print from F. M. Glass,
Long Creek Rifles, a Brief History

Capt. John B. Love, Co. A, 15th Mississippi Infantry, was also with Loring's troops as they prepared their defense at Morton. The Confederate command, however, was in some confusion about the size of Sherman's force and his objectives. After pulling troops from Mobile to Morton, Polk became convinced that Sherman was headed to Mobile. Informed by Loring that he did not have enough men to stop the Yankee advance at Morton, Polk ordered the troops from Mobile back to that city, and he ordered Loring and French's divisions to retreat toward Livingston and Demopolis, Alabama. Love and the other infantry began to withdraw during the evening of February 7, as their rearguard lit fires to convince the Federals that Loring's force was present and waiting a morning fight. The retreat undercut the morale of many Mississippians who saw the decision as one to abandon their state to the invaders. One Mississippi soldier among those sent back to Mobile wrote, "*Now* the whole State was to be abandoned without a single blow. No wonder the hearts of her sons burned within them; and no wonder if they learned to distrust the policy that gave their homes to the torch and their families to the tender mercies of the foe. . . . We started on our return but so many had left the regiment that some companies were slimly represented. . . . I doubt if I ever see one of them again but these men are neither traitors nor deserters."[5]

MARION ROBINSON
carte de visite

After the Confederate army withdrew from Morton, the Federal columns were able to march to Meridian with little opposition other than cavalry harassment of their flanks. Pvt. Marion Robinson of Co. D, 20th Illinois Infantry, was one of the twenty thousand infantrymen who marched along with Sherman's army. The 20th was one of some fifty-seven Union regiments. Such a large force devastated the path of its march. Another soldier with the XVII Corps, Lucius W. Barber of the 15th Illinois Infantry, described the road to Meridian and back: "Large [foraging] parties were sent out daily . . . Sherman's army left fire and famine in its track. The country was one lurid blaze of fire; burning cotton gins and deserted dwellings were seen on every hand. I regret to say it, but oft-times habitations were burned down over the heads of occupants, but not by orders. . . . I have seen the cabin of the poor entered and the last mouthful taken from almost starving children. . . . The wretches who caused this suffering were brought to punishment as often as caught, but the most vigorous measures could not always stop it."[6] *Photo courtesy of U.S.A.M.H.I., Richard Tibbals Collection*

309

ABNER STEEDE
copy of unknown original

As Sherman's men moved leisurely toward Meridian, only the Confederate cavalry resisted. They had tried to block the Yankees west of Jackson, and then to raid their columns as they moved east. Maj. Abner C. Steede led one group who snipped at the Federal flanks and also reported their movements. On February 13, Steede reported that the Yankees had left Decatur and definitely were moving on Meridian. Steede and other units tried to delay Sherman's movement by obstructing the route of march so that Gen. Stephen D. Lee's main cavalry force could get between the Yankees and Meridian. Lee's units could not achieve this goal, however, and on the evening of the thirteenth Lee was ordered to use the forces that he could get to Meridian to cover the evacuation of the town. *Photo courtesy of Thomas Wixon*

RICHARD McGUIRE
copy of unknown original

General Starke's brigade was the only part of Lee's force that was able to reach Meridian. On February 14 Starke's regiments waited for Sherman's men in a line across the main road into town. Sgt. T. Richard McGuire, the son of a wealthy planter from Bolivar County, was with Co. H (Bolivar Troop) of the 1st Mississippi Cavalry that day, deployed across the road. Col. Edward F. Winslow's Federal cavalry found the Confederates early that morning, and Winslow ordered the 5th Illinois Cavalry to charge the position of the 1st Mississippi. The Confederate line broke, and the troopers moved to the rear behind the 20th Mississippi. At the same time Winslow's men moved against the Confederate right with the same result. Starke saw the outcome as inevitable and ordered his men to retreat. The fight outside of Meridian could not stop Sherman, but it did give Polk's infantry and artillery additional time to escape. *Photo courtesy of Herb Peck*

Edward H. Wolfe
carte de visite

Col. Edward H. Wolfe, as commander of the Third Brigade in Gen. A. J. Smith's Third Division, XVI Corps, was part of the army that moved into Meridian on February 14 and 15. The Third Division was assigned the task of destroying the Alabama & Mississippi Railroad out of Meridian; the troops tore up some six miles of track. Another soldier on the expedition, Lucius Barber, described the work of the army during the next three days: "Each division was assigned a certain portion of track to destroy, which they effectually did by tearing up the ties, piling them on the rails and then setting them on fire. After the rails were red hot, they would twist them around the trees, utterly unfitting them for further use. In this raid our army destroyed four hundred miles of railroad and burned over twenty engines and a large number of cars."[7] In addition, the Yankees destroyed the town of Meridian. On February 20, with no word from Gen. Sooy Smith's cavalry, which was supposed to have joined Sherman at Meridian, the Federals began to march back to Vicksburg. *Photo courtesy of U.S.A.M.H.I., MOLLUS, Mass., Collection*

W. SOOY SMITH
carte de visite

Smith's cavalry column had not reached Meridian because it was in trouble. Smith, a West Pointer from Ohio who had shown considerable promise as a commander, had been slow to start from Memphis, and the progress of his column had also been slower than planned. His column did not reach the Mobile & Ohio at Okolona until February 18. The Yankees then spent two more days moving down the railroad tracks toward West Point, destroying the rail line and much of the other property in the neighborhood. By February 19, however, Smith was becoming increasingly concerned with the presence of Nathan Bedford Forrest's cavalry, which he feared outnumbered his own command. Forrest was present and laying a trap for Smith below West Point. Confederate cavalry was being hastened from Meridian under Gen. Stephen D. Lee to try to make the battle with Smith decisive. *Photo courtesy of the Library of Congress, LC US812-9093*

314

Nathan Bedford Forrest
carte de visite

Forrest's command was much smaller than Smith's. When Lee arrived, however, the Confederate force would have numerical superiority. Forrest's plan was to draw Smith into a pocket bounded by Sakatonchee and Oktibbeha creeks and the Tombigbee River, cut off his escape route, and then destroy his force. Smith became wary, however, and on February 21 began to withdraw. In action typical of his leadership, Forrest threw his smaller force at the rear of the Yankee column, driving them rapidly through West Point, Okolona, and then on back to Collierville. With Forrest at their rear, the Federals marched in five days the same distance that had taken them ten days to cover as they advanced toward Meridian. *Photo courtesy of U.S.A.M.H.I., MOLLUS, Mass., Collection*

WILLIAM M. PRINCE
copy print of unknown original

Forrest's movement against Smith had been carried out by raw recruits and state troops who had seen little battle before. William M. Prince of the 1st Partisan Rangers was typical of the men Forrest had at hand. Prince, a thirty-two-year-old farmer from Prentiss County, was part of a regiment that had shown notoriously bad discipline. In January 1864, a large number had deserted rather than submit to a new commander following the loss of Lt. Col. Lawson B. Hovis to disabling wounds. With Forrest at Sakatonchee Creek, however, Prince, his unit, and the other troops were inspired with new purpose and discipline by their general. As the Confederate troops chased Smith, one of the many untried troopers fled from the line of battle only to run into Forrest. Forrest thrashed him with a stick and then pushed him back into battle shouting, "Now, God Damn you, go back to the front and fight! . . . You might as well be killed there as here, for if you ever run away again you'll not get off so easy."[8] With such troopers, Forrest sent Smith reeling backward. *Photo courtesy of Edwin H. Davis*

Lee's cavalry, no longer needed by Forrest, received orders to return to central Mississippi to harass Sherman's columns as he marched back to Vicksburg. Lt. Addison Harvey of Madison County led his small contingent of cavalry known as Harvey's Scouts in such attacks. In his official report Harvey noted that his 23 men had carried out their mission by "attacking his [Sherman's] foraging parties and pickets, and firing into the main column whenever a favorable opportunity was offered."[9] His unit lost three men killed, two wounded, and one captured. In turn, he claimed to have killed and captured one officer, 109 men, forty-seven horses and mules, and two wagons. *Photo courtesy of the Old Court House Museum, Vicksburg*

Pvt. F. M. Lassiter, a resident of Vicksburg, was another of the troopers set upon Sherman's columns as the 28th Mississippi Cavalry joined in the pursuit. As part of Starke's brigade, the 28th had marched nearly eighty miles from the vicinity of Meridian to Starkville to meet Smith's column, only to be ordered back south some ninety miles to Canton. Arriving in the vicinity of Canton on February 27, the 28th and the other units of Starke's brigade engaged the enemy for four days before the Federals withdrew across the Big Black. With too few men and with men and horses tired from the campaign, the Confederates could do little but hasten Sherman's men on. *Photo courtesy of the Old Court House Museum, Vicksburg*

William L. Nugent
copy print of unknown original

William Lewis Nugent, a prominent planter, attorney, and politician from Washington County, was another member of Starke's cavalry, serving as an officer in the 18th Mississippi Cavalry. In a letter to his wife, written from a station on the rail line north of Jackson on March 8, he captured something of the conditions experienced by these troopers in the fighting between February 3 and March 2. He wrote: "We have had a hard time of it. Our wagons were sent back to Demopolis, Alabama, and I haven't had a change of clothing for more than a month. I have my underclothes washed at night & have managed to get along very well considering. I am almost without a shirt; bought a homespun shirt the other day for twelve dollars, and rely upon it a lot together. I have to get another soon, but if I cannot succeed it makes very little difference. I think we will whip the Yankees this year anyhow and I can afford to transport a scanty wardrobe until then."[10] Mississippians would not see the end of the war soon, however, and the state would experience continued raids by Federals in the subsequent months. *Photo courtesy of M.D.A.H.*

SAMUEL G. STURGIS
carte de visite

Following the Meridian Expedition, the next major sortie against Confederate troops in Mississippi began with the advance of Brig. Gen. Samuel G. Sturgis into the state from Memphis on June 1, 1864. Its purpose, according to Maj. Gen. Cadwallader C. Washburn, was prompted by reports that Forrest was at Tupelo preparing for an expedition. "It was regarded," wrote Washburn, "as of the first importance to engage him, and if possible to whip and disperse his forces, as also to destroy the Mobile and Ohio Railroad."[11] To "whip" Forrest, Sturgis was sent out with a force of thirty-three hundred cavalry, five thousand infantry, and sixteen pieces of artillery. From the beginning Sturgis's progress was slow because of heavy rains. Nine days after it moved out it had reached Ripley, about seventy miles away from their starting point. The slow movement of the Federal column allowed Confederate forces in Mississippi to move toward Ripley to resist the Yankee advance. *Photo courtesy of U.S.A.M.H.I., MOLLUS, Mass., Collection*

STEPHEN D. LEE
albumen print

Command of Confederate forces in Mississippi had been assigned to Maj. Gen. Stephen D. Lee following Joseph Johnston's departure for Georgia in the spring of 1864. Lee had only about sixteen thousand men in the entire state, primarily Forrest in northern Mississippi, Wirt Adams' brigade near Jackson, a contingent of cavalry in northern Alabama, and Samuel Gholson's brigade of state cavalry. Forrest had left Tupelo on June 1 for a raid into Tennessee, but with the appearance of Sturgis, Lee recalled him and ordered the rest of his cavalry to converge at Okolona. As in the previous February, Forrest struck before all of the Confederate forces were arrayed. A change in the direction of the Federal column brought Sturgis and Forrest face to face to the south of Tishomingo Creek at Brice's Crossroads, where the Baldwin-Pontotoc and Ripley-Guntown roads crossed. *Photo courtesy of L.L.M.V.C., L.S.U., Civil War Album*

321

BIRD C. CARRADINE
copy print of unknown original

Sgt. Bird C. Carradine of a Clay County farming family was with his unit, Co. C, 8th Mississippi Cavalry, on the morning of June 10 when Forrest's advance units ran into Gen. Benjamin Grierson's cavalry on the Baldwin-Pontotoc road a mile to the east of Brice's Crossroads. Forrest moved up his force and threw Carradine's unit to the south of the Baldwin-Pontotoc road, roughly the center of the Confederate line. The Confederate line advanced slowly, and Grierson was forced back toward the crossroads in hard fighting. Along with some forty-eight other men, Carradine fell, wounded severely in the arm, as the 8th moved against the Federal line. By 1:30 P.M. Grierson's cavalry was almost out of ammunition and on the verge of defeat. At that point Sturgis's infantry began to arrive on the field after an exhausting march from the rear, allowing the Federals to resist the Rebel advance and allowing Grierson to retire to replenish his ammunition. *Photo courtesy of Joyce Aycock*

Capt. Elliott N. Bush of Co. G, 95th Illinois Infantry, was part of Sturgis's Second Brigade, the first infantry unit to arrive on the field to relieve Grierson. The brigade deployed across the Baldwin-Pontotoc road, on the Federal left, and was immediately engaged in battle. As the afternoon progressed, Confederate pressure continued all along the line. By 5 P.M., however, both the Federal right and left began to give way, and Forrest threatened to cut off any possibility of retreat by driving on the bridge across Tishomingo Creek. Sturgis later reported that the Federal force "now drifted toward the rear, and was soon altogether beyond control."[12] Sturgis shored up his line, only to have it disintegrate again. Sturgis ordered a retreat, which quickly turned into a rout that fell back to Ripley before any resistance could be reorganized. Captain Bush was one of the 441 casualties suffered by the Second Brigade that day, killed by a gunshot while resisting the Confederate attack. *Photo courtesy of U.S.A.M.H.I., Richard Tibbals Collection*

FELEN FELIX ADEN
albumen print

Capt. Felen Felix Aden was with Co. G, 7th Tennessee Cavalry, at Brice's Crossroads. The 7th Tennessee had been engaged from the earliest moment of the battle on June 10. Forrest regrouped his force following Sturgis's withdrawal from the field, then threw his cavalry after the fleeing Yankees at 1 A.M. on June 11. At Ripley, Sturgis tried to stand, but an assault by the 7th Tennessee and Forrest's own escort company renewed the rout. Sturgis's troops did not stop their flight until they reached the Memphis and Charleston Railroad. Captain Aden was unable to continue the pursuit after being wounded in the battle on the eleventh. The battle was a complete victory for Forrest. The general reported seizing 250 wagons and ambulances, eighteen pieces of artillery, five thousand stands of small arms, and five hundred thousand rounds of ammunition. Forrest remained a formidable force in northern Mississippi. *Photo courtesy of U.S.A.M.H.I., Rose Haley Collection*

ANDREW J. SMITH
carte de visite

On July 5, 1864, Maj. Gen. Andrew J. Smith left the Federal Sixteenth Army Corps from La Grange, Tennessee; he had been ordered by General Sherman to "go out and follow Forrest to the death if it cost 10,000 lives and breaks the treasury. There will never be peace in Tennessee till Forrest is dead."[13] Once again a Union army was marching into Mississippi to engage Forrest's Confederates. Smith's force consisted of some fourteen thousand infantry, cavalry, and artillery and moved in two parallel columns toward Ripley. By July 12 Smith was beyond Pontotoc and headed toward Okolona. The next day he surprised Confederate forces rushing to stop him by shifting his line of march to Tupelo, setting the stage for the most important battle of the campaign on July 14 and 15. *Photo courtesy of U.S.A.M.H.I., MOLLUS, Mass., Collection*

JOE WALKER
sixth-plate ambrotype

General Forrest arrived on the scene that evening, deployed his troops in line of battle, and ordered a dismounted assault along Smith's entire front for the next morning. Although outnumbered two to one, the Confederate commanders felt that they had to do battle or risk giving up the entire region, an important corn-producing area. Most of the Mississippians present were part of Col. Hinche P. Mabry's brigade on the Confederate left. The attack went badly, however, with the Confederate right moving forward before the left. It was cut up and began to withdraw before the left moved. Twenty-year-old Joe Walker had joined the 3rd Mississippi State Cavalry in April 1863, and his unit had become part of the 38th Mounted Infantry prior to the battle. The clerk from Holly Springs advanced in an attack described by Brig. Gen. A. Buford: "Arriving at the open space and having to cross a cornfield, they slowly advanced, but so deadly was the concentrated fire that, after penetrating some fifty steps, they retired to the cover of the timber, where they kept up a heavy and continual fire upon the enemy for three hours."[14] Eighteen men and officers were killed and fifty-two were wounded in the deadly encounter, but Private Walker escaped. *Photo courtesy of the Marshall County Museum*

ROBERT C. MCCAY
carte de visite

Maj. Robert C. McCay was also with the 38th Mississippi as it advanced on July 14. Col. Hinche P. Mabry reported, "the heat was so intense and the distance so great that some men and officers fell exhausted and fainting along my line, while the fire from the enemy's line of works by both artillery and small-arms was so heavy and well directed that many were killed and wounded. . . . At about sixty yards from the enemy's works, seeing that my line was too much weakened to drive the enemy, I halted and directed the men to protect themselves."[15] Major McCay was one of three officers in the unit who were killed in the frontal assault. *Photo courtesy of the Mississippi State Museum*

WILLIAM H. BLANCHARD
carte de visite

Receiving the attack of the Confederate line on the morning of the fourteenth was the right of the Union army, and a part of the command at that point was the 12th Iowa Infantry. Lying behind a heavy rail fence, Pvt. William H. Blanchard and the other members of the regiment fired at the advancing Confederates for nearly two hours until their ammunition was exhausted. Retiring for forty-five minutes, the unit then returned to the firing line for the rest of the battle. During the engagement the regiment used almost one hundred rounds of ammunition per man. Of the 295 men with the regiment, 7 were killed and 39 were wounded. Private Blanchard was struck in the leg by a shell and the leg was subsequently amputated. *Photo courtesy of Roger Davis*

When A. J. Smith's lines did not break under a frontal assault, Forrest began to probe the Federal flanks. Confederates faced men such as Sgt. George A. Jackson of the 3rd Iowa Cavalry. Part of Brig. Gen. Benjamin Grierson's cavalry command, the men had been picketed to uncover just such a move by Forrest, and that evening they successfully foiled the Confederate maneuver. Smith had already decided to return to Tennessee, however, and during the evening of July 15 he began to withdraw his command from position. Jackson's unit and the rest of Grierson's cavalry stymied Forrest's efforts to hasten Smith's departure. The withdrawal brought an end to the engagement at Tupelo, the last major battle that would be fought on the soil of Mississippi.
Photo courtesy of Roger Davis

WILLIAM WIRT ADAMS
carte de visite

A. J. Smith's withdrawal from Mississippi did not end the agony of the state. Mississipians would not see any more major battles, but the skirmishes and clashes that took place would be violent nonetheless. Smith returned again in August 1864, but with-drew after reaching Oxford. Cavalry raids struck from Vicksburg and Baton Rouge in November and from Memphis in December. Confederate forces were incapable of resisting these raids after Forrest withdrew into Alabama. Only the cavalry command of Gen. Wirt Adams and a few state troops were left. A Mississippi attorney, Adams had commanded a cavalry regiment at the beginning of the war and was promoted to brigadier general following his service at Vicksburg. By the autumn of 1864 his forces were spread thin across the state. One of his brigades turned back Embury D. Osband's raid from Vicksburg. In December, they faced thirty-five hundred cavalry led by General Grierson. *Photo courtesy of the Library of Congress, LC B812-3240*

BENJAMIN GRIERSON
carte de visite

The Federal cavalryman Benjamin Grierson may have been the one Yankee most closely connected to Mississippi during the war. In the spring of 1863 he had led a successful cavalry raid from La Grange, Tennessee, to Baton Rouge, Louisiana, which was designed to divert Confederate attention from preparations along the Mississippi River to attack Vicksburg. His men had been involved in actions throughout northern Mississippi after that. In December 1864, he was moving again. The Yankees destroyed the Mobile & Ohio Railroad from Booneville to Egypt, then marched to the Mississippi Central at Grenada and destroyed it from Grenada to Durant. On the way they burned everything. Grierson, moving from Durant toward Vicksburg, ran into Adams' command at Franklin. Adams' force was crushed. The battle at Franklin showed that the Confederacy had little left to prevent victory after victory by the Yankees. While the war continued until the following April, for all purposes it was over in Mississippi by the new year. *Photo courtesy of U.S.A.M.H.I., MOLLUS, Mass., Collection*

Chapter 10

After the War

In the spring of 1865, the military struggle to resolve the issues raised in 1861 came to an end. Growing out of the Northern victory, however, were new issues that meant the conflict of 1861–1865 would continue on other fields for much of the rest of the century. The loss and destruction caused by the war presented Mississippi and the rest of the South with a massive problem of social and economic restoration. Political Reconstruction raised questions concerning who would ultimately govern the state. The outcome of the war posed the question of where exactly those who supported the Confederacy and the very history of that lost cause fit within the postwar nation. The ultimate end of the Civil War conflict would require a resolution of those questions. By the end of the nineteenth century most were resolved, although the role of former slaves would await a future solution.

The human and material loss caused by the Civil War represented the most immediate problem felt by the vast majority of Mississippians.

Thousands of lives had been lost. One estimate concluded that approximately one-fourth of the white males aged fifteen and above in 1860 had died in the service, some twenty-seven thousand men. The loss among the civilian population was immeasurable. Those who survived, both soldiers and civilians, often suffered from the effects of wounds and disease for the rest of their lives. The material impact on individuals was also large. Homes, businesses, and farms had been destroyed by invading armies. Even property that escaped the torches of soldiers was often neglected during the war years. In addition, the wealth invested in slaves was liquidated completely with the war's end. The overall economic loss suffered during the war years was reflected in the 1870 census figures, which showed that Mississippi farms had 17 percent fewer acres of improved farmland than they had in 1860. The cotton crop shrank by 53 percent.[1]

In the decades following the war new immigrants would arrive in the state to supplement the natural increase of population, and the towns and fields would be rebuilt as well. By the end of the century much of the material loss caused by the war had been restored. An agricultural depression that began in the 1870s and continued into the next century, however, meant that more people, more farms, and more crops did not bring about renewed prosperity.

While Mississippians worked to rebuild their state, another issue that had to be resolved was the change in political leadership. President Andrew Johnson's proclamation for the reorganization of Mississippi provided for a general amnesty and pardon for most of the state's citizens if they took an oath of loyalty to the Union, but this excluded most Confederate officials and property owners with wealth in excess of twenty thousand dollars. Participation in postwar politics for many of the prewar elite was limited, although the program did allow these persons to apply for individual pardons from the president.

The first attempt to establish a postwar order came in May 1865 when President Johnson appointed William L. Sharkey provisional governor. Sharkey, a planter and prewar Whig, had opposed secession and stayed out of public affairs once Mississippi left the Union. Sharkey called for a convention of delegates to repudiate secession and accept the results of the war—particularly the abolition of slavery. In the July election, prewar Whigs won the majority of seats in the convention, portending a shift in political power. These delegates were men who had supported the Union in 1861 or who had been lukewarm secessionists. They provoked congressional outrage against white Southerners' responses to the war's end. The convention's members engaged in an unseemly debate over whether or not the state had any obligation to make concessions to the president or the North and adjourned after conceding that since the war had destroyed slavery that institution no longer existed.

In the subsequent state elections the Whigs again won control of the state government, but their actions aided further the forces ready to bring an end to President Johnson's plan of Reconstruction. Many of the elected officials, even though they had been Unionists during the secession crisis, had played active roles in the Confederate government and military. Benjamin G. Humphreys, the successful candidate for governor, was typical. Although he had been a prewar Whig, Humphreys had served as a brigadier general in the Confederate army. The new legislature caused serious complaints in the North when it passed the South's first Black Code, a vagrant law, an apprentice law, and other legislation that seriously limited the freedom of Mississippi blacks.

Mississippi's Whig government hastened the imposition of a more rigorous and potentially more revolutionary congressional program in 1867. Convinced that the South was trying to thwart the results of the war, Congress divided the region into military districts. Mississippi, with Arkansas, became part of a district commanded by Gen. E. O. C. Ord. The military supervised a new registration of voters that for the first time included blacks. The new electorate then chose delegates to a constitutional convention charged with writing a new constitution that would accept the results of the war. This convention met from January 8 to May 18, 1868, and produced a constitution that could have permanently changed the basis for political power in the state. The new constitution enfranchised all adult black males and disfranchised some twenty-five hundred individuals who had sworn oaths of allegiance to the United States as public officials before the war and then supported the Confederacy. It also excluded from political office all who had voluntarily supported secession and the Confederate cause.

In the election held in June 1868, opponents

managed to defeat the new constitution, leaving the state in the hands of a military commander. After considerable maneuvering, the constitution was resubmitted to the electorate in December 1869, minus the disfranchisement clauses, and supported by a unified Republican party, headed by the prewar Whig leader James L. Alcorn. This time it was adopted easily, paving the way for the inauguration in January 1870 of a government that promised a new order for the state.

The new state government was quickly readmitted to the Union. The state legislature rapidly demonstrated what the new political leadership of the state promised. It ratified the Fourteenth and Fifteenth amendments. When it selected United States Senators, it chose General Adelbert Ames, who had been military commander in the state, and, more significant, Hiram R. Revels, a black minister from Natchez. In its legislative program, the new Republican leadership promised policies that would work to the benefit of all Mississippians, white and black, rich and poor. In the next years they tried to promote economic diversification, development of transportation facilities, and creation of a system of public schools. However, the promised new day never arrived. Persistent economic problems connected with agriculture ensured that Republican policies produced few real changes.

Ultimately, the failure to change economic and social conditions in the state, factional splits among the Republicans, and the persistent opposition of antebellum conservative leaders brought an end to the Republican regime. Conservatives emphasized the issues of taxation and race in their attacks upon the Republican government. They did not hesitate to use violence to manipulate white voters and intimidate blacks. Using the "Mississippi Plan," in 1875 the Democrats regained control of the state legislature, and in 1876 they "redeemed" the state. Their renewed control was marked by the election of L. Q. C.

Lamar to Congress in January 1876, and in March by the impeachment of the Republican governor, who resigned his office, and the impeachment and conviction of the Republican lieutenant governor, allowing John M. Stone, the Democratic president pro tempore of the Senate, to take over the executive office.

Redemption marked the political triumph of Mississippi's antebellum political leaders. In part, it reflected the reassertion of control over Mississippi by those people who had led the state to secession in 1861, and it justified their course during the war. Their triumph made possible the subsequent integration of former Confederates and the Confederate experience into the mainstream of postwar white life. Much of this reconciliation would take place through the development of Confederate veterans' and memorial associations. Among the earliest of such associations in Mississippi was the Baldwyn Confederate Memorial Association organized in 1866 at Baldwyn. Its original purpose was to decorate the graves of Confederate soldiers and to construct a monument to their memory. This group later became the Northeast Mississippi Confederate Veterans Association. After 1889 this and many other such groups would join the larger United Confederate Veterans organization.[2]

The veterans' organizations worked hard not only to commemorate their fallen comrades, but also to justify their actions, the Confederacy, and the war itself. They produced their own history, emphasizing ideological motives as the basis of the war and deemphasizing the role of slavery in the conflict. The constitution of the United Confederate Veterans (UCV) indicated the importance of this goal, posing as one of its major objects the gathering of "authentic data for an impartial history of the war between the States." In Mississippi this activity was marked by the appearance of works such as John Rietti's *Military Annals of Mississippi*. The *Publications* of the

Mississippi Historical Society, reorganized in the 1890s and directed by Prof. Franklin L. Riley of the University of Mississippi, became a major conduit for the presentation of the views and defenses of ex-Confederates such as Gen. Stephen D. Lee.[3]

Southern apologists created pressure for the acceptance of their story as the truth about the war, and they worked for the dismissal of Yankee-inspired history. As late as 1920 the UCV in Mississippi lobbied the state textbook commission to adopt "correct" textbooks in the public schools and were successful in obtaining the adoption of "histories from which the young will be taught the truths of Confederate history . . . books fair to the south."[4]

As the veterans themselves lessened in numbers, their ranks were filled by members of the United Daughters of the Confederacy—the Mississippi division created in 1898 for the purpose of collecting and preserving material for a "truthful" history of the Confederate states, honoring the memory of those who served and died in service of the Confederacy, recording the part taken by Southern women, cherishing friendships among members of the society, and fulfilling duties of charity to the war's survivors. With the UCV they helped create archives and museums for Confederate relics, memorials throughout the state, and the preservation of burial sites at major battlefields. Their work would be furthered by later chapters of the Children, Daughters, and Sons of the Confederacy.[5]

In many ways the success of the former Confederates in influencing the writing of the war's history helped bring about the ultimate end of the conflict. At the same time that blacks who had been freed by the war found themselves segregated and disfranchised, the ex-Confederates were able to make their own role in the war a part of the mainstream of American history. They legitimized their rebellion and regained their place in the American experience. That represented the final reintegration of Mississippi and the rest of the South into the nation.

Elected governor under the constitution of 1869, James L. Alcorn was one of the few leaders of the old order who attempted to play a role in reconstructing Mississippi on a different basis. A Unionist in 1861, he had supported the Confederate cause during the war. Now, in 1870, he pledged that his new government would concede full citizenship to blacks, and he also promised a new policy for poor whites. Alcorn went on to the United States Senate in 1871, but he and his Republican successors worked to bring about economic change, education, and protection of the rights of blacks to the state during the next four years. *Photo courtesy of Mrs. Barry Vaught*

JAMES L. ALCORN
copy print of unknown original

338

HIRAM R. REVELS
copy print from glass plate

An indication of the new era promised by
the Republicans of 1870 was the election of
Hiram R. Revels to the United States Senate.
Revels had been born a free black in North
Carolina and had moved to the North,
where he was educated at a seminary in
Ohio and at Knox College in Illinois. An
ordained minister of the African Methodist
Episcopal Church, he recruited blacks for
the Union army at St. Louis during the
war and joined the army as a chaplain of
a Mississippi regiment. He remained in
Natchez after the war and was active in
Republican politics. In 1870 he was elected
by the state senate to fill the seat of Jefferson
Davis. Clearly, power appeared to have
shifted within Mississippi. *Photo courtesy of
the Library of Congress, no. LC BH 8301-1823*

The new political day in Mississippi was not to last long. The old leadership began to reassert itself by 1872. L. Q. C. Lamar represented that return to power. A professor from the University of Mississippi, Lamar had served in the United States Congress before the war, the state Secession Convention, the 8th Mississippi Infantry, and the Confederate government. In 1872 he was elected once again to the United States House of Representatives. In 1876 he was elected by the state legislature to the United States Senate, where he became one of the South's national leaders, working for sectional reconciliation and at the same time promoting the economic development of the region. *Photo courtesy of the Library of Congress, no. LC BH 826-28955*

L. Q. C. LAMAR
copy print from unknown original

ALEXANDER TRAVIS HARVEY
cabinet card

The return of conservative rule in Mississippi was not a peaceful one. At the local level the struggle for "redemption" continued into the 1880s. Alexander T. Harvey had been a color bearer for Co. K, 13th Mississippi Infantry, at Gettysburg. After the war, he was elected tax assessor of Lauderdale County. In the midst of a county reelection campaign in 1881, Harvey was killed in an election riot at Marion. A local white newspaper reported that blacks had come to the polls armed and that they "were insolent, abusive and insulting to the whites." Then one white struck one of the black voters, and in the ensuing fight three whites were killed and three wounded, while one black was wounded. The county sheriff and a mob pursued the blacks, and there was extensive subsequent bloodshed in the black community, disruption of the polls, and a conservative election victory.[6] *Photo courtesy of J. B. Harvey*

SURVIVORS OF THE LAMAR RIFLES
copy print from *Thomas P. Buford, comp., Lamar Rifles, a History of Company G, Eleventh Mississippi Regiment, C.S.A.*

A major part of the rehealing of the split between Mississippians and the nation was the organization of veterans' groups some years after the war had ended. These provided the vehicles within which the Confederate cause could be romanticized and justified. Annual reunions were well covered by newspapers, and ultimately they became the means to celebrate the Confederate cause. One typical group was the Survivors Association of Lamar Rifles, shown in a reunion in 1901 at Oxford.

341

342

SILAS C. BUCK
copy print

Seventeen-year-old Pvt. Silas C. Buck was
the color bearer for the 12th Mississippi
Cavalry when the unit surrendered at
Citronelle, Alabama, on May 4, 1865. Buck
hid the flag shown in this picture and later
gave it to an officer of the regiment for safe-
keeping. In ca. 1902 Buck and a few of the
remaining survivors of the 12th Mississippi
Cavalry gathered in Dallas, Texas, for the
annual reunion of the United Confederate
Veterans. There Buck had his picture made
with the flag that he had saved almost thirty-
seven years before. In the war, colors such
as these served as a symbol of honor for the
soldiers who fought to protect them. The
old flags served the same purpose for the
aging veterans who periodically gathered
to remember the war. *Photo courtesy of the
Kentucky Historical Society*

In Mississippi, veterans' organizations did not exist just among former Confederates. Black Union army veterans organized posts of the Grand Army of the Republic (GAR) in Mississippi beginning immediately after the war, and these units continued with the support of the national organization through the rest of the century. Here one group of veterans commemorates Freedom Day in 1890. *Photo courtesy of the Grand Gulf Military Monument Park*

FREEDOM DAY, CLAIBORNE COUNTY, 1890
copy print of unknown original

For black veterans such as these lined up for a parade in Natchez, the politics of the GAR were much like the civil politics of the state. White Union veterans in the South tried to exclude blacks from the GAR during the 1880s. The black veterans resisted, urging the national organization to take a moral stand on the issue and insist on black membership. As a result, in the deep South most GAR posts became primarily black by the 1890s. The history of these men, however, was left largely unwritten. *Photo courtesy of William E. Stewart*

GAR PARADE, NATCHEZ, 1890S
copy from original glass negative
Robert Livingston Stewart

The writing of Confederate history did not begin until the 1890s. John C. Rietti proposed one of the first projects. Published in 1894, Rietti's *Military Annals of Mississippi* was a compilation of published company rosters of Mississippi infantry units, but it also contained details of the service of individual units and was the beginning of efforts to write an overall history of the state's wartime experience.

Perhaps no individual was more responsible for the writing of Confederate history in Mississippi and elsewhere than Stephen D. Lee. Settling in Mississippi after the war, Lee became involved in Confederate veterans' organizations in the 1880s and then in the writing of war history in subsequent years. He published articles on battles in Mississippi in the *Confederate Veteran* and *Southern Historical Society Papers*. He helped reorganize the Mississippi Historical Association and was a major force behind the creation of the Mississippi Department of Archives and History. Lee hoped to see the development of a history fair to the South and to the cause for which he had fought. In one speech advocating such a history he summed up the reasons for his advocacy, concluding, "The South has suffered much at the hands of school histories."[7]
Photo courtesy of the Columbus and Lowndes County Historical Society

348

DEDICATION OF THE MISSISSIPPI *(right)*
AND ILLINOIS MONUMENTS
copy prints

Reflective of the healing of wartime divisions and the reintegration of the South into the national experience was the creation of national military parks such as the one at Vicksburg. The Vicksburg National Military Park Association was organized in 1895 with Stephen D. Lee as its head. In February 1899, the association finally secured legislation from Congress creating this park. In 1904 Massachusetts erected within the park the first state monument to its troops. The dedication of each subsequent monument gave cause for public expressions of admiration by each side for the other. *Photo courtesy of the Old Court House Museum, Vicksburg*

JEFFERSON DAVIS AND FAMILY AT BEAUVOIR
copy print

No single individual represented the merging of the Confederate experience into that of the nation better than Mississippi's best-known Confederate, Jefferson Davis. Arrested at the end of the war, Davis suffered from economic adversity in the postwar world. By the 1880s, he had settled on the Beauvoir plantation to write his memoirs; he became a popular symbol of the Confederacy, despite his unpopularity during the war itself. His acceptance throughout the nation indicated the healing of war wounds. An editor of the *Atlanta Constitution* summed up Davis's significance during one of the former Confederate leader's trips across the nation. The purposes of secession and the Confederacy were less important than the character shown by the Southern leaders. The editor wrote: "Ours is one country; all that has been done in it to the credit of the American character is the heritage of the whole country, not solely of one section."[8] *Photo courtesy of M.D.A.H.*

349

Appendix

Adams, Walter W.

Adams remained with the 21st Mississippi until the Battle of Cedar Creek on October 19, 1864. During the fight, his left femur was fractured, and Adams was sent to the hospital in Richmond, where he was captured when the city fell. The authors could find no record of his activities after the war.

Adams, William Wirt

After the war Wirt Adams settled in Vicksburg and later moved to Jackson. There he served as state revenue agent before becoming postmaster in 1885. On May 1, 1888, a newspaper editor who had been quarreling with the general killed Adams in a street brawl. He is buried in the capital city.

Aden, Felen Felix

The authors found no information on Aden's activities after the war.

Alcorn, James Lusk

Alcorn retired from the U.S. Senate in 1877, and returned to Friars Point, Mississippi, to manage his farm and practice law. He died on December 20, 1894, and is buried on his plantation, Eagle's Nest, in Coahoma County.

Anderson, Patton

Anderson surrendered in North Carolina with the Army of Tennessee and later settled in Memphis. He edited a farm journal and served as collector of state taxes for Shelby County. Anderson died in Memphis on September 20, 1872, and is buried in Elmwood Cemetery.

Baker, Robert Enos

Baker died of camp fever at the residence of Governor Winston in Madison County, Alabama, on August 14, 1862.

Baldwin, William

Baldwin was captured at Vicksburg and subsequently exchanged. He then served briefly with the Army of Tennessee before being transferred to the District of Mobile. On February 19, 1864, Baldwin was killed in a fall from his horse. He is buried in Friendship Cemetery, Columbus, Mississippi.

Barksdale, William

Barksdale died at Gettysburg from the wound that he received on July 2, 1863. He is buried in Greenwood Cemetery in Jackson, Mississippi.

Barry, William

Barry helped organize the 35th Mississippi Infantry and served as colonel of the regiment. He was seriously wounded at Allatoona Pass, Georgia, on October 5, 1864. Barry died of disease at Columbus, Mississippi, on January 29, 1868.

Barton, Seth

Barton was paroled after surrendering at Vicksburg, and he returned to duty in the East. Barton's later career was unexceptional, and he was captured a second time at Sayler's Creek on April 6, 1865. He was released from prison in July 1865 and moved to Fredericksburg, Virginia. Barton died in Washington, D.C., on April 11, 1900. He is buried in Fredericksburg.

Beauregard, P. G. T.

Beauregard spent much of his subsequent military career in South Carolina, Georgia, and Virginia. His timely action near Petersburg in June 1864 saved Richmond from capture. He returned to his home in New Orleans after the war and was involved with several railroad companies. Beauregard also served as adjutant general of Louisiana, and published several military studies. He died in New Orleans on February 20, 1893, and is buried in Metairie Cemetery.

Bell, James R.

Major Bell remained in prison until the war ended and then returned to his home in Yazoo County, Mississippi. He died there on February 12, 1906, at the age of seventy-five. For many years Bell was an active member of the Yazoo Camp of the United Confederate Veterans.

Benton, Samuel

Benton died from his wounds on July 28, 1864. He is buried in Holly Springs, Mississippi.

Blake, Billy

Blake was discharged from the army after losing his leg at Gettysburg. After the war he lived most of his life in New Orleans. Blake died at Waveland, Mississippi, on September 23, 1902.

Blanchard, William H.

The authors found no information on Blanchard's activities after the war.

Bowen, Jerome

Jerome Bowen died on May 15, 1864, at the Battle of Resaca, Georgia.

Bowen, John

John Bowen died of disease near Raymond, Mississippi, on July 13, 1863, less than two weeks after he had surrendered at Vicksburg. Twenty-four years later Bowen's remains were reinterred in the Confederate Cemetery at Vicksburg.

Bowman, Thornton H.

Bowman was exchanged after his capture at Britton's Lane, and transferred to Cameron's Louisiana Battery. He was later commissioned and assigned to the 4th Louisiana Cavalry. Bowman served with the unit until sometime in 1864 when he fell from his horse and was permanently disabled. After the war he studied in

France before returning to Louisiana to teach. In 1871 Bowman moved to Belton, Texas, where he taught school and practiced law until January 1874 when he went to work in Austin as a clerk in the Texas Department of State. For the next twenty years Bowman held a number of political offices. After being defeated for Congress in the 1896 Democratic caucus, he moved to Coke County. In 1898 he was appointed superintendent of the state orphans' home and served until around 1900. Bowman died on November 7, 1905. He was married twice and had four children with his second wife.

Brandon, William L.

Brandon returned to his farm in Wilkinson County, Mississippi, and died there on October 8, 1890. He is buried in the family cemetery at Arcole Plantation.

Bringhurst, Thomas H.

Bringhurst mustered out of the service at Louisville, Kentucky, on September 4, 1865. His regiment, the 46th Indiana, had lost 264 men to wounds or sickness. He returned to Indiana and was a businessman in Logansport for most of his life. Bringhurst, who was also a Mexican War veteran, died on May 26, 1899, at the age of seventy-nine. He is buried in Mt. Hope Cemetery. His second wife, Elizabeth, who had married Bringhurst in 1857, died on March 25, 1915.

Brown, Albert Gallatin

Albert G. Brown resigned from the U.S. Senate on January 6, 1861, and returned to Mississippi. He raised a company which fought with the 8th Mississippi Infantry at First Bull Run. In December 1861 Brown was elected to the Confederate Senate and served until the end of the war. He eventually broke with Davis, arguing that the unlimited power to make war rested with the Confederate Congress. He favored expanding the draft and freeing those slaves who would serve in the army. After the war

Brown supported reconciliation with the Union, a position that made him a political pariah in Mississippi. He died on his plantation in Hinds County, Mississippi, on June 12, 1880.

Brown, Charles

Charles Brown of the 33rd Illinois Infantry mustered out with his unit in Chicago on December 6, 1865. He lived in Illinois until 1869; then Brown and his wife, Celia, moved to Nebraska. The two had ten children, and Brown farmed for most of his life. He died of cancer in Lincoln, Nebraska, on August 8, 1914. His wife was still drawing a pension as late as 1929.

Brown, Charles

Charles Brown of the 11th Indiana Infantry died at Champion's Hill on May 16, 1863.

Brownlee, James

Brownlee was paroled after the fall of Vicksburg and returned to the 35th Mississippi in late 1863. He rose to the rank of second lieutenant and was captured at Fort Blakely, Alabama, near the end of the war. Brownlee eventually settled in Madisonville, Texas, and died there in 1927.

Buck, Silas

Buck was living in Kentucky in 1902, but the authors found no other information about him.

Buford, Thomas

On March 25, 1865, Buford was wounded and disabled while serving in the Siege of Petersburg. He returned to College Hill, Mississippi, after the war and farmed there until 1873. Buford then moved to Big Lick (Roanoke), Virginia, where he continued farming. He was a founding member of the William Watts Camp of the United Confederate Veterans, and served as the post commander. Around the turn of the century, he helped compile material for a history of the Lamar Rifles, which was published in 1903.

Buford died on January 16, 1915, and is buried in the Fast Hill Cemetery in Salem, Virginia.

Buford, Walter Scott

Private Buford was seriously wounded on August 30, 1862, during the Second Battle of Bull Run. He died on September 15, 1862.

Bullard, Arthur N.

Arthur Bullard became ill while serving with the 10th Mississippi and returned to his home at Baldwin. He died of measles on April 27, 1862.

Bullard, James

Arthur's father, James Bullard, served with the 10th Mississippi at Shiloh. On September 14, 1862, he was mortally wounded at the Battle of Munfordville, Kentucky.

Bush, Elliott N.

Bush was killed at Brice's Crossroads on June 10, 1864.

Byers, John Alemeth

On October 19, 1864, Byers was shot and killed during the Battle of Cedar Creek, Virginia.

Calvert, Metellus

Calvert died on May 19, 1863, in Grant's first assault against Vicksburg.

Capers, Ellison

Capers recovered from the wound he received during the Battle of Jackson and later fought in the Army of Tennessee. On March 1, 1865, he was appointed brigadier general in the Confederate army. After the war Capers became an Episcopal priest, and was eventually elected bishop of South Carolina. He also served as chaplain general of the United Confederate Veterans and wrote the South Carolina volume

of Clement Evans' *Confederate Military History*. Capers died in Columbia, South Carolina, on April 22, 1908, and is buried in the Trinity Cathedral churchyard.

Carradine, Bird Calhoun

Carradine survived the war and returned to his home in Clay County, Mississippi, near West Point. He later served on the County Board of Supervisors and managed his plantation. Carradine died on January 9, 1924.

Carter, Sinclair B.

Carter served during the Atlanta Campaign and probably surrendered in North Carolina with the 15th Mississippi Infantry. He returned to Mississippi and farmed there until moving to Milam County, Texas, in 1877. Carter died at Rockdale, Texas, on January 17, 1918.

Chalmers, James R.

Chalmers transferred to the cavalry shortly after the Battle of Stones River, and saw extensive action in Mississippi and Tennessee. After the war Chalmers returned to Mississippi and served in the U.S. House of Representatives from 1877 until he was unseated in a contested election in 1882. He was elected to Congress as an Independent in 1884, but was defeated for a second term. Chalmers then moved to Memphis and practiced law until his death on April 9, 1898. He is buried in Elmwood Cemetery.

Chandler, William H.

Chandler was discharged from the service at Mobile, Alabama, on July 7, 1865. He returned to Columbus, Ohio, to pursue his craft as a carriage maker. On February 19, 1867, Chandler married Mary Neven, and the couple had three children. The family later moved to Bellefontaine, Ohio, where Chandler was a merchant. Mary died on May 1, 1921, and William lived until March 9, 1924.

Childs, George

Childs survived the war and returned to his home in Iowa, where he lived until 1867. The next year he married Mary McNair, and the couple moved to Minnesota, where they lived until 1875. Childs then lived in Illinois and Kentucky, before returning to Iowa in 1903. In 1913 he moved to the Iowa soldiers' home, but the authors did not find the date of his death.

Chilton, Thomas

Chilton served with the 11th Mississippi until he was captured at Petersburg on April 2, 1865. He lived in Memphis after the war and married Blanche M. Blair in 1871. For several years Chilton was a business partner with W. M. Wilkerson & Co., and later became involved with several financial institutions. Chilton's wife died on June 7, 1899, and Chilton survived until December 11, 1911. At the time of his death Chilton was president of the Tontine Savings Association.

Clark, Charles

Clark was confined at Fort Pulaski, Georgia, for a brief period after the war. After his release he practiced law in Mississippi, until he was appointed chancery judge in 1876. Clark died the following year on December 18, 1877, and is buried in Bolivar County on the Doro plantation.

Clayton, Rufus

Clayton died on November 15, 1862, from the wound he received during the Battle of Iuka.

Code, James

Code was released from Andersonville Prison when the war ended and returned to Iowa. He died in Keokuk on September 20, 1895.

Cosby, Lemuel Prior

The authors found no information on Cosby's activities after the war.

Courtney, Alonzo

Courtney served with the 63rd Ohio until he was captured during the Atlanta Campaign on July 22, 1864. He was sent to Andersonville, Georgia, and later transferred to Florence, South Carolina. Courtney died in prison on February 11, 1865.

Cunningham, Joseph

Cunningham was paroled at Camp Douglas, Illinois, on February 13, 1865, and returned to his home in Holly Springs, Mississippi. Cunningham farmed and worked as a furniture maker for many years. In 1900 he moved to Warren, Arkansas, and worked for the Southern Lumber Company. Cunningham later relocated to Fordyce, Arkansas, where he lived with his daughter until he died on March 21, 1920.

Dabney, Frederick Y.

Dabney was sent to Johnson's Island after surrendering at Port Hudson and remained in captivity until the war was over. He later worked as a civil engineer for various railroads until ill health forced him to retire around 1894. Dabney died at his home in Crystal Springs, Mississippi, on March 15, 1900.

Davenport, Henry

Henry Davenport died in a Federal hospital near Gettysburg on July 17, 1863. After the war Samuel Weaver located the body for Davenport's mother; it was buried about four miles south of town. Weaver remarked in his letter that there would be "nothing left but the bones," but he offered to reinter the remains in a private cemetery for twenty-five dollars.[1] Mrs. Davenport apparently declined his offer. In 1872 many

Confederate bodies were exhumed and moved to the Hollywood Cemetery in Richmond, Virginia. Davenport's remains were transferred to that location on June 15, 1872.

Davenport, Stephen

Henry's brother, Stephen Davenport, was assassinated in Mississippi on November 8, 1863.

Davis, Claudius Virginius Hughes

C. V. H. Davis was killed in action at Peachtree Creek, Georgia, on July 22, 1864.

Davis, Jefferson

Jefferson Davis became president of the Confederacy, but his rigid attitudes and constant interference with military operations often hindered the war effort. After the war Davis was charged with treason and imprisoned at Fort Monroe, Virginia, for two years. He was finally released on bail, but never brought to trial. Davis eventually returned to Beauvoir, his plantation in southern Mississippi. In 1881 he published *The Rise and Fall of the Confederate Government*, which recounted Davis's version of his role in the rebellion. Davis remained an unreconstructed Southerner and never asked to have his citizenship restored. He died at his home on December 9, 1889.

Davis, Joseph R.

Joseph Davis led his brigade through the remaining battles in Virginia and surrendered at Appomattox Court House. He returned to Biloxi, Mississippi, after the war and practiced law there until his death on September 15, 1896. Davis is buried in the Biloxi Cemetery.

Dilley, Robert W.

Dilley was admitted to the hospital in Richmond for diarrhea in May 1862, but was released in time to fight with the 12th Mississippi Infantry during the Peninsular Campaign. He was hospitalized again for diarrhea and missed the battles of Second Bull Run and Antietam. Dilley returned to duty on November 1, 1862, but he was hospitalized for a third time in April 1863. He died of pneumonia at General Hospital No. 2, in Lynchburg, Virginia, on April 23, 1863.

Dilley, Samuel W.

Robert's brother, Samuel Dilley, died of typhoid fever near Centreville, Virginia, on September 12, 1861.

Dockery, Thomas

Dockery surrendered with the Vicksburg garrison. He was promoted to brigadier general shortly after being paroled, and later commanded a brigade in Arkansas. After the war, Dockery eventually moved to Houston, Texas, where he worked as a civil engineer. He died on February 27, 1898, while visiting New York City.

Duval, Henderson

Henderson Duval was killed at Champion's Hill on May 16, 1863.

Duval, Thomas Isaac

Thomas Isaac Duval died at Champion's Hill on May 16, 1863.

Duval, William Russel

William Duval was killed at Corinth on October 4, 1862.

Eisele, George T.

Eisele was in the hospital at Citronelle, Alabama, when the war ended. He was paroled at Meridian, Mississippi, on May 12, 1865. The authors found no information about Eisele's activities after the war.

Evans, William D.

Evans was wounded at Champion's Hill and later captured with the 7th Mississippi Battalion at Vicksburg. His unit was paroled and subsequently served in the Atlanta Campaign where Evans was again wounded. Evans, who had since been promoted to first lieutenant, was wounded a third time at the Battle of Franklin. After the war he settled in Newton County, Mississippi, and on November 24, 1865, he married Mary E. Phelps. Mary died on February 28, 1875. Nine months later Evans married his sister-in-law, Nancy Jane Phelps, who died on March 27, 1877. On February 24, 1878, Evans married Diana Jones; they purchased a farm and moved to Leake County, Mississippi. During the war Evans had written several verses about his experiences, and he continued to publish poems, letters, and articles in many local newspapers throughout his life. He was also active in several Confederate veterans' organizations. Evans died near Hillsboro, Mississippi, on June 1, 1934, at the age of ninety-four. He is buried in Pleasant Hill Cemetery near Carthage in Leake County.

Eves, Clarkson

Eves was exchanged shortly after being captured at Palo Alto and rejoined his regiment. He mustered out of the service on September 9, 1865, and eventually farmed near Vermillion in the Dakota Territory. On December 31, 1875, he began receiving a pension of four dollars per month for a service-related disability. In 1905 Eves moved to San Jose, California. Eves' first wife, Rebecca, died on January 31, 1891. He married his second wife, Emma, on June 22, 1892. At the time of his death on December 10, 1921, Eves was living in Long Beach, California. He was eighty-two years old. Emma received a government pension until her death on September 14, 1929.

Farmer, Andoniram J.

Farmer was mortally wounded at Gettysburg on July 3, 1863. He was buried on the battlefield.

Farmer, De Witt

Farmer surrendered with the Army of Northern Virginia and returned to his home in Noxubee County, Mississippi. He died there in November 1871.

Farragut, David

Farragut continued to command the West Gulf Blockading Squadron after the fall of Vicksburg. On August 5, 1864, he ran several Union ships by two forts protecting Mobile Bay and seized the last major Confederate seaport on the gulf. In December 1864, Farragut was promoted to vice-admiral, but because of failing health he saw little action. In July 1866 he was promoted to admiral. Farragut died on August 14, 1870, while visiting the Portsmouth, New Hampshire, Navy Yard.

Fayard, Sylvester

The authors found no information on Fayard's activities after the war.

Featherston, Winfield Scott

Featherston returned to Mississippi after the war and was an unsuccessful candidate for the U.S. Senate in 1865. In 1876 he was elected to the Mississippi House of Representatives and served until 1880. Featherston then practiced law in Holly Springs, Mississippi, and remained active in Democratic politics until his death on May 28, 1891. He is buried in Holly Springs.

Fontaine, Lamar

Fontaine returned to Mississippi after the war and married L. S. Brickell of Yazoo County. The Fontaines had eight children and settled in Coahoma County, where he pursued his profession as a civil engineer. Fontaine also wrote several verses and songs about the Civil War, including "All Is Quiet along the Potomac Tonight," "Only a Soldier," and "Oenone." As did many old veterans, Fontaine tended to embellish his role in the war, claiming, on more than one instance, that he was wounded sixty-seven times and killed sixty men in one hour. Fontaine died in 1921.

Forrest, Nathan Bedford

Forrest was promoted to lieutenant general to rank from February 28, 1865. On April 2, 1865, at Selma, Alabama, he suffered one of his few defeats, but he eluded capture until the end of the war. Forrest lived in Memphis after the war; he helped organize the Ku Klux Klan and served as the organization's Grand Wizard. He also continued to manage his farm and served for several years as president of the Selma, Marion, & Memphis Railroad. Forrest died in Memphis on October 29, 1877, and is buried there.

Foules, Henry Luse

Foules was killed in a skirmish near Atlanta, Georgia, on July 16, 1864. He is buried in the Kingston Cemetery in Adams County, Mississippi.

French, Samuel Gibbs

French surrendered near Mobile, Alabama, in April 1865. He returned to Mississippi and managed his wife's plantation. French later retired to Florida where in 1901 he published his memoirs, *Two Wars: An Autobiography.* French died on April 20, 1910, at the age of ninety-two. He is buried in Pensacola, Florida.

Fullwood, William H.

After the Battle of Corinth, Fullwood served at various times under generals Nathan Bedford Forrest and Joseph Wheeler. When the war ended he returned to his father's farm near Shiloh, Tennessee. Fullwood inherited the land when his father died and continued to farm it until his own death in 1891 at the age of fifty.

Gage, Jeremiah

Gage was mortally wounded at Gettysburg on July 3, 1863.

Garrott, Isham

Garrott later fought at Champion's Hill and withdrew into the Vicksburg defenses with the beaten Confederate army. He was killed by a sharpshooter on June 17, 1863.

Geer, Morgan

Geer mustered out of the 20th Illinois on July 16, 1865. He moved to Lexington, Missouri, and married Eliza Ann Roberts in May 1866. The couple settled in Warrensburg, Missouri, and he began practicing law. Geer was active in local politics, serving at various times as mayor, a member of the school board, and prosecuting attorney. He was a charter member in the Colonel Grover Chapter of the Grand Army of the Republic. Geer died in Warrensburg in 1926 at age eighty-five. The bullet that had struck him in the neck over sixty-three years before at the battle of Raymond was still lodged near his spine.

Gerrard, Alexander J.

Gerrard surrendered with the 39th Mississippi at Port Hudson, Louisiana, on July 8, 1863, and was a prisoner until the war ended. He is not listed in the 1870 Mississippi Census and may not have returned to his home after the war. The authors found no other information on Lieutenant Gerrard.

Gholson, Samuel J.

Gholson commanded a cavalry brigade which operated in Alabama, Mississippi, and eastern Louisiana during most of the war. In December 1864 he was severely wounded in an engagement at Egypt, Mississippi, and lost an arm. After the war Gholson served in the state legislature from

1865 to 1868, and again from 1878 to 1880. He died in Aberdeen, Mississippi, on October 16, 1883, and is buried in the Odd Fellows Cemetery.

Gooch, Alphonso

Alphonso Gooch rejoined the 20th Mississippi after his capture at Fort Donelson and served with the regiment until the end of the war. Gooch apparently returned to Mississippi, but he moved to Little Rock, Arkansas, around 1873. Gooch subsequently worked as a carpenter, machinist, and pump repairer for the railroad. Around the turn of the century Gooch started a general contracting firm which he owned at the time of his death on March 10, 1915.

Gooch, Thomas

Alphonso's brother, Thomas Gooch, also rejoined the 20th Mississippi after his capture at Fort Donelson. Thomas was captured a second time at Edward's Depot on June 10, 1863, while scouting the Union forces surrounding Vicksburg. He was imprisoned at Fort Delaware until the war ended. Gooch returned to Mississippi after the war and was there in 1870. The authors found no other information about Thomas Gooch.

Grammer, George A.

In the fall of 1862, Grammer wrote in his diary that "I resolved by the grace of God to lead a better life and if possible to atone for the past."[2] Early the next year he joined the Soldiers Christian Association. When the war ended Grammer returned to Warren County and was elected assessor in 1866. However, his real interest was in pursuing his religious proclivities. He became a minister and remained in Vicksburg until approximately 1877. Grammer then moved to Tennessee where he continued to preach in the Baptist church and was a member of the Hiram S. Bradford Bivouac, No. 28, of the United Confederate Veterans. Grammer died at Brownsville, Tennessee, on June 27, 1902.

Grant, Ulysses Simpson

When the Civil War ended Grant was a lieutenant general and commander-in-chief of the United States Army. Grant's personal popularity and his support for the congressional radicals made him an ideal candidate for the presidency in 1868. Grant easily defeated his Democratic rival, but his two terms were marred by financial scandals that reached into the highest levels of government. Grant left office in 1877 and settled in New York City four years later. Shortly afterward, he was victimized by a fraudulent banking scheme and was left practically penniless. Grant, with the encouragement of his friend, Mark Twain, began writing his memoirs. The manuscript was finished shortly before the general died of throat cancer on July 23, 1885. His volume, *The Personal Memoirs of U.S. Grant*, earned nearly $450,000 for Grant's family and became one of the great works of military autobiography. Grant's tomb is on Riverside Drive in New York City.

Green, Martin E.

Martin Green led his brigade during the Vicksburg Campaign and retreated into the city after the Battle of Champion's Hill. On June 27, 1863, Green was shot and killed by an enemy sharpshooter.

Green, Nathaniel

Green served in the West Gulf Coast Blockading Squadron throughout the remainder of the war and took part in the Union attack against Mobile Bay. He died in Reading, Pennsylvania, on March 22, 1873, at the age of thirty-seven. He was still on active duty with the rank of commander in the U.S. Navy.

Gregg, John

Gregg later fought at Chickamauga, Georgia, where he was wounded. He was then assigned to command the Texas brigade in the Army of

Northern Virginia. Gregg led his Texans until he was killed at Darbytown Road near Richmond on October 7, 1864. He is buried in Aberdeen, Mississippi.

Grierson, Benjamin

Grierson remained in the army after the war and was appointed colonel of the 10th U.S. Cavalry. He saw extensive service in the West and was promoted to brigadier general on April 5, 1890. Grierson retired three months later and moved to Jacksonville, Illinois. He died in Omena, Michigan, on September 1, 1911, and is buried at Jacksonville.

Hadley, John S.

Hadley mustered out of the service with the 47th Illinois Infantry on January 21, 1866. The authors found no death date on Hadley, although he did begin receiving a pension on September 1, 1871. His wife was still alive and living in Wisconsin in 1920.

Haines, William

Haines was badly wounded in Grant's May 22, 1863, assault at Vicksburg. He recovered from his wound and served until being discharged at Savannah, Georgia, on July 25, 1865. After the war Haines farmed in Iowa and later in Illinois. Haines was living in Springfield, Illinois, when he died on May 13, 1935.

Hall, Levi

After the Siege of Vicksburg, Levi Hall was transferred to Louisiana. On May 26, 1864, he was arrested for raping a black woman at knife point. Hall was convicted of assault with intent to rape and sentenced to fifteen days hard labor and forfeited twenty-four dollars in pay. The rape charge was reduced "in consideration of the fact that the complainant did not make any vigorous physical resistance to the embraces of the prisoner."[3] Hall was discharged at Vicksburg

on November 24, 1865, and resumed farming in Illinois. In November he married Almira Meek, and they had ten children. Hall later farmed in Missouri, Kansas, and Oklahoma. He died on his farm near Beaver, Oklahoma, on January 4, 1923, at the age of eighty-three.

Hall, Winchester

Hall was badly wounded in the leg during the siege of Vicksburg. He surrendered with the garrison and, after being exchanged, rejoined his regiment. Hall returned to Thibodaux, Louisiana, after the war and resumed his law practice. Conditions in postwar Louisiana were so bad that Hall could not make a living, and in 1868 he moved to Chicago, where he practiced law until retiring in 1882. He eventually settled at Pocomoke City on the eastern shore of Maryland. There he published his memoirs entitled *The Story of the 26th Louisiana Infantry*. Hall died on December 10, 1909, at the age of ninety.

Halleck, Henry Wager

Halleck remained in Washington, D.C., until the Civil War ended; he continued to enjoy a reputation as an able bureaucrat. The general was serving as commander of the Division of the South when he died at Louisville, Kentucky, on January 9, 1872. Halleck is buried in Green-Wood Cemetery in New York City.

Hamilton, Charles S.

After the Battle of Corinth, Hamilton tried to use his political influence to obtain command of a corps under Grant. When Grant learned about Hamilton's activities, he protested to Washington. Hamilton offered to resign, and Grant, on April 13, 1863, accepted his offer. Hamilton returned to Wisconsin where, ironically, President Grant appointed him to the post of U.S. Marshall. Hamilton became a prominent Milwaukee businessman and leader in the Military Order of the Loyal Legion. He died on

April 17, 1891, and is buried in Milwaukee at the Forest Home Cemetery.

Hardin, Thomas J.

Hardin was killed at Spotsylvania Courthouse on May 12, 1864.

Harris, John B.

On April 12, 1864, John Harris married Mary Ann Shidelar. He returned to the army, mustered out of the service on February 10, 1865, and rejoined his wife in Indiana. Except for a brief stay in Kansas during the mid-1870s, he spent his entire life in Indiana working as either a carpenter or a mechanic. Harris died in Rock Creek Township outside Huntington, Indiana, on March 29, 1932. His wife was eighty-two in 1937 and was still drawing a government pension. The authors did not find the date of her death.

Harris, Johnson

The authors found no information on Johnson Harris's activities after the war.

Harris, Marion

Marion Harris was mortally wounded at the Battle of Gaines' Mill on June 27, 1862.

Harris, Nathaniel

Nathaniel Harris continued to serve in the Army of Northern Virginia until the end of the war. He then practiced law in Vicksburg and was president of the Mississippi Valley & Ship Island Railroad. Harris later served as Registrar of Lands in South Dakota and eventually moved to California. Harris was on a business trip when he died at Malvern, England, on August 23, 1900. His body was cremated, and the ashes were buried in Green-Wood Cemetery in New York City.

Harris, Thomas

Thomas Harris was exchanged after surrendering at Vicksburg. Many soldiers of the 31st Louisiana never rejoined their command, but Harris apparently did report for duty at Minden, Louisiana. He was paroled at the end of the war and returned to his home in Claiborne Parish. Harris was serving as marshal in 1890, but the authors found no further record of his activities.

Harvey, Addison

Harvey was assassinated at Columbus, Georgia.

Heath, Albert

Heath was severely wounded at the Battle of Chattanooga, but he survived the war. Shortly after the conflict he and his wife, Caroline, moved to California. They first lived in Santa Cruz, but later moved to San Francisco. Heath died on September 19, 1887; his wife lived until September 26, 1923.

Henley, A. W.

The authors found no record of A. W. Henley after his surrender at Vicksburg on July 4, 1863.

Herrington, Isom D.

Herrington was sent to Camp Morton, Indiana, where he subsequently enlisted in the U.S. Army. After the war he returned to his home in Simpson County, Mississippi. Herrington eventually purchased his own farm before he died in 1908. He is buried in Husband Cemetery near Mage, Mississippi.

Hodges, Thomas P.

Captain Hodges died during the Battle of Ezra Church on July 28, 1864.

Holmes, John

Holmes recovered from the wound he received at Gaines' Mill and rejoined the 16th Mississippi. On August 24, 1864, Holmes was captured at Weldon Railroad and sent to Fort Delaware. He was exchanged and served with the Army of Northern Virginia until the end of the war. Holmes returned to Mississippi and married Miss A. M. Sparkman. He was a member of the Hattiesburg Camp No. 24, of the United Confederate Veterans. Holmes died at Bay St. Louis, Mississippi, in 1909 or 1910.

Hope, Frank L.

Frank Hope survived the war and returned to his home in College Hill, Mississippi. He died there on September 18, 1870.

Hope, George W.

Lieutenant Hope died in the Battle of Stones River on December 31, 1862.

Houston, Robert

Houston was still listed as a deserter at the end of the war, and he apparently returned to his home in Itawamba County. Houston is buried in Salem Baptist Cemetery in Itawamba County, but his headstone does not give a death date. He was, however, married three times, and his last wife did not die until June 18, 1941.

Hovey, Alvin Peterson

Hovey commanded his division during the Siege of Vicksburg. In the summer of 1864 he assumed command of the District of Indiana, and was brevetted to major general. Hovey's primary duty was to recruit soldiers for the Union armies. After the war Hovey served as minister to Peru between 1865 and 1870. He returned to his law practice in Mount Vernon, Indiana, and was elected to the U.S. Congress, serving from 1887 until 1889. Hovey was then elected governor of Indiana; he died in office on November 23, 1891. Hovey is buried in the Bellefontaine Cemetery in Mount Vernon.

Hughes, Felix

Hughes was killed on August 5, 1862, during the Battle of Baton Rouge.

Humphreys, Benjamin

Humphreys led his brigade until September 13, 1864, when he was badly wounded. The general recovered from his wound and was stationed in southern Mississippi when the war ended. Humphreys was Mississippi's first postwar governor, but he was removed from office on June 15, 1868, after President Andrew Johnson's reconstruction plan was superseded by that of the radicals. Humphreys died on his plantation in Leflore County, Mississippi, on December 20, 1882. He is buried in Port Gibson.

Ingram, Thomas

Ingram was exchanged after his capture at Vicksburg and became a member of the Whitworth Sharpshooters. He went on to fight in the Atlanta Campaign and was wounded on July 20, 1864. Ingram and several other members of the sharpshooters refused to surrender with Gen. Joseph Johnston in North Carolina and probably joined Lt. Gen. E. Kirby Smith's forces west of the Mississippi. Ingram lived in Bonham, Texas, after the war and engaged in the mercantile business until 1897. He then moved to Durant, Indiana, where he helped to organize a bank and served as an officer until his death on January 25, 1908. He is buried in Bonham.

Jackson, George A.

George Jackson survived the war and eventually settled in Kansas. In 1898 he began receiving an invalid's pension, which he drew until his death. Jackson died in Texas probably sometime in 1930, since his wife began drawing her pension that year.

Jackson, William H.

William H. Jackson continued to serve with the Confederate cavalry until the Civil War ended. He settled near Nashville, Tennessee, and spent the rest of his life raising thoroughbred horses. He was a proponent of improving Southern farming techniques and served as president of both the National Agricultural Congress and the Tennessee Bureau of Agriculture. Jackson died at Belle Meade plantation on March 30, 1903; he is buried at Nashville in the Mount Olivet Cemetery.

Jarman, Robert A.

Jarman's father was killed in a Federal raid in 1864, and after the war Jarman returned to manage the family plantation in Monroe County, Mississippi. On November 25, 1884, he married Minerva Huggins, and they had two daughters. Jarman died on May 9, 1893, after being thrown from a railroad car in Egypt, Mississippi.

Johnson, Henry P.

Colonel Johnson died at the Battle of Corinth on October 4, 1862.

Jones, John D.

Private Jones died at the Battle of Franklin on November 30, 1864.

Jordan, Fidel E.

Jordan died of disease at Mobile, Alabama, on July 12, 1862. His widow received $25.66 in back pay.

King, George W.

King died of disease at Yorktown, Virginia, on April 12, 1862.

Kinsman, William

Kinsman died in the engagement at Big Black River Bridge on May 17, 1863.

Lamar, Lucius Quintus Cincinnatus

After the war Lamar returned to teaching at the University of Mississippi. In 1872 he was elected to the U.S. House of Representatives and served until he took his seat in the U.S. Senate in 1877. Lamar held that office until 1885 when President Grover Cleveland appointed him Secretary of the Interior. Two years later Lamar was appointed to the U.S. Supreme Court, where he served until his death on January 23, 1893.

Lassiter, F. M.

Lassiter is listed in the 1870 Census as living in Warren County, Mississippi. The authors found no other information on Lassiter after that date.

LeCand, Frederick J. V.

LeCand returned to Natchez, Mississippi, after the war. He was, for many years, secretary and treasurer of the Rosalie Mills Company. As were many other ex-soldiers LeCand was active in a number of veterans' organizations. He also remained in his old militia unit, the Natchez Fencibles, and commanded the company for eighteen years. Several poems by LeCand appear in the *Confederate Veteran*, and he was named Poet Laureate of Mississippi. LeCand was still alive in 1917, but he had apparently left Natchez. The authors could not find out when or where he died.

Lee, Stephen D.

Lee was appointed lieutenant general on June 23, 1864; he was thirty-one and the youngest Confederate to hold that rank. He assumed command of a corps in the Army of Tennessee and served in Hood's 1864 offensive. Lee settled in Columbus, Mississippi, after the war. He farmed, served in the general assembly, and was the first president of Mississippi State College. Lee played a major role in encouraging the writing of Civil War history and published dozens of articles about the conflict. He also helped found the United Confederate Veterans and commanded the organization from 1904 until his death at Vicksburg on May 28, 1908. He is buried in Columbus.

Lewis, Andrew J.

Lewis was exchanged after his capture at Port Hudson and assumed command of a company in the 24th Mississippi Cavalry Battalion. He surrendered with his unit at Gainesville, Alabama, in May 1865. Lewis returned to his home at Edwards, Mississippi, where he was a merchant and farmer. He died on February 16, 1918, and is buried in the Edwards Cemetery.

Lindsey, Toliver

Lindsey served with the 6th Mississippi until he was wounded on July 17, 1864. He died at the Griffin, Georgia, Army Hospital on August 7, 1864.

Little, Lewis Henry

Little was killed on September 19, 1862, at the Battle of Iuka.

Love, John B.

Love was living in Attala County in 1870. The authors found no information about Love after that date.

Lovell, Mansfield

Lovell was relieved of command after his poor performance during the Battle of Corinth and held no other important post in the Confederate army. Lovell returned to New York City after the war and worked as a civil engineer. He died on June 1, 1884, and is buried in Woodlawn Cemetery, New York City.

Lowe, John C.

John Lowe was discharged from the army after losing his arm in the Battle of Antietam. The authors found no information about Lowe's activities after the war.

Lowe, William D.

William D. Lowe died of dysentery in a Richmond hospital on December 7, 1862.

Lowrey, Mark P.

Lowrey fought with the Army of Tennessee until he resigned his commission on March 14, 1865. In 1873 he founded the Blue Mountain Female Institute at Blue Mountain, Mississippi. Lowrey was president of the institute when he died unexpectedly at Middleton, Tennessee, on February 27, 1885. General Lowrey is buried at Blue Mountain.

Lyles, William D.

The authors found no additional information about Lyles.

McCay, Robert C.

McCay was killed at the Battle of Harrisburg, Mississippi, on July 14, 1863.

McClernand, John Alexander

McClernand continued to use his influence to push his own ambitions. His political interference led to conflict with Grant, who relieved him of command on June 19, 1863. McClernand briefly commanded a corps in Louisiana, prior to his resignation on November 30, 1864. He returned to Springfield, Illinois, and remained active in the Democratic party until his death on September 20, 1890. He is buried in Springfield.

McCollom, Albert O.

McCollom was exchanged after being captured at Hatchie Bridge. He rejoined his command and was captured a second time during the Vicksburg Campaign. McCollom was eventually transferred to the military prison in Little Rock, where he died on November 27, 1864. He is buried on the prison grounds in grave number 152.

McGuire, Thomas Richard

McGuire was captured early in 1865 while on furlough. He escaped on his way to the Alton, Illinois, prison and was captured again at the Battle of Selma, Alabama. McGuire returned to his farm in Bolivar County after the war and moved to Rosedale in 1877. The next year he was elected chancery clerk and held that office until at least 1896. He also served as postmaster from 1878 until 1891. McGuire died in 1903 and is buried in the Beulah Cemetery in Bolivar County.

McKie, Thomas Fondren

McKie was mortally wounded at Gettysburg. He died in a Federal hospital on October 16, 1863.

McMurtrie, Abner

McMurtrie was wounded on July 12, 1863, during the siege of Jackson. He died aboard the hospital ship *Nashville* on July 25, 1863.

McNair, Robert

McNair died on April 7, 1862, during the Battle of Shiloh.

McNulty, Samuel

McNulty was exchanged after his capture at Stones River and rejoined his command. McNulty fought in the Atlanta Campaign and was wounded. After the war McNulty returned to Mississippi and lived in Amite County in 1870. The authors found no other record of McNulty's postwar activities. It is likely that he was living in Louisiana at the time of his death, December 11, 1910.

McPherson, James B.

On March 26, 1864, McPherson assumed command of the Army of the Tennessee and led that command in the Atlanta Campaign. He was killed in action in front of Atlanta on July 22, 1864.

Malone, James D.

Malone does not appear in the 1870 Mississippi Census, and he may not have returned to the state after the war.

Martin, James J.

James Martin was sent to Johnson's Island, Ohio, after his capture at Big Black River Bridge; he was not exchanged for eighteen months. Martin did not return to the army, but joined his family, which had fled to Texas. He returned to his home near Little Rock, Arkansas, after the war and farmed there until his death on February 18, 1910.

Martin, Lyman

Lyman Martin was transferred to the Invalid Corps in November 1863 because of several wounds that he had previously received. He was discharged on August 1864 and was approved for a pension on June 17, 1865. The authors found no more information on Martin except that his wife was living in California and drawing a widow's pension as late as 1930.

Martin, William Thompson

William T. Martin was commissioned brigadier general on December 2, 1862, and transferred to the Western Theater. On November 10, 1863,

Martin was promoted to major general and commanded a cavalry division for the remainder of the war. He was later active in the Democratic party and served as trustee for both the University of Mississippi and Jefferson College. Martin also helped complete the construction of the Natchez, Jackson, & Columbus Railroad and served as the company's president. He died on March 16, 1910, and is buried in the Natchez City Cemetery.

Mathews, Joseph William

Mathews was exchanged after his surrender at Vicksburg and then served on the staff of Brig. Gen. Alexander Reynolds. He surrendered on May 8, 1865, at Athens, Georgia, and was immediately paroled. The authors found no information on Mathews' activities after the war.

Maury, Dabney

Maury was appointed major general to rank from November 4, 1862. In May 1863, he assumed command of the Department of the Gulf, which included the defense at Mobile. Maury skillfully protected the city until the closing months of the war. The war left Maury penniless, and he taught school for a few years before finally settling in Richmond, Virginia. Between 1885 and 1889 he served as U.S. Minister to Colombia. Maury played an important role in creating an interest in Southern history when, in 1868, he helped found the Southern Historical Society. Maury served as chairman of the Executive Committee of the society until 1886; he also contributed articles on the Civil War to dozens of different journals. In 1894 Maury published *Recollections of a Virginian in the Mexican, Indian, and Civil Wars,* which recounted his military service. Maury died at his son's home in Peoria, Illinois, on January 11, 1900.

Meriwether, Minor

Meriwether was transferred to Florida after the fall of Vicksburg. He surrendered at Meridian, Mississippi, in May 1865 and returned to his home in Memphis. He continued to work as an engineer for several years and then began practicing law. Meriwether later moved to St. Louis, where he practiced law and helped establish the Confederate Relief and Historical Association. He died in St. Louis in 1910.

Miller, Jacob

Miller mustered out of the service on November 24, 1865, and eventually began farming in Nebraska. After Miller's first wife died, he married Lovina M. Harrington on June 28, 1874. His second wife had lost her husband at the Battle of Chancellorsville. Sometime in the mid-1890s they moved to Texas and purchased 210 acres of farmland near Houston. On July 21, 1899, Miller suffered a massive stroke and died two days later. He was sixty-four years old. His wife died in Iowa on June 15, 1910.

Mitchell, Joseph Henry

Mitchell hauled logs in Arkansas and Texas after the war. When his third wife died in 1887, he moved to Tipton County, Tennessee, and began farming. He died at the age of sixty-five on August 6, 1904, and is buried in Milan, Gibson County, Tennessee.

Montgomery, Frank A.

Montgomery and most of his regiment were captured at Selma, Alabama, on April 2, 1865. Montgomery tried farming after the war, but his efforts failed, and he began practicing law. He also helped organize the Ku Klux Klan in Bolivar County and served in the Mississippi General Assembly from 1880 until 1886. In 1893 Montgomery moved to Coahoma County, where in 1895 he was again elected to the Mississippi House. At the close of the session he was appointed circuit judge of the 4th District. In 1901 Montgomery published *Reminiscences of a Mississippian in Peace and War.* He died on December 17, 1903, and is buried in the Beulah Cemetery in Bolivar County.

Moore, John R.

John Moore recovered from his illness and rejoined the army. He served until severely wounded in an engagement at Hernando, Mississippi. After the war he returned to Marshall County and resumed farming. Moore died on May 29, 1927, and is buried in the Wesley Chapel Cemetery in Marshall County.

Moore, Robert A.

Robert Moore later fought in the Chancellorsville and Gettysburg campaigns. He was killed September 20, 1863, at the Battle of Chickamauga.

Morgan, George W.

Morgan resigned from the army when the Union decided to employ black troops in the war. He supported George B. McClellan in the 1864 presidential election and was defeated the next year for the Ohio governorship. Morgan was then elected to the U.S. Congress and began serving his term on March 4, 1867. However, the election was contested, and he was unseated on June 3, 1868. Morgan was re-elected and served from March 4, 1869, until March 3, 1873. He was defeated for another term and returned to his law practice. Morgan died at Fort Monroe, Virginia, on July 26, 1893. He is buried in Mound View Cemetery in Mount Vernon, Ohio.

Mudge, Elliott

Mudge surrendered at Gainesville, Alabama, on May 12, 1865. The authors found no other record of Mudge's activities.

Murray, John T.

Murray mustered out of the service on March 20, 1866. He first lived in Kansas, where he married his first wife on September 29, 1871. She died shortly afterward, and Murray married again on March 11, 1873. The couple settled in Wilson County, Kansas, where Murray farmed until his death on September 25, 1884.

Nesmith, Cornelius Robinson

Nesmith was furloughed after being wounded at Weldon Railroad. While on leave he married Martha Rosina Trevilion. He returned to his unit sometime after March 15, 1865, and was likely captured in the assault on Fort Gregg on April 2, 1865. Nesmith returned to Claiborne County after the war and farmed in Martin Township. He died on November 10, 1917; his wife had died on July 22, 1917. They are buried in the Trevilion family cemetery in Claiborne County, Mississippi.

Nugent, William L.

Nugent survived the Civil War and became a successful attorney in Jackson, Mississippi. He died in January 1897.

Obert, Lewis

Obert returned to Iowa after the war and married Eliza Green in September 1867. They had six children. The family farmed in Iowa (1865–1875) and Minnesota (1875–1893). Obert and his wife then moved to Umatilla County, Oregon, where he died on May 5, 1925. His wife died two years later on May 25, 1927, in Reubens, Ohio.

Oglesby, Richard J.

Oglesby's wound was so severe that he did not return to active duty until April 1863. One month earlier he had been promoted to major general. Oglesby resigned from the army on May 26, 1864, and re-entered Illinois politics. He was elected governor in 1865 and U.S. Senator in 1873. Oglesby refused to run for a second term to the Senate, but served as governor from 1885 until 1889. He retired from politics after failing in a bid to return to the Senate in 1891. Oglesby settled on his farm, "Oglehurst," near Elkhart, Illinois, and died there on April 24, 1899. He is buried in the city cemetery.

O'Neil, James

No record of O'Neil could be found after his capture at Port Hudson, Louisiana, on July 8, 1863.

Ord, E. O. C.

Ord was severely wounded at Hatchie Bridge on October 5, 1862. He returned to duty near the end of the Vicksburg Campaign and later served in Louisiana and Virginia. Ord was seriously wounded again in September 1864 and was absent until January 1865. He commanded several military districts in the South after the war and retired from the army in 1881 as a major general. He was stricken with yellow fever on a trip to Vera Cruz, Mexico, and died in Havana on July 22, 1883. He is buried in Arlington National Cemetery.

Parker, James P.

Parker was sent to Johnson's Island, Ohio, after surrendering at Port Hudson, Louisiana, on July 8, 1863. The authors found no information on Parker after he was captured.

Parks, William F.

On August 1, 1862, Parks was discharged from the service because he was forty-four years old. He returned to Marshall County, where he died on July 16, 1901. He is buried in the Red Banks Cemetery.

Patton, William S., Jr.

Patton died at Malvern Hill on July 1, 1862.

Peel, Eli

Peel recovered from his wounds and rejoined the 11th Mississippi Infantry. He was killed at Gettysburg on July 3, 1863.

Pemberton, John C.

After the fall of Vicksburg, Pemberton was viewed with suspicion by many Southerners, some of who believed that his Northern roots led him to betray the garrison. In 1864 Pemberton resigned his commission as a lieutenant general; shortly afterward, he was recommissioned as a lieutenant colonel of artillery and served in the defense of Richmond. Pemberton lived on a farm near Warrenton, Virginia, after the war and later moved back to his home state of Pennsylvania. He died at Penllyn, Pennsylvania, on July 13, 1881, and is buried in Philadelphia.

Pettus, John

Pettus did not run for a second term as governor, but he did serve as a colonel in the state militia until the war ended. He moved to Arkansas and died there on January 25, 1867.

Posey, Carnot

Posey was slightly wounded in the leg at Bristoe Station on October 14, 1863. The injury became infected, and Posey died at Charlottesville, Virginia, on November 13, 1863. He is buried on the campus of the University of Virginia.

Pou, John Frank

Pou does not appear in the 1870 Mississippi Census, and the authors could find no information about his later life.

Price, Sterling

Price commanded the two divisions that bore the brunt of the fighting at Corinth. He was later transferred to the Trans-Mississippi District, where he fought at the Battle of Helena and in Frederick Steele's 1864 Camden Expedition. In September and October 1864, Price led an unsuccessful cavalry raid into Missouri. He fled to Mexico after the Civil War, but returned to Missouri in 1866. Price died in St. Louis on September 29, 1867, and is buried in Bellefontaine Cemetery.

Prince, William Mills

After the war Prince returned to his wife and his farm in Prentiss County, Mississippi. He died of a heart ailment on July 13, 1872, and is buried in the family cemetery on his farm.

Quitman, John A.

Quitman died in Natchez, Mississippi, on July 17, 1858.

Reynolds, Arthur E.

Reynolds and the 26th Mississippi Regiment were transferred to the Army of Northern Virginia in 1864. They fought at the Wilderness, Spotsylvania Courthouse, Cold Harbor, and Petersburg. After the war Reynolds resumed his law practice in Jacinto; he was elected to the U.S. Congress but did not take his seat because of the Radicals' position that Mississippi was not yet back in the Union. In 1868 he moved to Corinth and practiced law until his death in 1882.

Rietti, John C.

Rietti died on August 29, 1894.

Robinson, Marion

The authors found no information on Robinson's activities after the war.

Rosecrans, William Starke

After the Battle of Corinth, Rosecrans was promoted to major general and given command of the Army of the Cumberland. Rosecrans defeated Gen. Braxton Bragg at Stones River (December 31, 1862 to January 2, 1863), but was later defeated by Bragg at Chickamauga (September 19–20, 1863). Grant's dissatisfaction with Rosecrans' performance led to his removal

on October 19, 1863. Rosecrans remained in the army until March 28, 1867. The next year President Johnson appointed him minister to Mexico, but he was subsequently removed when Grant became president. Rosecrans moved to California and served in Congress from 1881 until 1885. He died on his ranch on March 11, 1898, and is buried in Arlington National Cemetery.

Rye, John C.

Rye was exchanged after surrendering at Vicksburg and served the remainder of the war in Arkansas. He returned to his home in Pope County, Arkansas, and in 1869, he married Nannie Dunbar of Kentucky. Rye died in Fort Smith, Arkansas, on December 19, 1907.

Seawell, W. B.

Seawell was imprisoned after surrendering at Port Hudson on July 8, 1863, and was not released until the war ended. He was living in Mobile in 1870, and apparently moved to New Orleans at a later date. He died there on February 27, 1897.

Sherman, William T.

Sherman assumed control of the Military Division of the Mississippi on March 18, 1864; his command contained most of the troops in the Western Theater. Sherman captured Atlanta, Georgia, in the fall of 1864 and then began his "March to the Sea," which ended with the capture of Savannah on December 21, 1864. He then led his armies into the Carolinas and accepted Gen. Joseph Johnston's surrender on April 26, 1865. Sherman was promoted to lieutenant general in 1866; three years later he became a full general and commander-in-chief of the U.S. Army. Sherman retired on February 8, 1884. In 1886 he moved to New York City and lived there until his death on February 14, 1891. He is buried in Calvary Cemetery, St. Louis.

Selfridge, Thomas O., Jr.

Selfridge served on the Red River Expedition and later commanded a vessel in the attacks on Fort Fisher, North Carolina. He remained in the navy after the war and retired as a rear admiral in 1898. Selfridge's autobiography, *Memoirs of Thomas O. Selfridge, Jr., Rear Admiral,* appeared in 1924. He died in Washington, D.C., on February 4, 1924.

Shaffer, John J.

Shaffer was exchanged after his capture at Vicksburg and served with the 26th Louisiana in his home state until the war ended. He then returned to his plantation near Thibodaux, Louisiana. Shaffer became an active member of the Braxton Bragg United Confederate Veteran Camp No. 196 and was president of the organization at the time of his death on September 24, 1918.

Shuler, James

James Shuler was living in Attala County in 1870. The authors could find no record of his activities after that date.

Shuler, Thomas

Shuler was killed at the Battle of Mill Springs, Kentucky, on January 19, 1862.

Smack, Findley

Smack rejoined his regiment after being wounded at Champion's Hill. On January 5, 1864, he transferred to the 5th Iowa Cavalry. The authors found no information on Smack's activities after the war.

Smith, Alfred Cox

Alfred Smith was shot to death in a personal dispute in May 1869.

Smith, Andrew Jackson

Andrew Smith later fought at Nashville and Mobile. After the war he became colonel of the 7th U.S. Cavalry, but he resigned his commission in 1869 to accept the postmaster's position at St. Louis. Smith served as city auditor from 1877 until 1889. He died in St. Louis on January 30, 1897, and is buried in Bellefontaine Cemetery.

Smith, Ashbel

Smith was paroled after surrendering at Vicksburg. He later commanded the Confederate forces on Matagorda (Texas) Peninsula and Galveston Island. Smith returned to his home near Galveston, Texas, when the war ended. He later served as president of the Board of Trustees of the Texas Medical College and helped to organize both Prairie View University and the University of Texas. He died at his home, Evergreen Plantation, on Galveston Bay on January 11, 1886. Smith is buried in the state cemetery at Austin, Texas.

Smith, Martin Luther

Martin Luther Smith was paroled after surrendering at Vicksburg. He later served as chief engineer for both the Army of Northern Virginia and the Army of Tennessee. Smith died in Savannah on July 29, 1866, at the age of forty-seven. He is buried in Athens, Georgia.

Smith, Robert A.

Robert Smith died in the assault at Munfordville, Kentucky, on September 14, 1862.

Smith, Thomas Kilby

Thomas K. Smith was promoted to brigadier general on August 11, 1863, and later served in the Red River Expedition. Ill health forced Smith to resign from the army in January 1865, but he was nevertheless breveted major general of volunteers on March 13, 1865. In 1866 Smith was appointed consul to Panama, but he returned to his home in Pennsylvania after only brief service. In 1887 he moved to New York, where he died on December 14. Smith is buried in Torresdale, Pennsylvania.

Smith, William P.

William P. Smith resigned from the 21st Mississippi Infantry because of a disability on August 1, 1862. The authors could find no other information on Smith's activities during or after the Civil War.

Smith, William Sooy

William Sooy Smith resigned from the army on July 15, 1864, and settled near Oak Park, Illinois. Smith, who was a professional engineer, went on to help develop many of the techniques that were used to construct steel bridges and skyscrapers. He died in Medford, Oregon, on March 4, 1916, and is buried in the Forest Home Cemetery in Riverside, Illinois.

Snow, George

Snow was killed at Champion's Hill on May 16, 1863.

Snyder, Napoleon

Snyder farmed in Illinois after the war. In March 1915 he wrote that he and his second wife had married in 1852 and "are living yet but getting old."[4] The next year, on November 14, 1916, Snyder, who was then eighty-six years old, moved into the Danville, Illinois, National Home for Disabled Volunteer Soldiers. His wife had apparently died shortly before then. Snyder remained in the home until his death on December 15, 1918.

Soule, Harrison

Soule mustered out of the service on September 5, 1865, at Jackson, Michigan. He lived in various towns in the state until 1883 when he settled in Ann Arbor. There he was treasurer for the University of Michigan for twenty-five years. When he died on January 2, 1922, the university flew the flag at half-mast in honor of his years of service. His wife, in a personal note to a friend, wrote that until Soule's death they had never been separated in sixty-seven years of marriage except for the Civil War.

Spell, John

John Spell surrendered with the 8th Mississippi Infantry in North Carolina and returned to Smith County, Mississippi. He lived in Sullivan's Hollow near Mize until his death in January 1913. Spell is buried in the Zion Hill Baptist Church Cemetery.

Spell, William

William Spell returned to Mississippi after the war and eventually settled in Covington County, where he farmed 455 acres of land. He died in December 1905.

Spinks, William L.

Spinks was killed on August 25, 1864, during the Siege of Atlanta.

Starke, Peter B.

Starke served under Forrest in Hood's 1864 Tennessee offensive, and he spent the last few months of the war fighting in Mississippi. After the war Starke served on the Mississippi Levee Commission Board from 1866 to 1872. He was also elected sheriff of Bolivar County for one term. Starke returned to Virginia in 1873 and settled in Brunswick County, near where he had been born. He died at Lawrenceville, Virginia, on July 13, 1888, and is buried in an unmarked grave on his second wife's family farm.

Starns, B. B.

Starns was captured with his battalion at Port Hudson, Louisiana, on July 8, 1863. He was sent to prison camp at Johnson's Island, Ohio, where he died of pneumonia on May 21, 1864. Starns is buried there.

Steede, Abner

After the war Steede returned to his home near Pascagoula, Mississippi. He died on October 17, 1901, and is buried in the family cemetery.

Steele, Joseph Theodore

Steele remained a prisoner of war after his capture at Gettysburg and was not released until June 11, 1865. He returned to Mississippi and farmed for a number of years near Olive Branch. Steele later moved to Sidney, Arkansas, where he continued to farm until his death on February 26, 1902.

Stewart, Benjamin

The authors found no additional information on Stewart.

Stockwell, Elisha, Jr.

Stockwell mustered out of the 14th Wisconsin on October 9, 1865. He lived in Alma, Wisconsin, until 1872, and then took up a homestead in Otter Tail County, Minnesota. He moved back to Wisconsin four years later and farmed near Black River Falls for the next thirty years. In 1906 Stockwell and his wife sold their land and moved to a new farm near Beach, North Dakota. He died on his farm on December 29, 1935, at the age of eighty-nine. Stockwell was the last survivor of his company and the next to last living member of the 14th Wisconsin Infantry.

Sturgis, Samuel G.

Sturgis mustered out of the volunteer army in August 1866 and accepted a lieutenant colonel's commission in the 6th U.S. Cavalry. He was promoted to colonel on May 6, 1869, and commanded the famous 7th Cavalry for several years. Sturgis retired from the army in 1886 and died in St. Paul, Minnesota, on September 28, 1889. He is buried in Arlington National Cemetery.

Swagerty, Lorenzo

Swagerty surrendered at Port Hudson on July 8, 1863, and was paroled at City Point, Virginia, on May 3, 1864, because he had chronic diarrhea. He served on detached duty in Arkansas until the end of the war. Swagerty lived in Clarksville, Arkansas, after the war, but the authors were unable to find the date of his death.

Swain, Andy

Swain served with the 5th Company of the Washington artillery at Missionary Ridge and in the Atlanta Campaign. When the fighting ended he was on detached duty as a steamboat pilot, the trade that he had followed before the Civil War. Swain returned to New Orleans and resumed his career. As late as 1899 he was still working on the river. Swain later moved to Rosedale, Louisiana, where he died on February 18, 1915. Sometime after the Civil War a member of the 5th Company bought the piano that Swain played at the siege of Jackson and later donated it to the Confederate Memorial Hall in New Orleans, where it remains to this day.

Swift, Halmer

Swift was discharged from the army in San Antonio, Texas, on February 12, 1866. After the war he farmed in Illinois, Missouri, and Michigan. Swift never married; he died in Michigan on May 12, 1912.

Taylor, Joseph

Taylor returned to Mississippi after he was discharged from the army. He married in 1870, but

Tilghman, Lloyd

Tilghman died at Champion's Hill on May 16, 1863. He is buried in Woodlawn Cemetery in New York City.

Trescott, Austin Augustus

When the 21st Mississippi surrendered, Trescott wrapped the regiment's colors around his waist and took the flag back to Vicksburg. Trescott was a small businessman in Vicksburg, and he died there on March 19, 1929.

Trimble, John T.

The authors found no information on John Trimble's life after the Civil War.

Trimble, William A.

The authors found no information on William Trimble's life after the Civil War.

Tucker, William F.

Tucker did not recover from the wound that he received at Resaca, Georgia, until near the end of the war. He returned to duty in the spring of 1865 and commanded the District of Southern Mississippi and East Louisiana. Tucker later resumed his law practice in Chickasaw County, Mississippi, and served two terms in the state legislature. On September 14, 1881, Tucker was assassinated at Okolona, Mississippi. The perpetrators were allegedly hired by a client against whom Tucker had filed suit. He is buried in Okolona.

Tunnard, William H.

Tunnard returned to Baton Rouge after the war and resumed his career as a journalist. In 1866 he published *A Southern Record*, which was one of the first regimental histories written about a Southern unit. In 1883 Tunnard moved to Shreveport, where for eighteen years he was editor of the *Shreveport Times*. Tunnard later edited the *Southern Journal* at Winnfield. Near the end of his life he wrote a friend, remarking that "I have been reviewing my memories of the war by reading my history. It seems the record of some early dream, yet its realities are, oh, so vivid."[5] Tunnard died on August 3, 1916.

Tuttle, James M.

Tuttle resigned from the army on June 14, 1864, and returned to Iowa. He owned several businesses and served in the state legislature. Tuttle, who had mining interests in the Southwest, died on October 24, 1892, while visiting one of his operations in Casa Grande, Arizona. He is buried in Des Moines in Woodlawn Cemetery.

Van Dorn, Earl

On May 7, 1863, Dr. George Peters killed Van Dorn, alleging that the general had been romantically involved with his wife. Van Dorn is buried in Port Gibson, Mississippi.

Vaughan, Alfred Jefferson

Vaughan returned to his farm in Mississippi after losing his leg at Vining Station, Georgia. In 1872 Vaughan moved to Memphis, where he became active in the United Confederate Veterans. At the time of his death on October 1, 1899, he was commander of the Tennessee Division of the U.C.V. Vaughan is buried in Memphis.

Wade, William

Wade was killed by a naval shell at Grand Gulf, Mississippi, on April 29, 1863.

Waldock, John

Waldock mustered out of the service on June 16, 1864, and returned to Illinois. The authors found no information about his activities after the war.

Walker, Joseph

The authors found no information on Walker's activities after the war.

Walthall, Edward C.

Walthall was promoted to major general on July 6, 1864, and led a division in the Army of Tennessee until it surrendered in North Carolina. Walthall returned to Mississippi where he practiced law and was instrumental in overthrowing the Republican rule in the state. He served in the U.S. Senate from 1885 until January 24, 1894, when he resigned because of ill health. Walthall recovered from his illness and was re-elected to the Senate on March 4, 1895. He served until his death in Washington, D.C., on April 21, 1898. Walthall is buried in Holly Springs, Mississippi.

Ward, Robert F.

Ward was wounded in the jaw during the Siege of Petersburg. After recuperating, he transferred to the cavalry and was serving in Mississippi with Henderson's Scouts when the war ended. Ward returned to his home in Tate County and served several years as circuit court clerk. He later moved to Marion, Arkansas, where he held the position of deputy clerk. Sometime after 1899 Ward moved to Jonesboro, Arkansas, where he owned a grocery store. In July 1915, Ward, who was seventy-four years old, applied for a pension, but it was never granted. The authors were unable to find the date of Ward's death, but it is likely that he died between 1920 and 1923.

Wells, Samuel H.

Wells was exchanged after his capture at Vicksburg and returned to his regiment. He lived in Bull Gap, Tennessee, after the war and died in 1900.

Whitaker, Isaac

Whitaker was paroled after being captured at Port Hudson, Louisiana. He returned to Mississippi and became captain of a company of guerrillas known as Whitaker's Scouts. Whitaker operated in the vicinity of Vicksburg and harassed the Federal garrison until the war ended. Whitaker eventually settled near Utica, Mississippi, and farmed there for many years. He died in 1909 and is buried in the Rittenhouse-Nutt family cemetery near Utica.

White, Joseph C.

White served with the Army of Northern Virginia until he was captured at Chester Station, Virginia, on April 3, 1865. He was released under oath on June 14, 1865, and returned to Mississippi. White apparently lived in Fellowship Community in Tippah County after the war. However, the authors were unable to verify that fact or locate the correct date of death for Joseph White.

Whiting, William Henry Chase

Whiting was transferred to North Carolina after the Peninsular Campaign and promoted to major general on April 22, 1863. Except for brief service in Virginia, he spent the remainder of his military career in North Carolina. Near the end of the war Whiting was severely wounded and taken prisoner. He died in New York on March 10, 1865, and is buried in Oakdale Cemetery in Wilmington, North Carolina.

Wilds, John Q.

Wilds succeeded to the command of the 24th Iowa on June 30, 1863, and was promoted to colonel on June 8, 1864. Colonel Wilds led the regiment until October 19, 1864, when he was mortally wounded during the Battle of Cedar Creek, Virginia. He died on November 8, 1864.

Williams, John LeRoy

Williams died fighting in the Muleshoe at Spotsylvania Courthouse, on May 12, 1864.

Wilson, David B.

On February 4, 1864, David Wilson married Jessie C. Fetter of Iowa. After the war he returned to Iowa and settled in Fairfield, where he practiced law and served as a justice of the peace for thirty years. In 1895 Wilson, who had been a widower since 1874, moved in with his only daughter. He lived there until his death on June 8, 1929, at the age of ninety.

Wilson, George H.

George Wilson mustered out of the service after the war and returned to his wife, Sarah, whom he had married in 1860. He lived in Illinois and worked as a laborer until the mid-1870s, when he moved to Nebraska and probably began farming. In 1890 Wilson began receiving an invalid pension because of chronic diarrhea that he had contracted during the Vicksburg Campaign. He and his wife eventually moved to Sheridan, Wyoming, where on June 27, 1903, Wilson died of cirrhosis and chronic peritonitis. His wife continued to draw a widow's pension until her death at Sheridan in May 1920. The couple had four children.

Wilson, John Frederick

Wilson settled in St. Helena Parish, Louisiana, after the war and raised cotton. In 1871 he moved back to Amite County, Mississippi, where he continued to farm. He and his wife had six children. He died at Liberty, Mississippi, on August 7, 1924; he is buried in the Amite River Cemetery.

Wolcott, Laurens

Wolcott was discharged from the service on July 6, 1865, and returned to Illinois. In 1869 he settled in Grand Rapids, Michigan, and began practicing law. Four years later he married Lucy Gallup, and they had two daughters. Wolcott continued to practice law until he died of heart failure on March 29, 1909. He was sixty-six years old.

Wolfe, Edward H.

Wolfe returned to Indiana after the war. He and his wife, Permelia Lindsay, whom he had married in 1860, had four children. Permelia died on December 19, 1897; Edward died at Rushville, Indiana, on August 17, 1916.

Work, George

Work mustered out of the 5th Iowa Infantry on October 11, 1865, and accepted a commission in the 60th Regiment, United States Colored Troops. He was discharged from the service on October 15, 1865 as a captain of Co. E. Work farmed in Iowa, Arkansas, and Nebraska after the war. He was granted a pension in 1874, because of the gunshot wound he had received at Iuka. The projectile had shattered the right side of his jaw. Work died in Chadron, Nebraska, on December 4, 1937.

Yates, L.

Yates was captured with the 18th Arkansas on July 8, 1863, at Port Hudson. The unit was paroled and eventually reorganized in Arkansas as mounted infantry. It is uncertain if Yates ever again served with the 18th Arkansas, but he apparently did live in the state after the war. The authors located no more information about Yates.

Notes

Chapter 1

1. Jackson *Weekly Mississippian,* 25 July 1860.

2. Material on photographers derived from the 1860 manuscript census.

3. Jackson *Weekly Mississippian,* 18 July 1860.

4. *Ibid.,* 19 September 1860.

5. Based on material in G. F. Witham, comp., *Catalogue of Civil War Photographers* (Portland, Or.: G. F. Witham, 1988).

6. *Harper's Weekly,* 12 July 1861, 395.

7. Vicksburg *Daily Herald,* 16 June 1864 (quote), 22 November 1864; Vicksburg *Weekly Citizen,* 3 June 1864.

8. Vicksburg *Daily Herald,* 1 June 1864 (quote), 3 January 1865.

9. Vicksburg *Weekly Citizen,* 3 June 1864 (quote); Vicksburg *Daily Herald,* 4 January 1865.

10. James B. Lloyd, *The University of Mississippi: The Formative Years, 1848–1906* (Oxford: John Davis Williams Library, Department of Archives and Special Collections, 1979).

Chapter 2

1. James W. Silver, ed., *A Life for the Confederacy, As Recorded in Pocket Diaries of Pvt. Robert A. Moore. Co. G, 17th Mississippi Regiment* (Jackson, Tenn.: McCowat-Mercer Press, 1959), 6; Garrett and McCaleb quoted in John Bettersworth, ed., *Mississippi in the Confederacy: As They Saw It* (Baton Rouge: Louisiana State University Press, 1961), I, 48, 49.

2. James W. Silver, ed., *The Confederate Soldier* (Memphis: Memphis State University Press, 1973), 30.

3. Garrett quoted in Bettersworth, *Mississippi in the Confederacy,* I, 48.

4. quote from Dunbar Rowland, *Military History of Mississippi, 1803–1898* (Spartanburg, S.C.: The Reprint Company, Publishers, 1988), 39.

5. Silver, *The Confederate Soldier,* 37; William F. Fox, *Regimental Losses in the American Civil War, 1861–1865* (Albany, N.Y.: Albany Publishing Co., 1893), 554.

6. quote from Rowland, *Military History of Mississippi,* 44; Fox, *Regimental Losses in the American Civil War,* 554, 556–57.

7. Russell quoted in Bettersworth, *Mississippi in the Confederacy,* I, 53.

8. 34th Cong., 2nd Sess., *Appendix to the Congressional Globe*, 118.

9. Jefferson Davis to "Our Constituents," 14 December 1860, in Lynda Lasswell Crist, ed., *The Papers of Jefferson Davis* (Baton Rouge: Louisiana State University Press, 1989), VI, 377.

10. quote from Allan Nevins, *The Emergence of Lincoln: Prologue to Civil War, 1859–1861* (New York: Charles Scribner's Sons, 1950), 425.

11. *Mississippi Senate Journal* (1860): 12.

12. quote from Bettersworth, *Mississippi in the Confederacy*, I, 43–44.

13. *Ibid.*, 26.

14. *Ibid.*, 27–28.

15. *Proceedings of the Mississippi State Convention* (Jackson: Power and Cadwalader, 1861), 13.

16. *Ibid.*, 90.

17. Lamar Fontaine, *My Life and My Lectures* (New York: The Neale Publishing Company, 1908), 65.

18. Silver, *A Life for the Confederacy*, 28.

19. Vicksburg *Weekly Citizen*, 21 April 1861.

20. William Howard Russell, *My Diary North and South* (Boston: T. O. H. P. Burnham, 1863), 213.

21. James G. Bullard to My Dear Ann, 10 April 1861, manuscript in family possession.

22. *Ibid.*

23. Natchez *Daily Courier*, 18 May 1861.

24. Braxton Bragg to Governor Moore, 2 August 1861, in G. P. Whittington, ed., "Papers of Thomas O. Moore, Governor of Louisiana, 1860–64," *Louisiana Historical Quarterly*, XIII (January 1930): 25.

Chapter 3

1. William L. Huettel, ed., "Letters from Private Richard C. Bridges, C.S.A. 1861–1864," *Journal of Mississippi History*, XXXIII (November 1971), 358–61. (Hereafter cited as Huettel, "Letters from Private Richard C. Bridges.")

2. Charles E. Hooker, *Mississippi*, Vol. IX, *Confederate Military History: Extended Edition* (Wilmington: Broadfoot Publishing Co., 1987), 115.

3. U.S. War Department, *The War of the Rebellion: A Compilation of the Official Records of the Union and Confederate Armies*, 128 vols. (Washington: Government Printing Office, 1880–1901), Ser. I, Vol. XI, pt. 2, 751. (Hereafter cited as *O.R.*; all references unless otherwise noted are from Series I.)

4. *Ibid.*, 973–84.

5. Rowland, *Military History of Mississippi*, 124.

6. J. S. McNeilly, "Barksdale's Mississippi Brigade at Gettysburg," *Publications of the Mississippi Historical Society*, XIV (1914): 241.

7. Horace Porter, *Campaigning with Grant* (New York: The Century Co., 1897), 37.

8. Heuttel, "Letters from Private Richard C. Bridges," 371.

9. Silver, *A Life for the Confederacy*, 269–70.

10. *Ibid.*, 270.

11. *O.R.*, Vol. XI, pt. 1, 1045.

12. *Ibid.*, pt. 2, 616.

13. Letter from Frank R. Johnson to *The Woodville Republican*, 6 February 1985, Northeast Mississippi Museum Association.

14. *O.R.*, Vol. XI, pt. 2, 755.

15. Terry L. Jones, *Lee's Tigers* (Baton Rouge: Louisiana State University Press, 1987), 110, 235; William S. Patton, Jr., to Ma & Onie, 12 May 1862, photocopy in possession of J. B. Harvey, Marion, Mississippi.

16. *O.R.*, Vol. XII, pt. 2, 623.

17. J. Harvey Mathes, *The Old Guard in Grey* (Memphis: Press of S. C. Toof & Co., 1897), 73–74.

18. U.S. National Archives, "Compiled Service Records of Confederate Soldiers who Served in Organizations from Mississippi," 11th Mississippi Infantry, Taylor, Joseph L. (Hereafter cited as U.S. National Archives, "Compiled Service Records.")

19. *O.R.*, Vol. XIX, pt. 1, 858, 862.

20. U.S. National Archives, "Compiled Service Records," 13th Mississippi Infantry, Lowe, George W.

21. Maud Morrow Brown, *The University Greys* (Richmond: Garrett and Massie, 1940), 33.

22. Silver, *A Life for the Confederacy*, 332–34.

23. *O.R.*, Vol. XXV, pt. 1, 872.

24. *Ibid.*, 840.

25. McNeilly, "Barksdale's Mississippi Brigade," 236, 239, 241.

26. Lloyd, *The University of Mississippi*, 35; William A. Lowe, "Mississippi at Gettysburg," *Publications of the Mississippi Historical Society*, IX (1906): 43.

27. *Ibid.*, 46–47.

28. *Ibid.*, 46; *O.R.*, Vol. XXVII, pt. 2, 651.

29. Rowland, *Military History of Mississippi*, 105.

30. Bruce Catton, *A Stillness at Appomattox* (New York: Doubleday Co., 1953), 124.

31. *O.R.*, XXXVI, pt. 1, 1092.

32. U.S. National Archives, "Compiled Service Records," 12th Mississippi Infantry, Nesmith, Cornelius Robinson.

33. *Ibid.*, Bell, James B.

34. Hartman McIntosh, ed., "The Civil War Letters of John Alemeth Byers, 17th Mississippi Infantry," *Military Images*, IX (May–June 1988): 11.

35. J. S. McNeilly, "A Mississippi Brigade in the Last Days

of the Confederacy," *Publications of the Mississippi Historical Society*, VII (1903): 55.

Chapter 4

1. William Chambers, "My Journal," in *Publications of the Mississippi Historical Society*, Centenary Series, V (1925): 375–79.

2. Hooker, *Mississippi*, Vol. IX, 40.

3. *O.R.*, Vol. X, pt. 1, 382–84.

4. *Ibid.*, 581.

5. *The Confederate Soldier in the Civil War* (n.p.: Fairfax Press, n.d.), 376.

6. *O.R.*, Vol. XX, pt. 1, 658–60, 676–81.

7. *Ibid.*, Vol. XXX, pt. 2, 11–20.

8. *Ibid.*, 86, 243, 291, 319.

9. Longstreet's command, including Humphreys' Mississippians, failed to strangle Burnside's force and on 4 December 1863, the Confederates ended the siege. Longstreet's Corps remained in East Tennessee until March 1864 when the troops received orders to rejoin the Army of Northern Virginia.

10. Sherman actually had three separate armies under his command. At the beginning of the campaign, Maj. Gen. George Thomas commanded the Army of the Cumberland; Maj. Gen. James McPherson led the Army of Tennessee; and Maj. Gen. John M. Schofield headed the Army of the Ohio. Therefore Sherman technically had an Army Group under his control, but the term was not yet in popular use as a military organization.

11. Hooker, *Mississippi*, 214–16.

12. Weymouth T. Jordon, ed., "Mathew Andrew Dunn Letters," *Journal of Mississippi History*, I (January–October 1939): 126.

13. Chambers, "My Journal," 338.

14. Rowland, *Military History of Mississippi*, 367.

15. *Ibid.*

16. Chambers, "My Journal," 379–80.

17. Arthur W. Bergeron, Jr., and Lawrence L. Hewitt *Miles Legion: A History & Roster* (Baton Rouge: Elliott's Bookshop Press, 1983), vii, 79–84.

18. Dee Brown, *Bold Cavaliers* (Philadelphia: J. B. Lippincott Co., 1959), 68, 223–29.

19. *O.R.*, Vol. VII, 379–80.

20. *Ibid.*, 381.

21. H. Grady Howell, Jr., *Going to Meet the Yankees* (Jackson: Chickasaw Bayou Press, 1981), 79–87; The Confederate Soldier, 376.

22. *O.R.*, Vol. X, pt. 1, 603–4.

23. E. T. Sykes, "An Incident of the Battle of Munfordville, Ky., September 14th, 1862," *Publications of the Mississippi Historical Society*, Centenary Series, II (1918): 539.

24. *O.R.*, Vol. XX, pt. 1, 763, 767.

25. *Ibid.*, 764.

26. *Ibid.*, 906–7.

27. *Ibid.*, Vol. XXX, pt. 2, 366–67.

28. *Ibid.*, 509–10.

29. *Ibid.*, 325.

30. E. T. Sykes, "Walthall's Brigade," *Publications of the Mississippi Historical Society*, Centenary Series, I (1916): 537–42.

31. *O.R.*, Vol. XXXI, pt. 2, 757–58.

32. *Ibid.*, Vol. XXXVIII, pt. 3, 798.

33. *Ibid.*, 809; *Arkansas Gazette*, 30 August 1936.

34. Franklin A. Montgomery, *Reminiscences of a Mississippian in Peace and War* (Cincinnati: Robert Clarke Co., 1901), 4, 37, 172–74.

35. *O.R.*, Vol. XXXVIII, pt. 3, 726.

36. *Ibid.*, 883–84.

37. Rowland, *Military History of Mississippi*, 497.

38. R. W. Banks, *The Battle of Franklin* (Dayton: Morningside Bookshop, 1982), 60–66.

39. Samuel G. French, *Two Wars: An Autobiography of Gen. Samuel G. French* (Nashville: Confederate Veteran, 1901), 295.

40. *Ibid.*; *O.R.*, Vol. XLV, pt. 1, 716–19.

41. Richard M. McMurry, ed., "A Mississippian at Nashville," *Civil War Times Illustrated*, XII (May 1973): 14–15.

Chapter 5

1. Margaret Greene Rogers, *Civil War Corinth, 1861–1865* (Corinth: Rankin Printery, 1989), 2.

2. Richard Barksdale Harwell, ed., *Kate: The Journal of a Confederate Nurse* (Baton Rouge: Louisiana State University Press, 1959), 13–14.

3. On 11 July 1862, President Lincoln named Halleck General in Chief of the Federal armies, and he took up his new duties in Washington. Halleck's promotion left the Union armies in the west divided between major generals Ulysses S. Grant and Don Carlos Buell. This split command made cooperation difficult if not impossible to achieve.

4. Dabney H. Maury, "Campaigning against Grant in North Mississippi," *Southern Historical Society Papers*, XII (1885): 288.

5. Ord always claimed that he never heard the fighting, but Rosecrans continued to doubt his explanation. However, on more than one instance during the Civil War, an atmospheric phenomenon prevented soldiers from hearing gunfire that was only several thousand yards away. This

phenomenon, known as "acoustic shadow" apparently occurred because of unusual atmospheric pressure which inhibited the transmission of sound over relatively short distances. This condition may well have existed on 19 September 1862, and could account for Ord's inaction during the day.

6. Maury, "Campaigning against Grant," 290–91.

7. William S. Rosecrans, "The Battle of Corinth," in Robert U. Johnson and Clarence C. Buel, eds., *Battles and Leaders of the Civil War* (New York: Thomas Yoseloff, Inc., 1956), Vol. II, 744–55.

8. William W. Cluett, *History of the 57th Regiment Illinois Volunteer Infantry* (Princeton: T. P. Streeter, Printer, 1886), 40. (Hereafter cited as Cluett, *57th Illinois Volunteer Infantry*.)

9. *Ibid.*, 41–42; Maury, "Campaigning against Grant," 295.

10. Cluett, *57th Illinois Volunteer Infantry*, 42–43.

11. *Ibid.*, 44; Maury, "Campaigning against Grant," 296.

12. Byron R. Abernathy, ed., *Private Elisha Stockwell, Jr., Sees the Civil War* (Norman: University of Oklahoma Press, 1958), 200.

13. Harwell, *Kate*, 14.

14. *O.R.*, Vol. X, pt. 1, 667.

15. Thomas L. Snead, "With Price East of the Mississippi," *Battles and Leaders of the Civil War*, Vol. II, 719–20.

16. *O.R.*, Vol. XVII, pt. 1, 51; Thornton H. Bowman, *Reminiscences of an ex-Confederate Soldier* (Austin: Gammel-Statesman Pub. Co., 1904), 24.

17. *O.R.*, Vol. XVII, pt. 1, 66, 118.

18. Charles S. Hamilton, "The Battle of Iuka," *Battles and Leaders of the Civil War*, Vol. II, 735.

19. William H. Tunnard, *A Southern Record: The History of the Third Regiment, Louisiana Infantry* (Baton Rouge: n.p., 1866), 182–83.

20. William H. Tunnard Papers, L.L.M.V.C., LSU.

21. *O.R.*, Vol. XVII, pt. 1, 99.

22. Albert Casteel, ed., "The Diary of General Henry Little, C.S.A.," *Civil War Times Illustrated*, XI (October 1972): 43–46.

23. Lawrence T. Jones, *Confederate Calendar*, July 1981.

24. Rosecrans, "The Battle of Corinth," 740–43.

25. *Ibid.*, 740–41.

26. Abernathy, *Private Elisha Stockwell*, 43–49.

27. Maury, "Campaigning against Grant," 294.

28. Ezra Warner, *Generals in Blue* (Baton Rouge: Louisiana State University Press, 1981), 347.

29. *O.R.*, Vol. XVII, pt. 1, 278–79.

30. *Ibid.*, 401.

31. William Denson Evans letter to his brother, 4 September 1933, in the possession of Mary Johnson.

32. R. S. Bevier, *History of the First and Second Missouri Confederate Brigades* (St. Louis: Bryan, Brand, & Co., 1879), 153; U.S. National Archives, "Compiled Service Records," 3rd Missouri Infantry, Duval, William.

33. *Ibid.*, 3rd Arkansas Cavalry, Fullwood, William H.; Letter to the authors from Dr. Ronnie Fullwood; Maury, "Campaigning against Grant," 300.

34. Laurens W. Wolcott, "The Battle of Corinth," *War Papers Read before the Michigan Commandery of the Military Order of the Loyal Legion of the United States*, Vol. II, (Detroit: n.p., 1898?), 271–72.

35. *The Athens Messenger*, 23 October 1862.

36. Walter J. Lemke, ed., *The War-time Letters of Albert O. McCollom* (Fayetteville: Washington County Historical Society, 1961), letter no. 17.

37. *O.R.*, Vol. XVII, pt. 1, 406.

38. Lucius Barber, *Army Memoirs of Lucius W. Barber* (Chicago: J. M. W. Jones Stationery and Printing Co., 1894), 79–83.

Chapter 6

1. Peter F. Walker, *Vicksburg: A People at War, 1860–1865* (Wilmington: Broadfoot Publishing Company, 1987), 6–10.

2. Samuel Carter III, *The Final Fortress* (New York: St. Martin's Press, 1980), 21–22.

3. *O.R.*, Vol. XV, 7.

4. E. B. Long, ed., *Personal Memoirs of U.S. Grant* (Cleveland: The World Publishing Company, 1952), 237–39. (Hereafter cited as Long, *Memoirs*.)

5. Carter, *Final Fortress*, 19.

6. Walker, *Vicksburg*, 8–9.

7. *Ibid.*, 7–9, 13–16.

8. Harrison Soule, "From the Gulf to Vicksburg," *War Papers Read before the Michigan Commandery of the Military Order of the Loyal Legion of the United States*, Vol. II (1894), 64–66.

9. *O.R.*, Vol. XV, 6–8.

10. U.S. Navy Department, *Official Records of the Union and Confederate Navies in the War of the Rebellion*, 31 vols. (Washington: U.S. Government Printing Office, 1894–1922), Ser. I, Vol. XVIII, 588. (Hereafter cited as *Naval Records*; all references unless otherwise noted are from Series I.)

11. *Ibid.*, 789–90.

12. *Ibid.*, Vol. XXIII, 685–86.

13. Patricia L. Faust, ed., *Historical Times Illustrated Encyclopedia of the Civil War* (New York: Harper & Row, 1986), 320.

14. *Ibid.*, p. 569.

15. *O.R.*, Vol. XVII, pt. 1, 494–95.

16. J. G. Dupree, "The Capture of Holly Springs,

Mississippi, Dec. 20, 1862," *Publications of the Mississippi Historical Society,* IV (1901): 51–54.

17. *O.R.,* Vol. XVII, pt. 1, 512–13, 516.

18. Long, *Memoirs,* 222–23; *O.R.,* Vol. XVII, pt. 2, 420.

19. Thomas O. Selfridge, Jr., *Memoirs of Thomas O. Selfridge, Jr., Rear Admiral* (New York: G. P. Putnam, 1924), 74–75.

20. George W. Morgan, "The Assault on Chickasaw Bluffs," *Battles and Leaders of the Civil War,* Vol. II, 468.

21. Winchester Hall, *The Story of the 26th Louisiana Infantry* (Gaithersburg: Butternut Press, 1984), 42–49

22. A. R. Munn, et al., *Military History and Reminiscences of the Thirteenth Regiment of Illinois Volunteer Infantry . . .* (Chicago: Woman's Temperance Pub. Association, 1892), 243, 247–48.

23. *O.R.,* Vol. XVII, pt. 1, 625, 671, 697; John Cauthron, ed., "Letters of a North Louisiana Private to His Wife, 1862–1865," *Mississippi Valley Historical Review,* XXX (June 1943): 538.

24. *O.R.,* Vol. XXIV, pt. 1, 374–75.

25. *Ibid.,* 415.

26. Order of the Regimental Association, comp., *History of the Forty-Sixth Regiment Indiana Volunteer Infantry* (Longsport: Press of Wilson, Humphreys & Co., 1888), 48–50.

27. *Naval Records,* Vol. XXIV, 489.

Chapter 7

1. Long, *Memoirs,* 238.

2. *Ibid.,* 239–40.

3. On 22 April 1863, Porter ran five more transports by the Vicksburg batteries. The seven steamers that were now below Vicksburg ferried supplies from the Louisiana shore to Grand Gulf until Grant invested Vicksburg. However, this supply route was tenuous, and Grant had no safe line of communications until 18 May 1863, when he established a secure supply depot on the Yazoo River.

4. Long, *Memoirs,* 252.

5. *Ibid.,* 257–58.

6. *O.R.,* Vol. XXIV, pt. 3, 842–43.

7. *Ibid.,* 870.

8. *Ibid.,* 876–77.

9. Carter, *Final Fortress,* 209.

10. George C. Osborn, ed., "A Tennessean at the Siege of Vicksburg: The Diary of Samuel Alexander Ramsey Swan (May–July, 1863)," *Tennessee Historical Quarterly,* XIV (March 1955): 357. (Hereafter cited as Osborn, "Diary.")

11. Paul H. Hass, ed., "The Vicksburg Diary of Henry Clay Warmoth: Part II (April 28, 1863–May 26, 1863)," *Journal of Mississippi History,* XXXII (February 1970): 72.

12. Stephen D. Lee, "The Siege of Vicksburg," *Publications of the Mississippi Historical Society,* III (1900): 60.

13. Osborn, "Diary," 364.

14. Lida Lord Reed, "A Woman's Experiences during the Siege of Vicksburg," *The Century Magazine,* LXI (April 1901): 923, 926.

15. Hosea Whitford Rood, *Story of the Service of Company E, and of the Twelfth Wisconsin Regiment, Veteran Volunteer Infantry* (Milwaukee: Swain & Tate Co., 1893), 192. (Hereafter cited as Rood, *Twelfth Wisconsin Regiment.*)

16. Richard Lewis to Dear Cousin Lizzie, Vicksburg, Miss., 5 July 1863, original in the possession of Roger Davis.

17. J. T. Woods, *Services of the Ninety-sixth Ohio Volunteers* (Toledo: Blade Printing, 1874), 27–28.

18. *O.R.,* Vol. XXIV, pt. 1, 527–29, 539.

19. *Ibid.,* 627.

20. *Ibid.,* 675–78.

21. Simeon Barnett, *History of the Twenty-second Regiment Iowa Volunteer Infantry* (Iowa City: N. H. Brainerd Publisher, 1865), 4, 27.

22. *O.R.,* Vol. XXIV, pt. 1, 679–82.

23. *O.R.,* Vol. XXIV, pt. 1, 736–39.

24. Mary Ann Andersen, ed., *The Civil War Diary of Allen Morgan Geer* (New York: Cosmos Press, 1977), 99.

25. Long, *Memoirs,* p. 262.

26. Edwin C. Bearss and Warren Grabau, *The Battle of Jackson* (Baltimore: Gateway Press, Inc., 1981), 23–24.

27. *O.R.,* Vol. XXIV, pt. 2, 8.

28. *Ibid.,* 98.

29. *Ibid.,* 55; Charles L. Longley, "Champion's Hill," *War Sketches and Incidents, Iowa Commandery Military Order of the Loyal Legion,* Vol. I (Des Moines: Press of P. C. Kenyon, 1893), 213.

30. *O.R.,* Vol. XXIV, pt. 2, 49–51.

31. Edwin C. Bearss, *Decision in Mississippi* (Little Rock: Pioneer Press, 1962), 266–68.

32. *O.R.,* Vol. XXIV, pt. 2, 315–16.

33. *Ibid.,* 100.

34. Photocopy of George A. Snow's Diary, The South Carolina Relic Room and Museum; original in the possession of Sarah M. Escott.

35. *O.R.,* Vol. XXIV, pt. 2, 80.

36. quoted in Jerry Korn, *War on the Mississippi,* Time-Life Civil War Series (Alexandria: Time-Life Books, 1985), 119.

37. A. A. Stuart, *Iowa Colonels and Regiments* (Des Moines: Mills & Co., 1865), 383–87.

38. Isaac H. Elliott, *History of the Thirty-third Illinois Veteran Volunteer Infantry* (Gibson City: Published by the Association, 1902), 194. (Hereafter cited as Elliott, *Thirty-Third Illinois.*)

39. Long, *Memoirs,* 276. Neither the Confederates nor the

Federals consistently used the correct military engineering terms to describe certain important features of the Vicksburg fortifications. The Stockade Redan is, properly speaking, a bastion which is a fortified position that projects outward from a main line. Similarly, the 3rd Louisiana Redan, is not a redan but a bastion. A redan is a fortified position in advance of a main line of fortifications. One of the few true redans along the Vicksburg fortifications was a small earthern fortification that protected the point where the Southern Railroad of Mississippi entered the Confederate works. That structure is usually identified as the Railroad Redoubt. In fact a redoubt is a small work that usually projects outward from a bastion. Rather than try to straighten out these terms, the authors have decided to use the common names and not worry about the niceties of military engineering terminology. The source for these common names is *The Official Military Atlas of the Civil War.*

40. *O.R.,* Vol. XXIV, pt. 2, 268; J. Crecian, *History of the Eighty-third Indiana Volunteer Infantry* (Cincinnati: John F. Uhlhorn, Printer, 1865), p. 30.

41. *O.R.,* Vol. XXIV, pt. 2, 376; Edwin C. Bearss, "A Special Portfolio of Maps on the Vicksburg Campaign," *Civil War Times Illustrated,* VI (July 1967): 41.

42. Hall, *The Story of the 26th Louisiana Infantry,* 67–68.

43. *O.R.,* Vol. XXIV, pt. 2, 415.

44. *Ibid.,* 254, 398, 407.

45. Kenneth Urquhart, ed., *Vicksburg: Southern City under Siege* (New Orleans: The Historic New Orleans Collection, 1980), 13–14.

46. Elliott, *Thirty-third Illinois,* 134.

47. *O.R.,* Vol. XXIV, pt. 2, 386–89.

48. *Ibid.,* 140–41, 241–42.

49. *Ibid.,* 420.

50. Lee, "Siege of Vicksburg," 50.

51. Barber, *Army Memoirs of Lucius W. Barber,* 113; Francis T. Miller, *The Photographic History of the Civil War,* 10 vols. (New York: The Review of Reviews Co., 1911), Vol. II, 201.

52. Wilbur F. Crummer, *With Grant at Fort Donelson, Shiloh and Vicksburg* (Oak Park: E. C. Crummer & Co., 1915), 120, 143.

53. Rood, *Twelfth Wisconsin Regiment,* 194–96.

54. U.S. National Archives. "Compiled Service Records," 39th Tennessee Infantry, Wells, Samuel H.

55. Osborn, "Diary," 368.

56. Stephen E. Ambrose, "A Wisconsin Boy at Vicksburg: The Letters of James K. Newton," *Journal of Mississippi History,* XXIII (January 1961), 4; Elliott, *Thirty-third Illinois,* 45.

57. *O.R.,* Vol. XXIV, pt. 2, 372–73.

58. *Ibid.,* 313; Inscription on the back of Code's photo, in the possession of Richard Holloway.

59. Long, *Memoirs,* 290–94; Polly Huling, "Missourians at Vicksburg," *Missouri Historical Review,* L (October 1955), 4.

60. *O.R.,* Vol. XXIV, pt. 2, 634; E. J. Sherlock, *Memorabilia of the Marches and Battles in which the One Hundredth Regiment of Indiana Infantry Volunteers Took an Active Part* (Kansas City: Gerard-Woody Printing Co., 1896), 40.

61. *O.R.,* Vol. XXIV, pt. 2, 655.

62. William Owen, *In Camp and Battle with the Washington Artillery* (Boston: Ticknor and Company, 1885), 418.

Chapter 8

1. P. L. Rainwater, ed., "Letters of James Lusk Alcorn," *Journal of Southern History,* III (1937): 201–2.

2. Edgar L. Erickson, "Hunting for Cotton in Dixie: From the Civil War Diary of Captain Charles E. Wilcox," *Journal of Southern History,* IV (1938): 508.

3. R. L. Howard, *History of the 124th Regiment, Illinois Infantry Volunteers* (Springfield, Ill.: H. W. Rokker, 1880), 185.

4. William M. Cash, ed., *My Dear Nellie: The Civil War Letters of William L. Nugent to Eleanor Smith Nugent* (Jackson: University Press of Mississippi, 1977), 160–61.

5. Jeannie Marie Deen, ed., *Annie Harper's Journal: A Southern Mother's Legacy* (Denton, Miss.: Flour Mound Writing Company, 1983), 19.

6. Richard A. McLemore, ed., *A History of Mississippi* (Hattiesburg, Miss.: University & College Press of Mississippi, 1973), I, 502.

7. James W. Silver, ed., "The Breakdown of Morale in Central Mississippi in 1864: Letters of Judge Robert S. Hudson," *Journal of Mississippi History,* XVI (1954): 102.

8. *O.R.,* Vol. XXXIX, pt. 2, 570.

9. *Ibid.,* 725.

10. *Ibid.,* Vol. XXX, pt. 4, 577.

11. *Ibid.,* Vol. XXXIX, pt. 2, 777.

12. *Ibid.,* 571.

13. Ulysses S. Grant, *Personal Memoirs of Ulysses S. Grant* (New York: 1885–86), I, 436.

14. *O.R.,* Vol. XXXIX, pt.1, 400.

15. Rood, *Twelfth Wisconsin Regiment,* 217.

16. Kate D. Foster Diary, typescript in M.D.A.H.

17. Charles W. Wills, *Army Life of an Illinois Soldier* (Washington, D.C.: Globe Printing Co., 1906), 188.

18. Howard, *124th Regiment, Illinois Infantry Volunteers,* 216.

Chapter 9

1. *O.R.,* Vol. XXXI, pt. 1, 176.
2. *Ibid.,* Vol. XLIX, pt. 2, 1290.
3. *Ibid.,* Vol. XXX, pt. 2, 814.
4. *Ibid.,* 376.
5. Chambers quoted in Margie Riddle Bearrs, *Sherman's Forgotten Campaign: The Meridian Expedition* (Baltimore, Md.: Gateway Press, Inc., 1987), 109–10.
6. Barber, *Army Memoirs of Lucius W. Barber,* 138.
7. *Ibid.,* 137.
8. *O.R.,* Vol. XX, pt. 1, 381.
9. quoted in Shelby Foote, *The Civil War, A Narrative: Fredericksburg to Meridian* (New York: Vintage Books, 1986), 931.
10. Cash, *My Dear Nellie,* 158.
11. *O.R.,* Vol. XXXIX, pt. 1, 685.
12. *Ibid.,* 93.
13. quoted in Stephen D. Lee, "The Battle of Tupelo, or Harrisburg, July 14, 1863[4]," *Publications of the Mississippi Historical Society,* VI (1903): 40.
14. *O.R.,* Vol. XXXIX, pt. 1, 331.
15. *Ibid.,* 349.

Chapter 10

1. William C. Harris, "The Reconstruction of the Commonwealth, 1865–1870," in Richard A. McLemore, ed., *A History of Mississippi* (Hattiesburg: University and College Press of Mississippi, 1973), I, 542; *A Compendium of the Ninth Census (June 1, 1870)* (Washington, D.C.: Government Printing Office, 1872), Tables LXXXIV, LXXXVIII.
2. *Confederate Veteran,* II (1894): 180.
3. *Confederate Military History:* 512b.
4. *Confederate Veteran,* XXVIII (1924): 317.
5. Mrs. Albert G. Weems, "Work of the United Daughters of the Confederacy," *Publications of the Mississippi Historical Society,* IV(1901): 73–78.
6. *The Carthaginian* (Carthage, Mississippi), 19 November 1881.
7. quoted in Herman Hattaway, *General Stephen D. Lee* (Jackson: University Press of Mississippi, 1976), 214.
8. quoted in Hudson Strode, *Jefferson Davis, Tragic Hero* (New York: Harcourt, Brace, 1964), 484.

Appendix

1. Samuel Weaver to Mrs. Davenport, 6 April 1866. Original in the possession of Margaret Rogers, Corinth, Mississippi.
2. Gordon Cotton, "War Puts Vicksburg Soldier on Path to Righteousness," Vicksburg *Evening Post,* 21 April 1991.
3. U.S. National Archives. Compiled Service Records, 33rd Illinois, Hall, Levi.
4. U.S. National Archives. Pension Application Files, Snyder, Napoleon, 1st Mississippi Cavalry (U.S.), Application Number 1.014.148.
5. Will H. Tunnard to Dear Ione, 19 June 1913. Will H. Tunnard Papers, L.L.M.V.C., L.S.U.

Select Bibliography

The authors have compiled this bibliography for those persons who wish to learn more about Mississippi's role in the Civil War. We have included the major secondary sources on Mississippi, standard reference materials, and selected primary works that, in the opinion of the authors, represent some of the best firsthand accounts of the soldiers' experiences. We have not listed all the materials examined for this volume, nor have we included unpublished resources.

General Sources

Boatner, Mark III. *The Civil War Dictionary.* New York: David McKay Company, 1959.

Confederate Veteran

Crute, Joseph H., Jr. *Confederate Staff Officers, 1861–1865.* Powhatan: Derwent Books, 1982.

Esposito, Vincent J., ed. *The West Point Atlas of American Wars.* Vol. I. New York: Frederick A. Praeger, 1967.

Faust, Patricia L., ed. *Historical Times Illustrated Encyclopedia of the Civil War.* New York: Harper & Row, 1986.

Hooker, Charles E. *Mississippi*, Vol. IX, *Confederate Military History: Extended Edition.* Wilmington: Broadfoot Publishing Co., 1987.

Johnson, Robert U., and Buel, Clarence C. *Battles and Leaders of the Civil War.* 4 vols. New York: Thomas Yoseloff, 1956.

Long, E. B. *The Civil War Day by Day.* Garden City: Doubleday & Co., 1971.

Rietti, J. C. *Military Annals of Mississippi.* Spartanburg: Reprint Company, 1988.

Rowland, Dunbar. *Military History of Mississippi.* Spartanburg: Reprint Company, 1988.

Sifakis, Stewart. *Who Was Who in the Civil War.* New York: Facts on File Publications, 1988.

Southern Historical Society Papers

The Confederate Soldier in the Civil War. n.p. Fairfax Press, n.d.

U.S. National Archives. "Compiled Service Records of Confederate Soldiers who Served in Organizations from Mississippi."

U.S. Navy Department. *Official Records of the Union and Confederate Navies in the War of the Rebellion.* 31 vols. Washington: U.S. Government Printing Office, 1894–1922.

U.S. War Department. *The Official Military Atlas of the Civil War.* New York: Arno Press, 1978.

———. *The War of the Rebellion: A Compilation of the Official Records of the Union and Confederate Armies,* 128 vols. Washington: Government Printing Office, 1880–1901.

Warner, Ezra. *Generals in Blue.* Baton Rouge: Louisiana State University Press, 1964.

———. *Generals in Blue.* Baton Rouge: Louisiana State University Press, 1959.

Chapter 1

Kelbaugh, Ross J. *Introduction to Civil War Photography.* Gettysburg, Pennsylvania: Thomas Publications, 1991.

Ray, Frederic E. "The Photographers of the War," in William C. Davis, *The Image of War, 1861–1865.* Garden City, N.Y.: Doubleday, 1981. Vol. 1. *Shadows of the Storm,* I, 409–14.

Witham, George F., comp. *Catalogue of Civil War Photographers: A History of Civil War Photographic Imprints, 1861–1865.* Portland, OR: G. F. Witham, 1988.

Chapter 2

Bettersworth, John, ed. *Mississippi in the Confederacy.* Baton Rouge: Louisiana State University Press, 1961. 2 vols.

Rowland, Dunbar. *Military History of Mississippi, 1803–1898.* Spartanburg, S.C.: The Reprint Company, Publishers, 1988.

Woods, Thomas H. "A Sketch of the Mississippi Secession Convention of 1861—Its Membership and Work," *Publications of the Mississippi Historical Society,* VI (1902): 91–104.

Chapter 3

Brown, Maud Morrow. *The University Greys.* Richmond: Garrett and Massie, 1940.

Buford, Thomas P., comp. *Lamar Rifles, a History of Company G, Eleventh Mississippi Regiment, C.S.A.* Roanoke: Stone Printing and Manufacturing, 1903.

Huettel, William L. ed. "Letters from Private Richard C. Bridges, C.S.A. 1861–1864," *Journal of Mississippi History,* XXXIII (November 1971): 357–72.

Lowe, William A. "Mississippi at Gettysburg," *Publications of the Mississippi Historical Society,* IX (1906): 25–51.

McIntosh, Hartman, ed. "The Civil War Letters of John

Alemeth Byers, 17th Mississippi Infantry," *Military Images,* IX (May–June 1988): 6–11.

McNeilly, J. S. "Barksdale's Mississippi Brigade at Gettysburg," *Publications of the Mississippi Historical Society,* XIV (1914): 231–65.

———. "A Mississippi Brigade in the Last Days of the Confederacy," *Publications of the Mississippi Historical Society,* VII (1903): 33–55.

Silver, James W. ed. *A Life for the Confederacy.* Jackson: McCowat-Mercer Press, Inc., 1959.

Chapter 4

Banks, R. W. *The Battle of Franklin.* Dayton: Morningside Press, 1982.

Chambers, William. "My Journal," *Publications of the Mississippi Historical Society,* Centenary Series, V (1925): 225–385.

French, Samuel. *Two Wars: An Autobiography of Gen. Samuel G. French.* Nashville: Confederate Veteran, 1901.

Howell, Grady, Jr. *Going to Meet the Yankees.* Jackson: Chickasaw Bayou Press, 1981.

McMurry, Richard M., ed. "A Mississippian at Nashville," *Civil War Times Illustrated,* XII (May 1973): 9–15.

Montgomery, Franklin A. *Reminiscences of a Mississippian in Peace and War.* Cincinnati: Robert Clarke, Co., 1901.

Sykes, E. T. "Walthall's Brigade," *Publications of the Mississippi Historical Society,* Centenary Series, I (1916): 476–623.

Chapter 5

Casteel, Albert. "Victory at Corinth," in James M. McPherson, ed. *Battle Chronicles of the Civil War.* 6 vols. New York: Macmillan Publishing Company, 1989. Vol. II, 262–71.

Cluett, William W. *History of the 57th Regiment, Illinois Volunteer Infantry.* Princeton: T. P. Streeter Printer, 1886.

Maury, Dabney H. "Campaigning against Grant in North Mississippi," *Southern Historical Society Papers,* XII (1885): 285–311.

Rogers, Margaret Green. *Civil War Corinth, 1861–1865.* Corinth: Rankin Printery, 1989.

Tunnard, William H. *A Southern Record: The History of the Third Regiment, Louisiana Infantry.* Baton Rouge: n.p., 1866.

Chapter 6

Bearss, Edwin C. *Rebel Victory at Vicksburg*. Wilmington: Broadfoot Publishing Company, 1989.

Carter, Samuel III. *The Final Fortress*. New York: St. Martin's Press, 1980.

Dupree, J. G. "The Capture of Holly Springs, Mississippi, Dec. 20, 1862," *Publications of the Mississippi Historical Society*, IV (1901): 49–61.

Selfridge, Thomas O., Jr. *Memoirs of Thomas O. Selfridge, Jr., Rear Admiral*. New York: G. P. Putnam, 1924.

Walker, Peter F. *Vicksburg: A People at War, 1860–1865*. Wilmington: Broadfoot Publishing Company, 1987.

Chapter 7

Ambrose, Stephen. "Struggle for Vicksburg," *Civil War Times Illustrated*, VI (July 1967): 1–66.

Andersen, Mary Ann, ed. *The Civil War Diary of Allen Morgan Geer*. New York: Cosmos Press, 1977.

Barber, Lucius W. *Army Memoirs of Lucius W. Barber*. Chicago: J. M. W. Jones Stationery and Printing Co., 1894.

Bearss, Edwin C. *Decision in Mississippi*. Little Rock: Pioneer Press, 1962.

Bearss, Edwin C. and Grabau, Warren. *The Battle of Jackson*, and Bearss, Edwin C. *The Siege of Jackson*. Baltimore: Gateway Press, 1981.

Brown, D. Alexander. "Grierson's Raid," *Civil War Times Illustrated*, III (January 1965): 4–32.

Crummer, Wilbur F. *With Grant at Fort Donelson, Shiloh, and Vicksburg*. Oak Park: E. C. Crummer & Co., 1915.

Hall, Winchester. *The Story of the 26th Louisiana Infantry*. Gaithersburg: Butternut Press, 1984.

Korn, Jerry. *War on the Mississippi*. Alexandria: Time-Life Books, 1985.

Lee, Stephen D. "The Campaign of Vicksburg, Mississippi, in 1863 from April 15 to and including the battle of Champion's Hill, or Baker's Creek," *Publications of the Mississippi Historical Society*, III (1900): 21–53.

———. "The Siege of Vicksburg," *Publications of the Mississippi Historical Society*, III (1900): 55–71.

Long, E. B., ed. *Personal Memoirs of U. S. Grant*. Cleveland: World Publishing Co., 1952.

Osborn, George C., ed. "A Tennessean at the Siege of Vicksburg: The Diary of Samuel Alexander Ramsey Swan (May–July, 1863)," *Tennessee Historical Quarterly*, XIV (March 1955): 353–72.

Reed, Lida Lord. "A Woman's Experiences during the Siege of Vicksburg," *The Century Magazine*, LXI (April 1901): 922–28.

Urquhart, Kenneth, ed. *Vicksburg: Southern City under Siege*. New Orleans: The Historic New Orleans Collection, 1980.

Chapter 8

Bettersworth, John K. "The Home Front, 1861–1865," in Richard A. McLemore, ed., *A History of Mississippi*. Hattiesburg: University and College Press of Mississippi, 1973, 492–541.

Rainwater, P. L., ed. "Letters of James Lusk Alcorn," *Journal of Southern History*, III (1937): 196–209.

Silver, James W. "The Breakdown of Morale in Central Mississippi in 1864: Letters of Judge Robert S. Hudson," *Journal of Mississippi History*, XVI (1954): 99–120.

Chapter 9

Brown, D. Alexander. "The Battle of Brice's Cross Roads," *Civil War Times Illustrated*, VII (April 1968): 4–9, 44–48.

Carter, George Theodore. "The Tupelo Campaign. As Noted at the Time by a Line Officer of the Union Army," *Publications of the Mississippi Historical Society*, X (1909): 91–113.

Lee, Stephen D. "Sherman's Meridian Expedition from Vicksburg to Meridian, Feb. 3rd to March 6th, 1863 [sic]," *Publications of the Mississippi Historical Society*, IV (1901): 35–47.

———. "Battle of Brice's Cross Roads, or Tishomingo Creek, June 2nd to 12th, 1864," *Publications of the Mississippi Historical Society*, VI (1903): 17–37.

———. "The Battle of Tupelo, or Harrisburg, July 14th, 1863 [sic]," *Publications of the Mississippi Historical Society*, VI (1903): 39–52.

———. "The War in Mississippi after the Fall of Vicksburg, July 4, 1863," *Publications of the Mississippi Historical Society*, X (1909): 47–62.

Phillips, Lewis F. "A Gunner at Tupelo," *Civil War Times Illustrated*, XII (December 1973): 44–47.

Stinson, Byron. "Hot Work in Mississippi: The Battle of Tupelo," *Civil War Times Illustrated*, XI (July 1972): 4–9, 46–48.

Harris, William C. "The Reconstruction of the Common-wealth, 1865–1870," in Richard A. McLemore, ed., *A History of Mississippi*. Hattiesburg: University and College Press of Mississippi, 1973, I, 542–70.

Hattaway, Herman. "Clio's Southern Soldiers: The United Confederate Veterans and History," *Louisiana History*, XII (Summer 1971): 213–42.

———. *General Stephen D. Lee*. Jackson: University Press of Mississippi, 1976.

Sansing, David G. "Congressional Reconstruction," in Richard A. McLemore, ed., *A History of Mississippi*. Hattiesburg: University and College Press of Mississippi, 1973, I, 571–90.

Index

392